TRYING FREEDOM

RICHARD MEISLER

HARCOURT BRACE JOVANOVICH, PUBLISHERS

TRYING FREEDOM

FREEDOM

A Case for Liberating Education

SAN DIEGO   NEW YORK   LONDON

Requests for permission to make copies of any
part of the work should be mailed to:
Permissions, Harcourt Brace Jovanovich, Publishers,
Orlando, Florida 32887

Grateful acknowledgment is made to the following publishers for
permission to reprint excerpts: The lines on page vii are taken
from the song Little Boxes, words and music by Malvina Reynolds,
copyright 1962 Schroder Music Co. The lines by Doris Lessing
on page 135 are taken from The Golden Notebook, copyright 1974
by Doris Lessing, reprinted by permission of Simon & Schuster,
Inc. The excerpt by Margaret Mead on page 240 is taken from
Culture and Commitment, copyright 1970 by Margaret Mead, reprinted
by permission of Doubleday & Company, Inc.

Library of Congress Cataloging in Publication Data
Meisler, Richard.
    Trying freedom.
    1. Academic freedom—United States—Case studies.
2. Education, Higher—United States—Case studies.
I. Title.
LC72.2.M44   1984   378'.121   83-22543
ISBN 0-15-191358-7

Designed by Jacqueline Schuman

Printed in the United States of America

First edition

A B C D E

To my parents

And the people in the houses
All go to the university,
And they all get put in boxes,
Little boxes all the same.
—Malvina Reynolds

Contents

CONTENTS

Foreword

The struggle goes on, probably will ever go on: those who hold fast to the prerogatives and responsibilities of authority, as against those who argue for (and struggle long and hard for) what they call freedom—meaning, one hopes, the prerogatives and responsibilities of each person, including those who get called students. I must say I think it is not always helpful to polarize these two positions, turn teachers and pupils (among others) into antagonists. Still, there are quite real and important differences of opinion on the subjects of authority or freedom—abstractions, of course, which one ought to connect to concrete situations. For example, how ought school teachers or college professors to get along with those who study—*with* them or *under* them? How ought we who teach to regard those who come to our lectures and seminars— as colleagues, as innocent youths, as men and women who have a lot to teach *us,* as young people who will get an A or a B or a C or a D or an E, depending on how they do on their (our) tests?

A discussion of these questions, these alternative ways of thinking and seeing—of being?—is certainly not being pressed upon us today. Lord knows, during the 1960s a substantial body of discussion became part of our intellectual and educational history. The author of this book mentions many of his predecessors: Edgar Z. Freidenberg, Herbert Kohl, Paul Goodman, Jonathan Kozol, John Holt, and there were (are) others. What all these teachers, social theorists, educational critics (and Richard Meisler with this book is surely entitled to join their ranks as a full-fledged activist member) have in common is an insistence that the freedom side of the equation, so to speak, be emphasized, as against the requirements of authority. Put differently, Mr. Meisler and his spiritual kin worry about the minds that yearn to affirm their various and separate selves, the hearts that cry for expression, often in the face of stony silence if not outright cramped, punitive denial, and not least, the spiritual hunger that goes unaddressed by cold or self-important or plain stupid (and always officious) pedantry.

Yet, there is another way of approaching this subject, and I would think an introduction ought bring that divergent point of view to the reader's attention—the requirements of discipline, of a measure of respect for those who have preceded one in school and, yes, chosen to stay there as teachers. I realize that vain and morally insensitive professors can take for granted, even abuse, the trust their students accord, can resort to mean and brutish behavior in the name of their academic (bureaucratic) rights, can play favorites or use stupid and irrelevant criteria for their comparative evaluations of students, can betray the trust offered them by those they teach. On the other hand, let it be remembered, students can also be impossibly egotistical, manipulatively cunning, and in their own manner smug or nasty or petulant. It is ridiculous to stereotype either teachers or students and blame one or the other for any breakdown within the system. Indeed, one ought make every effort to ask more of both groups (or of any single human being) with some wariness, given the various messianic or utopian dreams which have foundered in past decades, centuries, no matter the earnest goodwill and passionate idealism spent.

This book offers concrete evidence of what can happen when a kind, sincere, hardworking, consistently sensitive, and thoughtful group of teachers involve themselves knowingly and affectionately with a group of students who are by no means without their "problems" and yet who become touched, engaged, and, at last, colleagues. There is, one can say, promising and endearing evidence here, and it deserves to be put on the record—in the mind of each reader, and on those imaginary scales which measure the pro and the con of one or another continuing argument. I felt somewhat nostalgic reading this book, found my mind remembering the 1960s, the early 1970s, other moments and other voices, but, all of them really, part of a grand Western tradition, centuries old: let the children, the young people, be our companions in this lifelong search for knowledge, for understanding, for wisdom; and in doing so, let us, the older ones, thereby earn a greater measure of freedom and dignity for ourselves. There ought be from us readers our cautionary responses—reminders of failures, excesses, blind spots, naïveté. Yet, we should also welcome the persistent reports of those brave souls who try hard, often against great bureaucratic (and social and economic) odds, to break away from the pack, explore new territory, and having done so, return to us with fresh and edifying news—which this book brings.

Robert Coles
Cambridge, Massachussetts
May, 1984

Acknowledgments

The love and confidence of Miriam, Joshua, and Daniel Meisler have bolstered me through several long years of writing and taking stock. It is to Miriam, too, that I owe the invaluable gifts of the time and freedom necessary to write. The wisdom and guidance of Keith McGary have been central to the story that is told in this book, to the work I have tried to do in the two decades since I met him.

Writing this book was for me the most recent stage of a longer process of exploring the possibilities of freedom in education. In this I have been fortunate in my friends and colleagues, many of whom are mentioned in the text. Mentioned not at all or only briefly, however, are several who have been so important, have shared successes and failures so fully, that I must acknowledge them here. They are Ken Huber, Sylvia Law, Barry Ensminger, Masao Yoshimasu, Charles and Florence Tate, Jane Van Nimmen-Adams, Richard Billow, Mel Tukman, Tom and Lena Langan, Ken and Bev Paigen, Albert Stewart, Joseph Piccillo, and Shirley Kassman.

I must also acknowledge the unique contributions of present and former members of the Buffalo State College faculty, Professors Ballowitz, Brennan, Cataldo, Clabeaux, Hulicka, Kury, Minahan, Morganti, R. Paterson, Randall, Riccards, and Roblin.

Excerpt from the song *Little Boxes*, words and music by Malvina Reynolds, © 1962 by Schroder Music Company, used by permission; all rights reserved.

The excerpt in Chapter 2 is from *The Academic Revolution* by Christopher Jencks and David Riesman, © 1968 by the authors, published by Doubleday and Company.

The excerpts in Chapter 3 and Chapter 27 are from *A Room of One's Own* by Virginia Woolf, © 1929 by Harcourt, Brace and Company.

The excerpt in Chapter 20 is from the Introduction to *The Golden Notebook* by Doris Lessing, © 1974 by the author, published by Simon & Schuster, Inc., used by permission.

TRYING FREEDOM

1

Introduction: Trying Freedom

During the fifteen years that I was a college teacher and administrator, the question of freedom for students became the central educational issue for me. I tried to use whatever influence and power I had, whether within a single classroom or a larger portion of the system, to expand the scope of students' control over their own education. I was not disappointed in the results.

I saw students take great strides toward autonomy as learners and people, even in the midst of powerful countervailing forces. They became actively engaged in the pursuit of knowledge, rejecting their accustomed roles as passive recipients or passive resisters of instruction in its familiar authoritarian trappings. I admired the raw courage of students who saw that it was necessary to confront stubborn shortcomings within themselves and then to act, mostly alone, to overcome them, often by slowly and painfully forming new habits. Students examined themselves and wondered about their futures. They began to make the risky decisions entailed by assuming responsibility for their own lives. This behavior was especially remarkable for taking place in a larger educational system in which they needed only to say the word in order to be presented with a complete package of certified educational tasks that could be pursued with hardly any risk and with comparatively little effort.

When entire programs were created to give students more freedom, faculty were affected too. Living without the authoritarian barriers that formerly separated them, students and teachers began working together, dealing with each other more fully as human beings, not as opponents in the intricate cat-and-mouse games of grading. I saw teachers with many years of experience reach new levels of involvement, effectiveness, and satisfaction in their work. The new settings finally allowed them to express in their work the love for students and learning that had always been in their hearts. As those students and teachers worked together, I would occasionally hear them laugh. It was the kind of spontaneous laughter that is rarely heard in classrooms. I think it could happen because teacher and student were free of other burdens and were able to experience the joy that is inherent in most learning and teaching.

There were bad experiences too. Some students could not give up the security of conventional education, in which progress toward a degree is virtually guaranteed to anyone willing to follow instructions. Many people felt that they did not have the time, or in some cases the inner resources, to struggle with old habits in order to achieve new levels of autonomy, especially since those habits were adapted to much of their environment, particularly to most formal education. Nervous parents, teachers, and friends encouraged students to believe that the investments of time and self required to use new freedoms would simply be too costly.

Some teachers found that, despite the attraction of rhetoric about freedom, the old authoritarian ways afforded them more gratification than they had realized. Others found that they did not value nontraditional types of learning as highly as they had thought, and therefore could not accept the implications of student choices. They too backed away from freedom for students. Teachers in the innovative programs also sometimes failed in skill or wisdom, often underestimating the difficulty of the task.

The major barrier to freedom in education is the large group of faculty that finds the concept abhorrent, at least when it is put into practice in any meaningful way. It is subversive of their basic educational philosophies, and they fight it vigorously. Campus conflicts, especially over liberal innovative programs, can become pretty dirty, and this was also part of my experience.

My experiments with educational freedom have encountered stubborn implicit difficulties and produced conflicts which led to defeats and unhappiness. Yet I have observed and been involved with students and teachers who used new freedoms spectacularly well. Their successes have been too heartening to allow for more than temporary pessimism on the question of educational freedom, even in an era in which it is out of style. When I waver, my mind returns to the smiles and enthusiasm of students and teachers working together outside conventional constraints. I think of significant substantive achievements of students and teachers collaborating in new ways. I remember my own two children and the hundreds of young adults who have been my students; I think of the quality of life I want them to have as they learn. It is thus with genuine optimism that I offer a memoir about some matters of freedom in education. It is the story of one person's encounter with an idea, the joys and problems of its implementation, and the reflections occasioned by dissonance between the idea and various parts of reality, including the nature of individual human beings and the educational institutions within which they live part of their lives.

*

The chapters that follow fall naturally into several categories, though they are interspersed with each other rather than separated. The point of this arrangement is to try to reflect the way in which diverse experiences and ideas actually entered the life of one educator.

One group of chapters amounts to a critique of certain customs and structures of our institutions of higher education. Another is autobiographical, describing my attempt to become a good teacher. A third category of chapters is primarily conceptual, dealing with ideas related to freedom in education. A few chapters deal with the possibilities of freedom in conventional classrooms. The largest portion of the book is, however, devoted to a description of a particular innovative program.

The program was the Individualized Degree Program at Buffalo State College. Most of these chapters deal with the experiences of particular students and teachers. I include many details of the personalities, problems, aspirations, and accomplishments of these people, for larger concepts like educational freedom enter life only in the form of such details.

The participants in this program were not chosen because they were extraordinarily gifted. A few were clearly blessed with outstanding talents. Others did special things when the program gave them special opportunities. In general we were ordinary people trying to take advantage of new freedoms. It is possible, of course, that ordinary people with new opportunities will often turn out not to be so ordinary.

In choosing faculty and students to include, I have attempted to avoid making an unfair case for a program to which I was deeply committed. As much as I believed in the IDP, I have tried to understand that these pages will be useful to the extent that they illuminate the dynamics of using *and* failing to use freedom. The strengths or weaknesses of a particular program and its participants are, in this context, incidental and unimportant.

These chapters include a slightly edited transcript of a talk I gave to the first group of students to enter the program. Most of us were flying high. Never have I been so hopeful and excited about my work and the prospects for being involved in good education. Such enthusiasm and idealism are necessary and important parts of this kind of story. There is also a description of the program and its institutional setting. The Individualized Degree Program may have been slightly more radical than most similar innovations, but it was far from unique. Programs with similar core values and academic structures have sprung up at dozens of colleges in the past ten or fifteen years. Entire institutions, especially those designed for adult learners like the Empire State College in New York and the various Universities Without Walls, are quite similar to the IDP.

I also include a brief history of the program and sketches of the administrators who influenced it. Just as a realistic treatment of an attempt to try educational freedom requires extensive reference to particular students and teachers, a program's history involves other events in the institution and the personalities, motives, and values of people with power. Again I feel that we are dealing here with people and developments that, although they have some idiosyncratic qualities, are not particularly unusual. Similar politics and personalities can be found on most campuses.

*

Because this book recommends significant alterations in educational practice, one must begin by considering an issue that arises in all advocacy of social change. How great a burden of proof or persuasion must be borne by a new idea such as educational freedom? I think it is proper to accept a conservative answer. As critical as I am of conventional schooling, I believe it is prudent to assume that existing institutions have incorporated some wisdom and efficiency into their structures and traditions. The argument for greatly increased educational freedom must therefore by strong indeed. I am satisfied that it is, and most of this book describes and reflects upon the experiences that led me to this position. Readers must make their own judgments.

Common discussions of freedom in education, however, usually don't reach basic questions. As an educator and parent I have engaged in hundreds of conversations over the years about open education. In a large number of cases, discourse tends to stop when a single negative story has been told. A student has "wasted" a year in an alternative program, or an aggressive or disturbed student has ruined the atmosphere of an open classroom. A sincere teacher who experimented with student freedom has been exploited by manipulative and unappreciative students. I don't wish to deny that such things happen or that they may be significant. There are plenty of horror stories to be told about both conventional and innovative educational programs. They are interesting, but should be taken for what they are. The concrete experiences of students and teachers should be invoked in arguments about educational forms, but they must be related to general or systematic issues. Otherwise we are reduced simply to swapping tales.

*

I would like to conclude these introductory remarks by mentioning the question that is raised most often in discussions about educational freedom. Is freedom best for everyone or only for a select group of students—the highly motivated or brilliant or off-beat or creative? The issue is frequently raised by parents who have some children who seem suited to an open system and others who do not. Conventional wisdom and common sense, of course, urge the recognition that students are different from one another and the selection of educational programs should follow accordingly.

The diversity to which this question refers is undeniable. Some students find it easier and more pleasurable to have educational freedom than others. My advocacy of open education, however, does not derive from this fact. As is evident in this book, I believe that conventional education is generally too rigid and authoritarian and that our school systems, colleges, and universities would do well to incorporate additional freedom everywhere. It is also possible that the students and teachers who find increased freedom most difficult are those who will profit from it and, in the end, enjoy it most.

2

Standard Conversation: First Day of the Semester

There are only a handful of colleges that make even nominal efforts to eliminate grades as the prime incentive for academic work. . . .

There is no reason for America to entrust both the education and certification of the young to the same institutions.

—Christopher Jencks and David Riesman

STUDENT A. What's this semester going to be like for you?

STUDENT B. Not too bad. I have quizzes every week in one course. I have to do term papers for three of the profs, and there are three midterms and five finals. Two of the finals are open book. The other three are machine-graded multiple-choice tests. It could be a lot worse.

3

Stories about Grades

No, delightful as the pastime of measuring may be, it is the most futile of all occupations, and to submit to the decrees of the measurers the most servile of attitudes. So long as you write what you wish to write, that is all that matters; and whether it matters for ages or only for hours, nobody can say. But to sacrifice a hair of the head of your vision, a shade of its color, in deference to some Headmaster with a silver pot in his hand or to some professor with a measuring-rod up his sleeve, is the most abject treachery, and the sacrifice of wealth and chastity which used to be said to be the greatest of human disasters, a mere flea-bite in comparison.

—Virginia Woolf

I

Student demonstrations after the Cambodian invasion and the Kent State killings blocked Elmwood Avenue, the main thoroughfare in front of Buffalo State College. Using tear gas, the police chased the students back on to campus. Some of the students fled into a dormitory. Police shot tear gas canisters through windows of the dorm, gassing demonstrators and bystanders alike. The next day the president of the college, fearing further violence, closed the college, declaring an early end to the semester. The remaining classes were canceled, offices were closed, and dormitory students given a day or two to move out. Things happened quickly. It was hard to make sense of them.

Chaos was followed by quiet. There was nothing much to do. I went to campus and wandered about, while it all drifted through my mind: the enormity of the war; shock at the violence at Kent State; the apparent inability of the antiwar movement to change government policy; the increasing polarization in thought and action of the opposing sides in our country; the hateful passions that were carrying the day; the combined exhilaration and repulsion at the increasing dangers entailed by our new rituals of confrontation.

I bumped into a few other people roaming the campus. We shook our heads, exchanged clichés and expressions of astonishment. Most people didn't want to talk much. There was one exception, a colleague who was raging mad and wanted to tell the world about it.

Anger was common enough in those days. People were angry at the students, the cops, and the college administration, to mention only a few of the more proximate targets. Just the previous day I had talked with a dean, an older man who prided himself on his carefully cultivated courtly manner. Taking me to be a troublemaker or provocateur, even though I had just spoken publicly against confrontations with a potential for violence and had been heckled by radicals as a Nixonian, the dean swore and shouted at me uncontrollably. My other colleague's anger, therefore, was no surprise, but it took me a minute to understand precisely what he was so angry about. When I understood, I simply didn't know what to say.

Of all the available reasons to be angry, many of which would have appealed to me, this professor's problem was that he had not been able to give the final examinations in his courses. This, however, he saw as unavoidable, and it was not what really made him furious. His anger was directed at the president of the college for what he thought would be done next. He was sure that faculty members would soon get a memorandum directing them to assign grades to students on the basis of work completed at the time classes were canceled. The professor was certain that the president would not choose one of the other options, like rescheduling final exams for the beginning of the next semester, or directing that they be administered by mail during the summer vacation, or simply leaving the arrangements to the discretion of individual instructors. (In fact, it was the latter choice that was actually made by the president.)

With tears of rage or frustration in his eyes, my colleague explained that his courses involved an intricate and delicate system of testing, of which the final exam was a critical element. One couldn't simply cancel the exam and rely upon what had gone before. The whole thing would be ruined. There would be no way to determine a fair and meaningful final grade with the system so distorted. And an administrative intrusion into the grading process, no matter how unusual the circumstances, was intolerable. The war, the violence, the politics, and all the rest were overshadowed by a potential violation of the core of this person's professional identity: autonomy and complete control in the matter of grading.

Stories about Grades

I am sure my colleague would have said that grading was only one of a teacher's jobs. But his lack of perspective in the midst of larger events, his rage, his watery eyes, and the pitch of his voice all suggested to me that the rest was almost insignificant to him. I felt that I was seeing, in the most extreme and pure form I would be likely to encounter, a concrete expression of a dominant view of teaching among college professors. The description of any pedagogical innovation, to give another example, is almost always followed by the immediate question, How would you grade in that system?

I had few other contacts with the man in the years that followed. On occasion we spoke about individual students whom we both knew. Not only did he know each student's grade-point average and classify him or her accordingly, but he also knew the extent to which the student had taken hard and easy courses and might thus be seen as the beneficiary of grade inflation or soft-touch teachers. My colleague spent a considerable amount of time reading transcripts.

I didn't like this man, and he liked me less. But there was something refreshing and honest about him. My liberal colleagues all talked about grading as a necessary evil, the white man's burden. They nevertheless behaved very much like my grade-obsessed colleague, and continued to exercise and enjoy the power of grading while righteously disagreeing with the system and confusing students with their mildly antiauthoritarian rhetoric. If one is going to behave that way, I came to believe, one might just as well come out of the closet, embrace and flaunt one's power in the open.

II

While working at Buffalo State College, I was able to go to Sicily with my wife. She attended a meeting and I had a vacation. Anticipating the trip, I sat in on Italian 101, Elementary Italian, at summer school. The class met five times each week. To encourage myself to keep up with the rapid pace of a summer course, I decided to take the examinations with the regular students. This was my first experience as a student in a graded course in ten years, and I learned some things about grades and education.

The teacher was a relaxed and charming older man who enjoyed the students and loved the Italian language. He was experienced and competent. The course began in an easy and good-humored fashion. It looked as though we'd all learn a lot and have fun doing so. During the first week, I developed a system of taking notes and identifying things that I thought would help me prepare for my trip. I managed to study a little almost every evening.

Toward the end of the second week, the professor talked about the first test. He tried to help us by indicating what we could expect. He was factual and did as little as he could to increase our anxiety. The classes, however, became more tense. He covered the material more systematically and spent less time pursuing the answers to our questions. He also stopped his digressions into interesting things like the connections of idioms to Italian culture. I especially missed these departures into discussions of life and customs because I felt that they'd help me on my trip. They were also useful in remembering points of language. The professor's personality and his love of Italy and its language were important to the class. As he became more systematic, these receded. Oddly it became slightly harder to learn because of the teacher's efforts to cover the material.

To my surprise I began to get nervous about the examination. It appeared to be very important to me to get an A, even though the grade in this undergraduate course could have no practical meaning for me. I had a Ph.D. I wasn't even registered for the course. I found, however, that I was still a bright kid hoping to get his kicks from being smarter, or at least from getting better grades, than the other kids.

My initial system of taking notes slowly gave way to another, an attempt to cover all the points in the text and the lectures. My study schedule became less regular; I studied a lot before the test and less after it, and this was repeated throughout the course. I'd sometimes fall behind the class schedule when I behaved in this way, so attending classes became less profitable. I did get A's on the tests. I was still bright, and I hadn't forgotten how to study for and take exams. Despite myself I got carefully hidden gratification from those grades, and I seemed to grow more rather than less concerned with them as the course went on.

The classes continued to change. Students left because they did poorly on the first exam and could see that their prospects were bad. Before the test they were learning some Italian, even if it was just a little; now they learned none. I had felt a real sense of community during the first two weeks of the class. It was fun to go to class, to mispronounce things, to have the teacher exhort, *"Corragio, corragio!"* This diminished. More seriously, there was a subtle division of the class into winners and losers. I even think that it grew hard for the winners to get low grades and for the losers to get high ones. The teacher and the students developed implicit theories of the work of each student. I saw small errors in the work of good students go unnoticed, while the same errors in the work of poor students were corrected. There was even physical segregation, with the students who got low grades drifting toward the back of the room.

My own consciousness remained divided between an interest in my grade and a desire to learn Italian. Although secretly embarrassed by it, I found pleasure in getting good grades as well as learning a bit of the language, so it was a pleasant experience for me in several ways. I watched with horror, however, as the losers began to act out their roles. Coming to class less frequently, sitting in the back, they were not prepared and were ashamed of their failures. Some of these students were simply not bright or talented, and I imagined that there was an extra measure of pain in the experience for them. For others the self-fulfilling prophecy of failure, once articulated by the first examination or two, seemed to operate powerfully. Small early failures produced later and larger ones. I had clear memories of some of the students who were uncomfortable, even suffering, at the end of the course. They were the same people who were learning and having fun at the beginning. Perhaps some of them were simply not equipped to learn Italian very quickly. But they did not begin as the sad creatures they were at the end.

Enjoyment aside, I tried to examine my own experience to see whether the pressures of examinations and grades helped me learn more. The answer is complex. I did learn most of the material on the tests. I forgot a lot of it by the time I got to Italy. I think that I retained a larger portion of the Italian I learned while following my own system of studying when it was not under the influence of the grading process. Those bits of knowledge were learned in association with my own ideas of what I wanted to know; the learning was more mine. I am also fairly sure that the testing removed energy from my continuing inquiry into the best way for me to learn a language. This quest was interrupted by the examination-defined task of "covering" the syllabus. I could not resist the idea that I was doing well if I got a good grade. I must add that even if there was more learning produced by the grading, I don't believe that the price—loss of joy in the class and the humiliation of some students—was worth it.

III

In a class I taught in Buffalo the discussion turned to the students' view of their education. One member of the group was a Vietnam veteran who had been seriously wounded in combat. He received a total disability pension from the government. He lived frugally, and his pension was adequate for all his foreseeable financial needs.

The veteran handled college differently from the other students. He concentrated on the courses in which he felt that he was learning something important. He didn't worry about or pay much attention to the others. He got some low grades, even some failing grades, but they didn't bother him. He went to school to learn, not to get grades, and he was very clear about it.

Other students in the class were envious. They wished that they could follow his example, for the young veteran's relationship to school seemed to them to be ideal. They discussed his situation at length. The tone of the conversation suggested that he was living out a common fantasy of a good education: if only one had the freedom to attend the stimulating classes and not the dull ones, to read the books that seemed most interesting and not the rest! The students talked, however, of being bogged down in endless busywork, of not having enough time to think because they were occupied with assignments of dubious value. None of them dared to do what the vet was doing. They feared that the low grades that would inevitably result would hurt their chances for employment in the future.

I have never seen a better demonstration of the true nature of grading in our schools. Grading has to do with money and power, not with learning.

4

Standard Conversation:
I'm Not Interested in Anything

STUDENT. Before I make up my course schedule, I need to know what I have to take.

ADVISER. Well, the requirements are very broad and flexible. Almost any course you'd be interested in would fulfill one of the basic requirements. (Explains broad distribution requirements in the humanities, natural sciences, and social sciences.) What do you think you might be interested in starting with?

STUDENT. I don't know. Aren't there any specific required courses?

ADVISER. No, not really. (Offers a short version of explanation of requirements.) What do you really enjoy?

STUDENT. I've always done well in English. Could I take an English course?

ADVISER (Relieved to be getting someplace). Yes. That sounds like a good idea. There are several literature courses still open. What kinds of books do you like to read?

STUDENT. Well, I don't read very much. It's just that I've always gotten good grades in English.

ADVISER. I see. But what are you really interested in? What do you really enjoy?

STUDENT. I've always done well in social studies too.

ADVISER. Do you enjoy social studies?

STUDENT. No, not particularly. I guess I'm not interested in very much.

ADVISER (Sooner or later). Well, to fulfill the social sciences requirement you might take sociology, and the biology course. . . .

5

Academic Treason: Abandoning Excellence and Rejecting Discipline

It is the business of a teacher to teach, not to judge.

—Maria Montessori

As a student I had few complaints about higher education and only a little clarity about what was happening to me. I did well, enjoyed the rewards, and had no reason to ask basic questions about a system that treated me kindly. I came to see what colleges do to students when I became a teacher, implicated in the doing.

Antioch College in the 1960s was an unlikely place to become convinced of the oppressive nature of higher education, and I was an unlikely recipient of that message. I am not one of those people who was born or raised to be a rebel, who by temperament or upbringing finds it natural to be in opposition to conventional ways. And Antioch was the most permissive of colleges. Before the turmoil of the decade reached a peak that was too much even for Antioch to handle, there was a certain smugness on campus that was rare in the disorientation of the sixties, a sense that the college's traditional liberalism was being vindicated, that the rest of the world was finally catching up with this small innovative college in Ohio.

By all available criteria Antioch was a progressive college, and as a loyal recent graduate, I accepted this image. The college's experimental tradition went back to its founder, Horace Mann, who had moved to the Midwest to start a new college and do things right from the beginning. The faculty and student body had been racially integrated for years, though at levels that were soon to be condemned as tokenist. There was extensive student participation in college governance long before this issue was raised seriously on most campuses. Antioch had pioneered in cooperative education, the program of alternating work and study. It added unusual breadth and worldliness to the experience of students and to the general life of a small and remote campus. The academic requirements gave students many choices, and the curriculum was aggressively experimental, offering instruction in a variety of unusual ways. There were interdisciplinary courses, courses about problems, team-taught courses, introspective courses, etc. It was almost embarrassing for an Antioch professor not to be involved in some sort of experimental course or teaching project. The atmosphere on campus was informal, collaborative, and egalitarian. Many professors were called by their first names; there were open houses at faculty members' homes on Sunday afternoons; instructors attended student social events and fielded teams in intramural sports. It was hard to imagine a college with less authoritarianism in the air.

I had gone to graduate school to study philosophy and returned to Antioch only three years later to join the philosophy department as an instructor. Becoming a colleague of my former teachers was exciting and full of the symbolism of success for me. I was eager to become an educator in Antioch's liberal innovative style. That ambition blended, in full consonance for a while, with the view of my profession that I had acquired in graduate school. I was writing my dissertation under the supervision of a distinguished scholar; I knew the current literature of philosophy, and I believed I could teach the subject and demonstrate its value, doing both in the Antioch style. I would be a good scholar and representative of my discipline. Being a good scholar meant continuing to study and write, and these were closely related to the ability to bring something of value, contemporary philosophy and its history, to students. Another part of the job would be to hold students to the discipline's highest standards of rigor appropriate to their academic level. A modicum of understanding and kindness would guarantee that the process would be pleasant and humane. Loyalty to the virtues of the discipline was part of the meaning of serving students well.

I was welcomed back to the campus warmly. There was no need to learn a new system or become oriented. I needed only to get on with the task, and the task was well-defined.

I worked at Antioch from 1963 through 1969. Antioch College was always a lively place, and the added turmoil and excitement of those years were fully expressed on its campus. The civil rights movement, the emerging counterculture, antiwar activities, and the student movement in education were all literally parts of daily life. It was a time of great growth for me, stimulated especially by experiences in a civil rights group. I was somewhere between the faculty and student generations. Living and working at Antioch College in that period was an education, a wonderful time for me. But I was startled to find that I had the most trouble in the area I expected to be easiest, my professional development as a teacher.

My teaching did not go well. As the junior member of the Philosophy Department, fresh from graduate school, I was assigned to teach technical courses like symbolic logic. They were supposed to be important, but nobody wanted to teach them. Their importance derived more from academic dogma than from reality. Even at Antioch a standard message of the curriculum was something like "Suffer through these courses in order to earn the right to take something more interesting." But it was not the nature of the curriculum that bothered me then. The focus of my problem was, at first, on basic skills.

Colleges and graduate schools operated then as now on the assumption, universally known to be false, that good teaching would automatically follow good scholarship. No preparation of young teachers, therefore, was necessary. I examined my work and found that part of my problem as a teacher was inexperience, the simple lack of many skills. I was disorganized and overwhelmed by the amount of material I had to teach. I did not lecture well, and despite my desperate desire to do so, I did not seem to be able to stimulate and lead an interesting discussion in class. I was not, unfortunately, one of those natural teachers, at home upon first entering a classroom, whose talent and charisma overcome the problems of inexperience. I soon realized that I was usually imitating my favorite professors. It was to be a while before I found my own voice and style as a teacher.

The trouble was reflected both in my relationships with students and in my experience in class. There was something missing in these classes, and it was not easy to accept the fact. As a student I had occasionally left a classroom with the feeling that something special had happened. I remembered a history professor who, on a certain day, had been eloquent and particularly clear about aspects of Greek culture. There had been an aesthetics class in which the students truly became engaged in a discussion of the significance of current avant-garde artists. And I recalled sitting in an elementary physics class, struck by the universal application of the laws of mechanics to the world around me. I remembered wondering, for the first time, about the nature of scientific knowledge. These special experiences had been rare, but their infrequency didn't affect the desire that I felt. I wanted the education that I offered to students to be real. I wanted to be doing more than going through the motions. Despite my various technical problems as a teacher, I felt it reasonable to expect that an occasional class would really be exciting, that things would soar. But I hardly ever felt the elation of genuine intellectual stimulation and the learning that follows it, and it was clear that the students in my classes didn't either. The classes were all duty, no joy. Even when things went well, the classes were flat. And Antioch was no different from other colleges: these things weren't easily discussed among faculty colleagues. Professors tell each other how well their classes are going, or they complain about the students, or they remain silent about teaching. The isolation didn't help. A young teacher with problems can be lonely, and even if there is someone to talk to, traditions and structures for getting help are absent. Professors are on their own.

At first I thought that most of my problems were practical and technical in nature, and I think I was correct to some extent. My deficiencies seemed as though they could be remedied by time and hard work. It was, in fact, a period in which I worked long hours. Students found me in my office even late at night, and I gave them individual help. These efforts partially neutralized my classroom shortcomings, and even in the latter area, both my students and I saw slow but real improvement. I was optimistic about learning the skills that I lacked, and I fully expected to become a good teacher with the passage of time. Despite improved skills, however, the classes didn't get much better. I understood the need for patience, but I also came to feel that there were deeper problems, problems that would be harder to solve and that somehow touched closer to the heart of good education.

I saw that I was having a problem with grading. I was committed to being fair and to maintaining high academic standards. These were basic parts of my job as both a teacher and scholar. I tried my best to help students, but at some point I knew that it was my responsibility to stop helping and to render a rigorous judgment on their performance. Or perhaps I accepted the standard professorial rhetoric that says one helps students *by* rendering such a judgment. Students seemed to appreciate my efforts to help, and none of them challenged the grading system. Partly because I wasn't a very good teacher, many students got low grades. We all worried.

My views on grading did not change suddenly, but I do remember one experience vividly, and perhaps it was important. One morning before I was to give an examination in my symbolic logic course, I walked into the college cafeteria. Groups of my students were eating breakfast together. I could see that some had been up all night studying. Others had gotten up early in order to do a little extra work to prepare for the exam. There were no unusual bad feelings between us, nothing I could see that was beyond the normal range of mutual likes and dislikes among individuals. People smiled and greeted me. There was a little bantering about exams and grades, some tension in the air. I knew most of the students were sincere, reasonably hardworking, willing to meet a teacher and a course at least halfway. Seeing these people before the exam was not particularly unpleasant, but there was something wrong. I knew how to prepare for and take examinations, just as these students did, and the scene I had just entered was very familiar. I also knew that it had little to do with learning symbolic logic. It was all about the game of testing, something that was quite different. I was also aware of the shift in my function with respect to these students. The time for helping was over, and the time for judging had come. This felt wrong and arbitrary. I had come to love the time I spent consulting with students, trying to assist them with the subject matter, trying to help. Why stop? And why judge? Some of their failures in mastering symbolic logic flowed directly from my failures as a teacher. Some of the students were bound to be penalized for my deficiencies. It didn't seem right.

I was troubled, and one ironic result was that I grew very sensitive to the small dishonesties of students who appeared to be trying to manipulate me in one way or another to get an advantage in the pursuit of grades. I have found these tricks to be almost pervasive. There are dozens of large and small moves that students make. Having recently been a good student, I knew the ropes and maintained vigilance. My pride was involved, for I was not eager to be played for a fool. I was determined to be fair but tough, and I was drawn ever deeper into the process of arranging for the proper assignment of grades. I fiddled with the grading systems in my courses, looking for an ingenious formula to do three quite different and important things: give all students the opportunity to do their best; eliminate the possibility of manipulation and of people getting unearned grades; and remain faithful to high standards. I never found the solution within this framework.

*

My slow progress and persistent problems as a teacher were bringing me closer to more basic questions of educational philosophy. At the same time these issues were being raised publicly and systematically on the Antioch campus. Soon after my return to the college, the planning started for a new program for freshmen. The structures of the program were to depart radically from conventional education, even from the conventions of innovative Antioch education. The First Year Program forced the institution to consider, in both conceptual and tangible terms, two central educational issues: the nature of the authority that is appropriate to the relationship between teachers and students, and the validity of the categories that shape the curriculum. I was fortunate to be present when these questions were being raised in a compelling fashion. It was also a moment in my own life when deeply felt goals and problems touched on these same matters. I was lucky too in the critical area of colleagues.

The chairman of the planners of the First Year Program was Keith McGary, a senior member of my own Philosophy Department. He was one of my former teachers, but I was not yet particularly close to him. Keith is an extraordinary person who, at a certain point in the midsixties, became the dominant influence in my intellectual and professional life, as well as my friend. Keith McGary is creative, original, and always surprising. A student of aesthetics, especially of the avant-garde, he approaches his life and work in a thoroughly experimental fashion. It was Keith who brought the artistic and educational uses of new media to the Antioch campus when they were just beginning to be glimpsed at only a few places around the country, where they were almost always overshadowed by the use of psychedelic drugs. It was Keith who, more than any of the art professors of that time at Antioch, inspired the college's exceptionally gifted group of art students to develop more fully the potential of their media and their ideas. It was Keith who saw, early in the game, that an educational system without computers had become outmoded, and who consistently opposed academia's bias against technology.

Keith's conversation is understated, paradoxical, strong, probing, provocative. His way of being a friend is to help when he is asked for help and always to be kind and empathic. My problems as a teacher sometimes caused me pain that I needed to share, and I could rely on Keith to understand and offer advice if it was appropriate. He could identify with my feelings even though these were often problems that he had not experienced.

Four or five years later, when we had become colleagues in the First Year Program and allies in the controversy that engulfed it, I sat with Keith on a bench on campus and told him that I felt the time had come for me to leave Antioch. Our informal division of labor within the program had delegated some of the work in faculty politics to me. I liked the discussions and explanations, the process of trying to build bridges to colleagues who disagreed, and I also liked some of the fighting. But as the battles about the program turned bitter and nasty, I saw myself becoming less effective. I began to leave meetings early, when previously I would have stayed to cast the deciding vote for our side or to help formulate a useful compromise. My anger was running too deep. The hostility produced by the controversy was unique in my experience, and I had no way of handling it well. It was becoming clear to me that the atmosphere of recrimination was hurting me more than I had previously realized and that I therefore had much less to learn and contribute by staying. Toward the end of the conversation I turned to look at Keith and found tears in his eyes for what had happened to me. It was not the only time in more than two decades as friends that I found my own feelings resonating sympathetically within Keith, and with great intensity and accuracy. Nor was it the only time that he understood my experience better than I, appreciating the uniqueness of opportunities we were losing. It was my first job, and I thought that the chance to change things in interesting ways would arise often. Keith knew that we were living through and losing something very special.

THE FIRST YEAR PROGRAM

At the beginning I had remained at the periphery of the planning of the new First Year Program. Youthful enthusiasm and serious conversation with Keith gradually drew me into the program, and by the time it started, I was deeply involved. The First Year Program attempted to make Antioch education more student centered and flexible. It seemed like the next step in the college's history of liberal experimentation. It was a period of innovation in education all over the country, and the First Year Program was a bold move, one that Antioch was especially qualified to attempt; it would keep the college in its accustomed position as a leader in experimental education.

The First Year Program eliminated semester-long courses for freshmen. They were replaced by a complex array of lectures, media presentations, short seminars, and independent study materials. Students were not locked into a fixed schedule or curriculum. The program's goal was to arrange learning resources, to the extent possible, in a randomly accessible fashion. Students could then use them to create their own programs, whose principles would be derived from an examination of their needs and goals. It was also possible for students to formulate a personal program of learning that drew little or not at all on scheduled and faculty-sponsored events. They would need to find their own resources in the library and elsewhere, and get help from individual faculty members willing to work with students in an independent study format.

The First Year Program also attempted to coordinate academic and cooperative job experiences more closely and to narrow the gap between the college's regular faculty and the staff that administered the co-op program. The goal was to make the latter group of faculty first-class citizens, despite the academic faculty's long-standing tradition of condescension. Many professors regarded the students' job experiences as interludes in their real educations. The new program tried to recognize the importance of co-op jobs and to exploit their potential further.

The most significant development for me was that a new faculty role, that of preceptor, was created to help students think about and make their educational choices. The preceptor would be both a teacher and adviser. The role arose from the new program's emphasis on personal definitions of the educational task. The student and preceptor would create an individualized freshman program for the student, a plan that could be revised and whose success would be constantly evaluated, formally and informally, as the year passed.

A preceptor worked with a group of students that lived together in a dormitory. The group had meetings and was expected to work on projects with academic content. Most preceptors announced the projects at the beginning of the year, and students chose preceptoral groups accordingly, but some simply said that the group would decide together about projects. The preceptoral group was, among other things, intended to provide students with the kinds of shared experiences that were no longer to be routinely provided in courses, but the sharing was to be more intimate and informal. Since the students lived together, this was also an attempt to use the normal social bonds within such a group to strengthen the educational program.

Grades were eliminated in the First Year Program in favor of written evaluations, discursive descriptions of the student's learning. On the premise that the student and preceptor knew most about the learning that was being sought, the two of them were given joint final control over the evaluation of the year's work. When a student worked with other faculty members, those professors submitted written evaluations, but the preceptor and the student made the ultimate decisions about what was to be included in the year's final evaluations. All students were guaranteed a minimum number of credits for the successful completion of the freshman year. The distribution of those credits among the degree requirements, along with the formulation of the written evaluations, was in the hands of the preceptor and student. In retrospect the program's structures for the evaluation of learning, in which power moved from course instructors to preceptors and students, was the critical change. It was sufficient to create an intramural controversy that did great damage to the institution and to many of the participants.

I worked in each of the program's major aspects. I taught philosophy by offering presentations and seminars, and I was a preceptor for several groups of freshmen. It was as a preceptor that I first began to experience the rewards of the career in which I had invested so much.

I spent a great deal of time with my preceptoral students, in both group meetings and individual conversations. The students were busy, animated, and productive. They had slumps, and they also had difficulty in defining projects. It was hard to adjust to a new system that didn't automatically provide a schedule for one's day. But they were serious about their education, for the most part, and they seemed to have most of the motivation and ability needed to overcome the problems of working on their own. More basically they appeared to be making progress in the direction of acquiring the skills of autonomous learners. This goal, always an implicit part of the Antioch approach, was now being addressed and realized more fully than ever before.

There was satisfaction for me in being a preceptor. I could see that I was helping the students and that our exchanges were often significant to both of us. My lack of conventional teaching skills was only a minor impediment in the process of bringing to preceptoral students whatever I had to offer in the realm of intellectual stimulation and problem solving. My interest in them and concern for their progress could be directly and productively expressed in the preceptoral relationship. Fifteen years later I can remember conversations with almost every one of the several dozen students for whom I was preceptor. I talked with them about their families, communities back home, and sometimes about their personal lives. I came to know what made them happy and what the sources of pain were in their lives. I knew about their goals or their search for goals or their inclination to live without goals. As a teacher/adviser I felt that the First Year Program's structures encouraged me to deal with whole people, not that segment of a person that happened to relate to my academic discipline. I also felt I could be myself. I could do my work naturally, without having to try to force myself into a professional role that was not right for me. The students and I could explicitly bring large portions of our histories —values, ambitions, fears, problems—to the educational exchange. No course syllabus filtered out parts of our lives, if those parts were implicated in the search for learning. My interactions with preceptoral students remain vivid memories, while my classes of that era are almost totally forgotten. I remember things that I learned from the preceptoral students and things that I thought I saw them learn from me. Best of all I found what had been missing in my work in the regular routine of teaching courses: a closeness that was not marred by the tension derived from grading, and an occasional, sometimes more than occasional, sense of genuine intellectual excitement.

Teaching philosophy in the seminars and presentations of the First Year Program was, however, a disaster for me. In contrast to my previous problems in teaching conventional classes, this time I was in plenty of good company. My experience was similar to that of most other professors offering their disciplinary subject matters in the program. A typical format was for a teacher to begin with a couple of lectures or media presentations, widely publicized on campus, intended to introduce an academic area to a large group of students. In the absence of freshman course requirements, these presentations were the main opportunities for a teacher or department to attract freshmen to further offerings in the field, especially to the seminars that usually followed. Professors would prepare their best, most dramatic introductions to their topics, hoping that the students would be influenced to include these areas in their educational plans.

The main problem was the students. Sometimes only a few of them would come to an initial presentation, and then even fewer would attend the seminars intended to probe the topic in greater depth. Students who attended the seminars might well disappear after a few meetings. When present they would not endear themselves to the professors, for they had often failed to read the assigned material. Sometimes they would resist the format and syllabus established for the seminar. In general, students in the presentations and seminars, the main arenas for contact between students and professors who were not preceptors, seemed bored, turned off, and mildly insubordinate. The orderly conduct of education appeared to be breaking down. Respect, not to mention affection, between student and teacher seemed to be vanishing rapidly.

The faculty was demoralized and stunned. Many of them had been teaching the same materials in courses for years and had been meeting with apparent success. These were the same people who were responsible for Antioch's reputation as a college at which excellent teaching in a liberal style was the norm. Now they were being placed in a position of having to try to sell themselves and their disciplines to freshmen, and finding themselves rejected. It was a humiliating experience.

Most members of the Antioch faculty experienced some measure of this pain of rejection by students in the First Year Program. Conversation in the faculty lounge was full of angry stories of professors who had spent weeks preparing a lecture or seminar that had been attended by only a handful of sulky, uninterested students. As the stories were repeated, of course, the preparation of the teachers became more extensive and the behavior of the students more outrageous. Ingrates.

A large faction of the faculty turned on the students and the preceptors, the group of their faculty colleagues most closely identified with the new program. They came to believe that the preceptors were influencing the students against them. They thought they saw the students being used as pawns by educationally radical faculty, the preceptors, who intended to gain control of the institution and reorganize things so that conventional teachers would be obsolete. It didn't help that one or two of the preceptors, most notably Keith McGary, were offering media presentations to packed houses. In fact, however, the preceptors were generally embarrassed by the failures of the presentations and seminars. We saw our program endangered by growing faculty resentment, and we tried to encourage students to attend.

During the controversy over the First Year Program, I had lunch one day with George Geiger, the chairman of the Philosophy Department, my colleague and former teacher. He was a highly respected member of the faculty and an opponent of the program. There were long-standing tensions between George and Keith, and I had been trying not to get in the middle, to stay on good terms with both older colleagues. The connections between George and me were significant. I had been one of his most successful students, attended graduate school at Columbia University as he had done, and had continued in the same general philosophical tradition. I was one of a small number of his former students who had gone on to teach philosophy, and the only one to return to teach at Antioch. As we talked at lunch, George said gravely that if the First Year Program was allowed to continue, its supporters, Keith and I and others like us, would move on to the creation of a Second Year Program and then a Third Year Program, and we'd soon be in control of the college. He and his allies were fighting for their survival. I gasped slightly at the power attributed to us by this fearful fantasy, and then I reasoned and laughed and cajoled. I told George that he must know he was exaggerating, that there was no such plot, and that we felt weak and vulnerable in the midst of the task of simply keeping the new program functioning. He didn't believe me, and he didn't crack a smile. Despite our past association, which had involved, I believe, a considerable psychological investment that he had made in me, George could no longer find it in himself to trust me. His implicit response to my attempts to reassure him was that I was a traitor and a liar.

One does not, of course, innovate without a certain amount of zeal, without being persuaded that new ways are sufficiently better to warrant the trouble of changing the system. The people involved in the First Year Program were enthusiastic. Nor does one innovate without bringing along substantive ideas. The interests of the faculty in the new program, influenced by McGary, reflected a fascination with McLuhan, technology, and youth culture, just as other professors organized thought by reference to concepts of the history of ideas or the principles of the "new" criticism. Other faculty members, many of whom had bad experiences giving presentations or seminars in the program, perceived us as arrogant. They didn't believe our protestations that we wished to preserve a full range of faculty styles and interests. We were, in fact, desperately looking for opportunities to involve other faculty in ways that would respect their identities as teachers and thinkers while still giving students the freedom to choose, a freedom that was basic to the program. And there were dozens of subtle ways, which I see more easily now in retrospect, that we preceptors tried to influence students to be a bit more conservative and conventional to please our colleagues. But early in the program's history it was too late; the battle was joined.

The conflict was seen not only as one for control of a small college. It was Bach versus the Beatles, Aristotle versus Stokely Carmichael. Many professors came to see the First Year Program as a battleground in a monumental cultural confrontation. The program was, to them, an expression of irrational political activism, drug culture, the rejection of the wisdom of generations by youth and its mindless followers. Faculty who, in my view, were actually defending themselves against the pain caused by freshmen who did not come to their lectures, decided that they were engaged instead in defending Western civilization against a barbarous new decadence. It did not seem as amusing then as it does now.

There was indeed a kind of cultural confrontation taking place at Antioch during those years. Using Margaret Mead's analysis of the postwar generation gap, I will discuss, in a later section of this book, the fact that innovations like the First Year Program were an expression of and a response to a new cultural situation. But that more general level of description is not required for an immediate understanding of what was happening at Antioch. Although the dynamics of the students' behavior were rather simple, it was hard to see them clearly because of Antioch's tradition of innovation and its unmatched past mastery of the art of producing the appearance of student freedom. When genuine student freedom and its consequences appeared on the scene, it was easier to think that civilization was crumbling than to disbelieve some of the local myths with which we had lived and flattered ourselves for some time.

As a preceptor I saw that the students were not intending to reject intellectual tradition and that, in fact, what they were doing was less grand. They were not trying to be provocative, inflict pain on their professors, or join other professors in a power struggle in the college. They were doing something rather natural. Suddenly free from the coercion of grades and course requirements, the students simply chose not to do what their professors wanted them to do. Large portions of the curriculum were boring or apparently useless. Assignments often seemed arbitrary. Teachers were sometimes inept or worse. In fact there were many large and small reasons for the students' response. Perhaps some were new and associated with the trends and fads of the 1960s. But most were not. The central fact was a single new condition that allowed a variety of other factors and perceptions to govern the behavior of students: a dramatic decrease in the power of professors to impose their judgments and wishes upon students. Students could and did take a walk. Professors had lost the power to punish absentees.

Antioch's tradition argued against this interpretation of events. Like elementary school students in open classrooms with "activity centers," Antioch students in conventional courses had always had many choices to make among a variety of options and activities and projects. Antioch education had indeed taken into account the students' wide variety of interests and styles. With all those choices to make, with all the arrangements made for the solution of the problems of individuals, it seemed as if there was plenty of educational freedom. And there was some, certainly a good bit more than was to be found at most colleges. In the end, however, a student who didn't perform well within one of the teacher-approved options was given a low grade, like all the schoolchildren who "can't handle open education." The options within a course were useful and enjoyable, but the grade was, as they say now, the bottom line. That was the universally accepted rule of the game. But the game as played at Antioch had special variations that were confusing. Many teachers would bend over backward to give students a chance to do better. And when a final grade was given, it was in the spirit of "This hurts me more than it does you." Students and professors even came to believe it.

The implications of student behavior in the First Year Program were disturbing to Antioch's collective self-image, but they were devastating in the lives of individual professors. The identities of many Antioch faculty members included, as a prominent element, the idea that they were excellent teachers. They got along well with students, and they taught courses that were innovative in structure and content. They were decent, effective, kind, and, understanding, perhaps even a little attractive and sexy. The friendly and collaborative behavior of students had always seemed to confirm this view. Suddenly the students acted differently, and all of this was challenged. It now appeared that students might have been acting out of fear and coercion all along, although these had been ingeniously disguised by liberal trappings. Instead of being pedagogical geniuses, Antioch professors might well have been authoritarian teachers after all, though perhaps they smiled more than most.

The whole thing surprised the planners of the First Year Program as much as it did everyone else. Given new freedom, the students had been expected to continue to learn the standard subject matters in partnership with the faculty, but with added creativity and intimacy. In preparation for the program, for example, I prepared independent study materials in symbolic logic. I also brought together the latest programmed texts in many fields. These were not acts intended to ovethrow the standard curriculum. There would, of course, be some additional room for the exploration of new fields, but this too was consistent with the Antioch tradition, and there was no new or radical intention to reject the standard curriculum or the principle of stu- dent-faculty collaboration. The idea had been to continue in the Antioch tradition, not to expose it as fraudulent. Those of us who were the innovators were as indebted to the special environment at Antioch as the others, perhaps more so.

I was, perhaps, a little less shaken than many faculty members. Although my First Year Program presentations and seminars did not go well, I already had my problems as a teacher, and I did not have decades invested in appar- ently successful teaching at Antioch. I also got considerable satisfaction from being a preceptor and from being a part of the program's faculty, especially in that it drew me closer to Keith McGary. I could not, however, escape the questions raised by the First Year Program with respect to my teaching of conventional upper-level philosophy courses.

I was coming to doubt my central assumption that either students wanted to learn philosophy or that I could persuade them that they should want to learn it. Students signed up for my courses, as they did for many courses, with basic misconceptions about the subject matter. Like many professors I began with a definition of the subdiscipline with particular stress on how it differed from the popular notions of the subject with which many students entered the class. ("Let me begin by telling you what ethics is not.") I dutifully presented the current graduate school definition of the area. I also offered an elaborate set of reasons for the utility and beauty of what I was forcing on the students. I've rarely met a professor who didn't have a similarly intricate construction and wasn't pleased to rehearse it with minimal provocation, especially at parties and other places where one is supposed to be having fun. But it was becoming clear to me that these rationales didn't persuade the students, partly because they didn't listen. There was little reason for them to follow the argument. Whether or not they were convinced, they knew that I intended to enforce the concept that I strained to justify. They complied with my syllabus because I would grade them at the end of the course. No wonder there was tension between us. No wonder things in class were never as good as they were supposed to be, even when we were all at our best. I was coercing them, and they were responding the way coerced people do: grudgingly, with ulterior motives, trying to make the best out of an undesirable situation. Many of my faculty colleagues pretended that this was not happening in their classes, but I had been their student only recently, and I knew better.

My specialty course was in the philosophy of science, the area in which I was writing a doctoral dissertation. The course had recently been added to the Antioch curriculum. In graduate school I had learned to deal with questions like the nature and variety of scientific explanations, the structure of theories, the existence of theoretical entities like electrons, the differences and connections between science and mathematics, and the status of laws of nature. I genuinely found these issues important and interesting, and I still do. Students entering the class often had other things in mind: the maverick theories of Velikovsky, the ideas of technological and scientific visionaries like Buckminster Fuller and Gregory Bateson, the moral issues confronting scientists, science in non-Western cultures, the relationship between science and the arts, the nature of scientific creativity. When students raised these questions with me, I gave standard answers, but I was beginning to believe them less. One answer was that some of their interests did not really belong in the realm of philosophy of science but fell, rather, within the domain of psychology or ethics or anthropology. I knew, however, that the courses in those fields wouldn't deal with their interests either. The students had an uncanny knack for being interested in things that fell between the disciplines or somehow beyond the scope of current academic inquiry. Another major answer was that in order to deal with their interests they would first have to get necessary background knowledge in the philosophy of science. "First you have to learn what science is." The more I gave this answer, the more I felt as though I were making a promise that wouldn't be kept. It was dogma. The exploration of a subject matter did not have to begin where I and my graduate professors said that it did. It could begin almost anyplace, and I knew this from my own experience in trying to learn about subjects in which I had no formal training.

The students' interests seemed valid and challenging, even though they did not fit my training or the standard definition of my subject matter. I knew that in some cases they would not get clear answers, but I also knew that academia selected questions for which clear answers were usually available, and that value and importance were sometimes sacrificed in the bargain. My arguments sounded increasingly hollow. Even when my replies did not sound weak or contrived, it occurred to me that the students probably should have the chance to make their own mistakes, to pursue dead ends, if that is what they were, and thus learn something about the process of inquiry. And they might surprise me. Their studies might be productive, even if they were initiated and governed by criteria different from those of my academic discipline. I tried to read widely and think in new ways and learn about new fields. I was proud of my breadth in these matters. My view of a good intellectual life was to be aware of issues in many areas without giving undue respect to the artificial boundary lines between fields. Yet I was discouraging my students from the same sort of intellectual exploration; indeed I was using my power to make it harder for them to live up to the ideals I aspired to.

It was my adherence to the standard behaviors of a professor of philosophy that helped to keep my students from straying, not my own best judgments about the life of the mind. The categories of my discipline and the expectations of my colleagues and teachers defined my job, and my students' work, to be duller than they had to be. I looked around at other faculty members, and I became aware of one of the most astonishing facts of academic life. Professors were offering dull pedantic courses that were far less interesting and lively than their personal intellectual lives as reflected in their conversations outside class. Our role as disciplinary professionals was hurting us. In the classroom we were imposing artificial limits on ourselves, and we were using our power to do the same thing to the students.

I was turning away from coercion for other reasons. It produced learning, but there had to be considerable truth to the cliché that a great deal was forgotten immediately after the exam. More importantly I was coming to feel that the central educational task was to learn how to learn freely, without being forced. I was just completing my schooling with the submission of my Ph.D. dissertation. I was acutely aware of the skills I had not learned under the academic, social, and economic pressures that act on graduate students. I was far from being the self-starting and self-disciplined learner that I wanted to be. It seemed to me that a coercive system could never teach these things. I wanted to be an educator who helped people acquire the skills needed to live the type of free ranging, adventurous intellectual life that was inconsistent with being governed by the wishes of others.

I believed that my relationships with students in my classes, indeed the whole educational venture in those classes, was being distorted by my power to grade. I therefore decided to stop grading in my classes. The institutional system was based on grades, and I realized that any arrangement that displaced them from their central role would be awkward and full of problems. I'd accept and try to solve the problems. I decided to have the students grade themselves. I would act as a conduit, passing the grades on to the registrar, formally maintaining the fiction that they came from me, although my new practice was no secret. Students might exploit the arrangement to give themselves unearned grades, or they might judge themselves with unnecessary harshness. Inequities would certainly develop in the competition among students. Believing that my highest loyalty was to the process of teaching, which was damaged by devoting time and energy to grading, not to mention by the subtler distortions in my relationships with students, I decided to ignore the inequities and focus on ways to help and stimulate students. As I have lived with that decision for almost twenty years, it has become increasingly clear to me that the concepts of fairness and equity, as they are applied to student performance rather than to ideas, have nothing to do with learning, even though faculty and students are virtually obsessed with them. Their introduction into an educational setting is inevitably distracting and harmful.

It would also be necessary for me to accept the fact that my graduate school definition of subject matters would have to compete freely in an open market with other definitions and interests. If I could not offer much help in an area because I did not have the necessary expertise, the student would have to work with less help. Teachers are normally constrained from letting students stray into foreign fields by the necessity of grading. How can a teacher, unqualified in a field, grade a student's work in it? The limitation vanishes when one abandons grading. I presented my views of the subject matter in class, and I was truly delighted when a student accepted and pursued them. But I would not punish students who rejected my orientation to a subject matter.

I had spent three or four years as a teacher before I stopped grading and forcing subject matters on my students. The day I walked into a classroom and abdicated my coercive power, however, felt like the beginning of a new career, one that was much closer to the ambitions and fantasies that I had been nurturing about teaching. The air cleared; communication between me and my students was better and more direct, not marred by petty dishonesties and suspicion. It felt to me as if the students and I were now on the same side, where we were supposed to be, no longer opponents. There was a sense of excitement, enjoyment, and shared intellectual pursuit in my classes. My decision on grading allowed me to be truly respectful of the students' interests, or rather to act on the respect I'd always felt. Just as they no longer felt obliged to manipulate me for better grades, I stopped feeling pressure to manipulate them away from their interests and toward mine.

I put my energy into teaching, not into being fair or preparing people for exams. Although I continued to work hard, there was a new sense of relaxation in my work and a better focus too. My shortcomings as a teacher seemed to be less damaging, and in fact I began to improve more rapidly. I still had a great deal to learn as a classroom teacher, just as I did as an educator functioning in a role like the preceptor's. But now I felt that everything would be all right, that I would indeed be able to make substantial progress toward fulfilling my potential as a teacher.

My colleagues, who called me and other easy graders or nongraders "short circuits," and some students were outraged. Students in my classes would give themselves good grades and do no work, they said, while students in other courses struggled to earn lower grades. This did happen, of course, though not on the scale my colleagues expected. That I could admit this was final proof to them of my perversity. But I had simply rejected the implicit economic model of education in which grades are money and the teacher's job is to see that people earn their living rather than steal.

Professors told me that I was abandoning my basic responsibility to uphold academic standards, or that I was desperately seeking popularity. Others said that I was passing my problem with grading on to students who were even less able to deal with it than I. My subtlest colleagues formulated tortured arguments to the effect that since I criticized and evaluated anyway, the new situation was identical to the old one in which grades were given, as if the infliction of harm mattered not at all. But I was already quite popular with students, and grading wasn't simply a personal problem that I was avoiding, it was a factor that affected an entire educational setting. I was not abandoning academic standards. If anything, paradoxically, I felt new freedom to assert standards, for I could do so without worrying about whether I was being fair.

I believed that I had one professional obligation that was prior to all others: to be the best teacher I could be for the students who wanted to learn from me. Grading and coerced allegiance to an academic discipline were barriers to achieving my goal. As a teacher I saw that I would have to subvert conventional academic structures while I worked within them. And I decided that if the opportunity arose, I would try to create new educational structures, as we had in the First Year Program, that did not have to be subverted in order to encourage learning.

6

Standard Conversation: You're Not Interested in Anything

And if a blight kill not a tree but it still bear fruit, let none say that the fruit was in consequence of the blight.

—William Blake

STUDENT. I thought I'd check with you before I handed in my registration materials.

ADVISER. Good. Do you know what courses you'd like to take?

STUDENT. Yes. I'd like to take psychology, philosophy, and political science. My friends and I love to sit around for hours talking about life and politics and what makes people do the things they do. So I thought those courses would be very interesting.

ADVISER. Yes, I think you might enjoy them. But you should be aware of the fact that our philosophy courses tend to focus on the way language is used. The political science and psychology courses place a heavy emphasis on research methodology and the results of empirical studies. They're quite scientific, and are probably different from the conversations you have with your friends. Before you sign up for courses, therefore, it might be best to go over to the library and look at the syllabi or go to the bookstore and look at the texts. It's important to know what to expect.

7

A Talk to New Students in a New Program: on the Best Uses of the IDP

THE SCENE. Buffalo State College in September, 1973, about ten years after the start of the First Year Program at Antioch. I am director of a new program, the Individualized Degree Program. I have been deeply involved in the planning and implementation of the program. The IDP consists almost entirely of independent projects pursued by students with the help of faculty. There are no courses or grades. It is a few weeks into the first semester. There are about eighty-five students. I am the speaker at our Weekly Academic Program.

It would be hard to overstate your importance to those of us who have worked on the Individualized Degree Program for the last two years. We have wondered, talked, and argued about you endlessly. We've tried to predict your goals, interests, feelings, and reactions. At last you're here, real people, not figments of our imaginations or constructs in our educational theories. We can finally get down to the business of talking and working with you. Just as coming to college may be a landmark experience in your lives, having you here is a landmark for me, the other faculty, and the students who have worked on the IDP. I doubt that there will ever be a program that we will be more committed to than the IDP or a group of students that means more to us than you do. I tell you this simply because it's true. I am not trying to add to your burden. I don't intend to launch into a sermon about the awesome responsibility that you bear because of our expectations. But you are special and important to us, and I want you to know it.

In spite of our excitement over your arrival, I know that we have already done some things that have been frustrating to you. During our orientation program and now during the first few weeks of the semester, we have failed to answer many of your questions. We have often turned your questions back to you without answers. We've been afraid that you might rely upon our answers too heavily. We want you to use the IDP's freedom to create your own education. We fear that you are in the habit of doing what you are told, for that is the main way most people have learned to survive in formal education. Put your name in the upper left-hand corner; write an introductory paragraph with four or five sentences; be sure that each subsequent paragraph presents a new thought; offer your conclusions only in the final paragraph; do not write in the first person; etc. This is the background of our unwillingness to answer some of your questions. If we have gone overboard, indulged ourselves in a bit of no-answer theater, I hope you will forgive our zeal in trying to act on one of our basic beliefs and in trying to make a point.

I've talked with most of you, and I think that someplace in the back of your minds you still don't fully believe the IDP or us. You're looking for the hooker. You think there might be two secret messages. The first is what we really want you to do; the second is what we'll do to you if you don't do it. Your expectations are reasonable, based upon a good deal of the education you've experienced. But the IDP has been created to try to make things different. The whole point is autonomy, for you to be in control. Our hope is to participate in education that is created by the student. You understand that intellectually, but it may be a while, for some of you, before old habits and expectations change. You are right to be suspicious. Teachers and administrators have lied to you before, especially on this very matter of freedom. But we are serious about it.

Now that the basic point has been repeated, there is no reason for me to hold back. Encouraging you to use your freedom doesn't imply withholding my thoughts from you. I hope you'll use the program in the way that is most productive for you. But I have ideas about how the IDP might be used. Here are my ideas; perhaps they will help you.

My thinking about education these days is very much influenced by life with my two children, little boys of two and four years old. The nature of learning is being clarified and made infinitely more vivid for me by these kids. First and foremost I see that learning is a joyous process. A giggle and a grin accompany each small achievement. Taking a step, saying a word, doing a new thing with a toy, and all the rest are fun. "Fun" is too weak a word. It is bliss. This does not mean that learning is easy. My children have sometimes screamed or wept with frustration at falling when they tried to walk or at not being understood when they tried to speak. They often choose things to learn that are difficult. *They choose for importance, not for ease.* Getting around better, manipulating a toy, communicating, these are all critically important in their lives, even though they can be hard. And perhaps the intensity of the joy of learning is connected with the difficulty of the tasks they attempt.

My children's learning seems to be almost entirely a result of their natural playfulness. Playing appears to consist of learning and having fun at the same time. They play virtually the whole time they are not sleeping or eating. That is why, I believe, children learn so much during their early years. When you stop to think about it, the amount of learning that occurs during those years is astonishing; imagine if we could keep it up, or even come a bit closer to maintaining in later years that rate of increasing competence and knowledge!

Somewhere along the line educators try to separate learning and playing. A lot of it happens between kindergarten and first grade. Learning, or work, belongs in the classroom, they say, and play takes place during recess. It is at that point that formal education has failed. Play *is* learning, and when we let its childish quality put us off, we make the biggest educational mistake of all. Of course teachers can never succeed in separating playing and learning for most of us, but they can transform schooling into something that is serious, solemn, and thus much less productive. Watch yourself and other people at play. Full energy is freely devoted to the activity. You don't want to stop. You push to your limits. Observe the typical classroom. People participate with a small fraction of themselves. They want to stop as soon as possible. Isn't it clear which type of activity will produce more learning?

The very best use of the IDP would be for each of you to turn back the clock to the time before playing and learning were supposed to be separate activities. If we recover the joy of learning, all else will follow. Learning will engage you more fully, and you will devote your energy to it more freely. You will work closer to your potential, as your parents and teachers have been urging you to do for all these years. A personal appreciation of your growth will be your reward, along with increasing competence, instead of a grade given to you by someone, a grade which you may or may not deserve. You will also, I think, be happier.

This makes me think of one of my new friends, Wendel Wickland, a member of our core faculty. Some of you are involved in a group project with Wendel down at college camp. Watch Wendel. He is intense, he works hard, and he has the time of his life. He loves those plants and bugs and animals. One of the great parts of the IDP for me has been to spend some time with him, after we have had a long meeting, walking in the woods or park. He tells me the names and characteristics of the trees and flowers. I forget most of them. But I try, and each time I remember a few more. I'm learning some botany. My learning is inseparable from the serenity I feel in the stillness of the woods, my enjoyment of the beauty of the plants and flowers, my awe at the evolved complexity of living things and their relationships, and the fun I derive from having a new friend and listening to him tell me about what he knows and how he came to know it. I am a city person, and the things that I can learn from Wendel come slowly to me. Yet I am learning because there is joy in the process. When I was in college, botany courses were incredibly dull. The professors made sure that all the joy was kept out of the classroom. Only the hard work remained. Now that I've discovered the rewards and can place the hard work in a context of adult play, I don't mind the difficulty at all. I know that I will continue to learn in this area.

Wendel is a very rare teacher. Even in the conventional classroom he is aware of and nurtures the connection between playing and learning. We are not usually lucky enough to find teachers like him, either outside or inside classrooms. The task thus becomes much harder. Many of our teachers are uncomfortable in the presence of joy; it makes them nervous. They think there is something unprofessional about the feeling. A laugh or a smile, they think, diminishes the dignity of their subjects or themselves. In the IDP we can stay out of their classrooms. We can try to relate to them in other ways, or we can do without them, trying to find the wisdom within ourselves to reunite play and learning. But it will not be easy. Most of our training has prepared us to be grim. We too will get nervous.

How does one do this after years of conventional schooling? Part of the process is to look within oneself. What are the different ways that you like to play? Where do you find your real enjoyment and challenge and excitement? Where does your energy naturally flow? These are key questions. The answers provide important clues to how you can structure your own education. Unfortunately you may answer these questions differently from the way your parents and teachers (and even yourself, in your more somber moods) would like you to. Even worse, you may have been listening to their answers for so long that you can't hear your own or don't recognize them or take them seriously. Formal education has a way of alienating people from themselves. You come to believe that you really enjoy certain things because you're supposed to enjoy them or because you got good grades in them once. You learn to reject things because your elders don't approve of them, no matter how much you really like them. You become separated from your own tastes and preferences.

Answering questions about who one really is and where one's playfulness lies may be a long and complex process because we are out of practice. It involves exploring the world as well as looking within oneself. You are on your own from the beginning. There are no external guidelines about where one starts exploring the world in order to find the important things. You probably have to begin with temporary answers to questions about your own nature, and these answers may change as you learn more about the world you live in. You may, for a while, be functioning on the basis of a view of yourself and the world that is very tentative, perhaps only dimly perceived. Self-knowledge and knowledge of the world will gradually lead to firmer answers. You will gain confidence. It may happen slowly. It requires patience and guts, the guts to wait and believe, and all the while to act on partial answers.

I hope you will be determined. It is easy to be intimidated by teachers and friends who tell you that if something is fun, then it can't produce learning. You will be besieged by people who think they know exactly what you should do. They will be glad to relieve you of responsibility for your own education. Do not be discouraged by your uncertainty. It is more genuine than their knowledge of what is best for you. Do not be discouraged by the time it takes to get significant new knowledge. If you settle for less, for the process of keeping busy with unimportant activities, you will simply be postponing, per-haps for many years, the time when you must confront yourself and the real questions of who you are and what you want to do. There are some people, of course, who never get to those questions, but I don't think they are the most productive or happiest among us.

Do not be influenced by me and the core faculty when we lose our nerve and become too eager to show the world that the IDP is producing concrete results. We are deeply committed to the success of our program, and we are sensitive to its critics. We will get nervous and be tempted to push you. Do not help us to commit the offenses we are trying to abolish.

The stakes are high. If you avoid the pitfalls, you may regain that state, trained out of you by much of your previous education, in which playing and learning are united again. You will derive joy from doing the most difficult things. You will be able to tap resources of energy and creativity that will astonish you.

This leads me to a closely related point: learning occurs in the course of real experience, all kinds of experience. It is not limited to a separate compartment of life, isolated and detached from everything else and labeled "education." We spend our time relating to other people, working, creating, playing, being political, worshipping, wondering, reading, imagining, and so on. In the course of all these activities, we learn most of the things that are important to us. Sometimes, in the midst of these experiences, the learning dimension becomes heightened; at other times it is negligible. The secret is to notice those moments of intensified learning, take a cue from them, and pursue them.

Formal education is usually thought of as a group of special experiences like going to lectures, participating in seminars, and working in laboratories and studios. These experiences are certainly intended to produce learning. But when we think of education as consisting solely of such activities, we forget about the learning that arises in most other parts of life. We can, however, approach formal education in another spirit. It can be seen both as an opportunity to learn from these specifically academic experiences as well as the opportunity to organize much more of our lives around the goal of increased learning. We can examine the various aspects of our lives more closely. We can reorganize the productive parts to make them even better. We can coordinate them in enriching ways. We can strengthen certain types of experience, possibly by adding new resources like teachers and books. We may add experiences with a particularly academic flavor, such as new reading and writing, but we may also find that our learning will be enhanced by adding or expanding experiences with other emphases, like political or volunteer work. As a college student you have unusual amounts of time and resources available to increase the learning that takes place in your whole life. The point is not only to participate in a new set of activities that begins when you step on to campus and that you leave behind when you complete your last homework assignment. The point is also to control and organize your life so that you learn more. The IDP allows and encourages this approach to education. Your learning contracts may include many different kinds of activities in addition to academic ones. Your task is to design a package of experiences to achieve as much learning as possible.

There are some rather dramatic implications of all this. Since learning begins with your experience, you must respect yourself. You must also respect your culture: the music you listen to and create; the poetry; the books you enjoy, including comic books, mysteries, science fiction, fantasy, and romances; the sports and other games you play; your dancing; your politics; your slang; your humor; your hobbies; your heroes and heroines; your television programs; your magazines; your movies; all of it. Most of it has been criticized by your teachers. College professors will continue the shameful tradition. They'll call it junk and trash, and they will ridicule it and by implication you. They will mock you and make you feel inferior. They will attack you with sneers and brows raised high. In a few years, of course, they will study the objects of your interests as folk art or popular culture. But that is not really what matters. It is imperative to respect what you love and who you are. It is all you have. You must not let anyone take your enjoyment and culture away from you. They are too precious. They contribute too heavily to your identity as a person. They are your starting points for further growth.

There are, of course, plenty of people on campus who want to teach you about new things. You will learn and enjoy many of these things, and perhaps you will even abandon some of your old enjoyments, or at least shift your attention to new areas. But for this to happen validly, you must come to new cultural elements in your own way, beginning with what is real to you. Otherwise you will be like some snob who listens to Bach but really loves country music. He ends up enjoying neither. He is a fool.

Insist on the integrity and value of your world. Do not let anyone put you down for the things you like. Be open to new experiences because you are secure in your appreciation of the old ones, not because you are afraid that someone will judge them to be unworthy. It is very unlikely that you can be helped by an educator who makes you feel bad about the things you know and love.

Work with your culture. Wallow in it. Push it further in order to see where it goes. This will make you more rather than less receptive to new things. This sort of approach will help you to put together an education within the freedom of the IDP.

The IDP gives you a related opportunity that is also very important. I think back to my own college education in the late 1950s. I see now that there were many exciting things happening in the world that were so new that they had not yet made their way into the college curriculum. The exciting classic period of molecular biology was beginning because the structure of DNA had just been worked out. The computer revolution was starting, and a few visionaries were realizing that almost nothing would remain untouched. Social scientists were doing interesting work focusing on group experiences as the loci for human growth and creative problem solving. It was also an extraordinary period in the history of American art, especially in my home city of New York. In later years I became intensely interested in all of these things, but I knew little or nothing about them during college. It takes a while for the curriculum to assimilate new developments. Now, fifteen or twenty years later, when all those things are history, there are courses dealing with them. There are, of course, new things happening today that will enter the formal curriculum only in a decade or two. People who are able to tune into these new things have wonderful opportunities for creative study and rewarding work. As IDP students you are less restricted by the standard curriculum than most students. You can keep your eyes and ears open for new things. You can study them. You can gamble heavily on your best judgment when most other students are not even allowed to place a bet. One can't know the future, so it is impossible to be sure that a particular new development will have lasting importance. In this matter, as in others, education in the IDP will be risky. Being autonomous is always a little risky, partly because the ultimate responsibility, along with the ultimate rewards, are yours. But even if you lose, you have won, because you will have learned from your efforts and taken your life into your own hands.

I'd like to say something about the social dimension of learning. Although the IDP emphasizes individual work, you are free to work with other people and to find ways of sharing your learning with others. This would be another important use of the IDP. It has already begun. We don't know how it will work out, but it is promising. A group of you is working on related science projects at college camp. Before you are through, I hope you'll work out some ways for the rest of us to go down there with you to learn from your work. Several IDP students plan to work at the art museum. I hope you'll take us over there some day and talk with us about the progress you've made. There is a poetry workshop being organized. Perhaps you'll present a poetry reading for the rest of us. Several people are working in the field of nutrition. You might look for ways to help the rest of us to understand the issues relevant to a healthy diet. There is a group working in and studying this year's local elections. Perhaps you'll offer an analysis of the results and a summary of your experiences at a Weekly Academic Program. The social aspect of learning can be very powerful. I suspect that if you looked back at your best educational experiences to date, you would find that many of them involved activities with groups of people. Some of you already have enough experience as teachers to know that one gains a much deeper knowledge of a subject when one tries to teach it. You need not, in the IDP, remain isolated. You may choose to work and interact with other people in such a way as to strengthen your learning and also enjoy yourself. Knowledge is also often useful. As you learn, you may put yourself in a position to help others as well as share with them. It makes sense to act on this fact.

Another important use of the IDP: structure your time to suit your personal needs and style. You are free to start projects at any time, and you may end them at any time. You are free to work on many things at one time, or you may work on a few. It is, however, hard to overestimate how accustomed we've become to academic calendars and to schedules of four or five courses, as if the year were really divided into semesters and knowledge is best acquired by following five course syllabi simultaneously. Already some IDP students have begun four or five contracts, each starting near the beginning of the semester and concluding at the end. It takes effort at first, not to duplicate the conventional structures without exploring the possible advantages of alternatives. I know that some of the faculty, including me, worry too much about whether you are doing enough work, and we encourage you, explicitly or implicitly, to mimic a conventional academic program. We are wrong to do this. It is important for all of us to shake loose from these habits, at least while we examine them to see if it would be better to do things in other ways. Structure your time and work so that you will be most productive. Structure them to exploit your own periods of enthusiasm and high energy. Arrange things so that you will be minimally hurt by your unproductive times. Do you work most effectively on one or two things intensively, or are you a juggler who works best when you have many things going at the same time? Create your program of work accordingly.

Don't be seduced by vacations. Life doesn't stop for Christmas, and neither does learning. Perhaps you'll need a vacation at another time. Take it then, when you need it, even though people aren't giving gifts. Work all night on New Year's Eve if things are going well. Be an opportunist. If there is a film festival or a political crisis or a guest speaker or symposium, drop every-thing for a while and do an intensive contract that will allow you to learn as much as possible from the unusual events or resources that have become available. If, like me, you occasionally become obsessed with the work of a particular author, let yourself go. Do a contract on his or her books. It's your time. Use it well.

I have some additional comments about avoiding practical problems that I think IDP students may face. Most of these remarks arise from experience I had with students in another free and innovative program about ten years ago at Antioch College. There are certain problems connected with indepen-dent work that seemed to arise over and over again.

The first suggestion is to try to figure out concrete ways to begin each project, ways that do not depend upon the cooperation of other people. There is nothing worse than sitting around with a good idea and not acting on it. Even if you intend to create a group project, it is critical to devise a starting activity that doesn't require the participation of others, either teachers or students. Professors may not show up for their office hours, or they may not have time for you on a particular day. Students may get involved elsewhere and not do what they said they would do. Unless you have some way to start without these other people, their failures in the matter, or the discrepancies between your priorities and theirs, will turn into major problems for you. After a week or two a dormant good idea will begin to seem a bit tedious. You will get demoralized. Your energy will be drained by annoyance and frustration. Even if your initial work turns out to be somehow wrong or unproductive, you will at least have learned something about getting started. It is better to be active and to learn a little than to be passive and to learn nothing. There may be no intellectual skill more important than the ability to move from a good idea to its implementation. Practice whenever you get the chance. Don't depend for your success in this area upon other people.

Another piece of advice concerns faculty: you need them. Neither Buffalo State nor any other accredited college is ready to allow you to progress toward a degree without being in some sort of close relationship with faculty mem-bers. Professors are not always wise and perfect (I know this will shock you!), but they are indispensable. This is sometimes too bad, but it's true. You can't do learning contracts in the IDP without minimal faculty cooperation. They will work with you if they wish to. You have no strong claim on their time.

You will be more successful in gaining their cooperation if you do several things. Be as clear as you can about what you want to do and what you want from them. If possible, be willing to make some changes in order to respond to the wishes of faculty members, but don't abandon the basic idea of a project or its personal meaning to you. Try to figure out what the individual instructor might be able to get out of working with you. One teacher might want assistance on a research project. Another might want to explore a new field, and your project might be the occasion to do so. Yet another might get a lot of satisfaction out of regularly tutoring an enthusiastic student, while another professor might be willing to sponsor a project only if committed to occasional consultation on very big problems, not on details. In a way it might be ideal if each faculty member were totally flexible and dedicated primarily to meeting your needs. You would only need to ask, and they would deliver their services. But it is not like that. They have their own needs, time pressures, and sources of satisfaction. To gain their cooperation, you must figure out how their work with you will help them get something they want, even if it is something as simple as the satisfaction of working with a good student. In the end this will make life harder for you, but possibly more interesting and profitable. In any case, whether it is better or not, it is necessary. I don't mean to be glum. You may have some bad experiences with faculty, but you will also have good ones, experiences in which together you enjoy the processes of teaching and learning. You have a gift to offer to your professors. If they are wise enough to accept it, you will both profit.

Another practical comment concerns contracts that do not work out, perhaps because they get blocked by major problems. It is also possible that a subject will not turn out to be as interesting as you thought it would. This is no crime. Ask for help or terminate the project as soon as possible. A major obstacle is the fact that it is hard for many of us to ask for help. It seems like an expression of weakness. We don't like to appear less than self-sufficient. It is also hard to leave something unfinished. We are taught that it is immoral not to finish something that we start. Such attitudes are not always rational, but they are deeply embedded within us. Whether the problem is to ask for help or to terminate a project, the longer we wait, the harder it becomes. Talk to the professor, even if it is embarrassing to do so. Cut your losses. Do not let problems fester. Make a clean break and move on. Sometimes, actually more often than you think, you will be surprised and find that things work out better than you thought they would. Simply by asking for it, you will get help that you didn't think was available.

One final piece of advice. My main message has been that you are central to the learning process in an active way. You are not going to be some sort of passive consumer of a commodity called education. Self-respect is vital. There are ways to act out such a stance. One is to take your work seriously by polishing it, saving it, collecting it. Keep the documents and creations that are associated with your learning and growth. Show them to people. Review them yourself. Be proud of them, even if they become slightly embarrassing in a few years because they seem naive. Look at them for the satisfaction they can give and for the growth they evidence. Cherish your work as if you were a fine craftsman or artist. You probably are.

8

Home for the Holidays: A Composite Sketch

Let us call her Susan, a name common in the generation of college students I knew best. I have heard the story of Susan's trip home for the holidays dozens of times. The variations reflect her personality, family, class, and sub-culture. The constants in the story are the nature of college education and the reactions of a student who cannot accept it easily. The occasion is most often Thanksgiving or Christmas. Easter is more relaxed because summer vacation is just a few weeks away. In any case, the holiday is ruined.

Susan returns home depressed. She wants to drop out of college. She may come right out and say so, or it may be implied by everything else she does say, though she lacks the nerve to make it explicit. In either case she has no alternative plans, or she suggests a period of travel, self-exploration, low-level employment, or informal apprenticeship in an art or craft in which she may or may not have talent or previous experience.

Susan's parents are shocked. A family crisis ensues. It consists of frustrating discussions and arguments, and it may dominate family life for months or even years. The response of Susan's parents is that she is irresponsible and unrealistic. She is willing to jeopardize an important opportunity, a college education, because of a passing adolescent malaise. They plead with her to respect their age and experience, to take their advice and refrain from making a mistake that could be irreversible. At least stay in college, they say, until you have developed realistic plans to do something else. Or sometimes they simply say, "Trust us." They may also decide that their continued financial support for her is contingent upon Susan's remaining in college.

Trying to explain herself, Susan talks of courses that have no meaning and seem to lead nowhere, indecision about an academic major and career, a sense of lacking direction, and about a longing to be truly on her own. College feels oppressive and dull. Somehow it opposes rather than encourages the development of a sense of oneself as an adult. It would make more sense, she thinks, and it would be much cheaper, to stay home and read the books that seem most interesting instead of the larger number of less stimulating ones that are assigned for courses. The textbooks, especially, are deadly. Susan understands that her parents see college as a privilege and an opportunity, but her experience feels quite different.

Susan and her parents go over the issues often, but they achieve little clarity about them, partly because there are so many, and they seem vast. Strong emotions are exposed, for the discussions touch upon some of the most highly charged issues in life: love between parent and child, along with the feelings of anger and resentment that are common to the relationship; growth into adulthood and independence; the differing hopes and aspirations of parents and their children; the place in life of financial security; the search for a proper balance between enjoyment and achievement; the advisability of taking the risks associated with unconventional choices. The decision to stay in college or drop out thus becomes the focal point of many issues between parents and their young adult children. The questions are difficult enough in theory, but they are not faced in the abstract. They are addressed by imperfect human beings with histories. The family members have made mistakes with each other, find their love distorted by fear and anger, and may not have discovered constructive ways of dealing with the ambiguous adulthood of a college student who is mature in some ways yet still dependent in others.

Susan may continue in college dutifully, genuinely undecided or insufficiently confident in her own judgments. Or perhaps she is just not brave enough to drop out. Her communication with her parents may improve, or it may degenerate to produce additional bad feelings. Susan and her parents will almost certainly blame each other for failures in understanding and sympathy. Back on campus, reviewing the holiday crisis with her and sometimes talking with her parents who have made the trip back with her to see if they could help her get "straightened out," I hear a familiar story. I have heard it too often to believe, as they do, that the fault lies with either Susan or her parents.

*

For several years at Buffalo State College I was in charge of academic advisement for all freshmen and for sophomores who had not decided upon majors.

It was in that capacity that I talked with hundreds of students and heard the stories of family crises like Susan's.

Although I aspired to much more, as did many other advisers I knew, an academic adviser in a conventional college program helps students select courses and sometimes discusses possible majors with them. Advisement means little more than answering the persistent question "What do I have to take?" The more I learned about students and discussed with them the important questions implicit in the educational decisions they faced, the more frustrating it was to conclude the conversations by reviewing the courses on the next semester's schedule. The conversations might have inherent value, but there was no escaping the fact that the function of advisement in the institution was trivial. It amounted to making sure that a student did not misunderstand the degree requirements.

I knew the courses, and I was getting to know the students. The idea that the latter would find what they were looking for in the former was a fiction. Even after Antioch, it took me a while to learn that the mismatch was inherent in the situation and that there was nothing the students and I, sitting in my office talking our hearts out, could do about it. In the interim I taxed my ingenuity to help students devise strategies for selecting majors and course sequences that might conceivably make contact with something real in their lives. There was little point to most of it, but our conversations were good, and I heard the stories of many family holiday crises. Sympathy and understanding were appreciated in the absence of concrete help.

My talks with bewildered freshmen were moving, for they told of betrayal. The students had believed the conventional wisdom about higher education they heard from their parents, teachers, and guidance counselors. They had studied college catalogs. The words and pictures suggested pleasant fantasies about the life of a college student. As college students they would be independent, thinking adults, using their own judgment to identify and deal with important issues. Professors would provide stimulation, guidance, and help. One would be drawn willingly to these teachers by their knowledge. One would wish to study with them and work hard, but the days of coercion and imposed authority would be over. The natural authority of knowledge and experience would suffice to motivate the collaboration between student and teacher. Higher education would, in many real senses, be the beginning of autonomous adult life.

Within six weeks many freshmen were deeply troubled, and they came back to my office to have another kind of conversation. Some saw that they had been deceived. Others believed, with a great deal of implicit encouragement from professors, that there was something wrong with themselves. There must, they said in many ways, be something in these courses that we are missing. The victims blame themselves.

English Composition, a required course, was regimented and boring. The writing assignments were artificial and, like the readings, remote from any impulses to communicate that the student might have. General Biology, the most attractive option to fulfill the science requirement, was too technical, emphasized the memorization of categories, and seemed by design to avoid the larger and more interesting questions. The occasional student who chose the course out of a genuine feeling for the natural world had to struggle to stay in contact with that feeling. The Humanities course required the reading of one Great Book each week, and that was more than even a Great Mind could absorb. The notion that one might do well to think about Plato for a couple of weeks before moving on to Aristotle would be regarded by most teachers of freshmen as a poorly disguised case for indolence. Introduction to Philosophy, concentrating on the analysis of language, turned out to have less to do with the meaning of life and the search for wisdom than the average dormitory bull session. Introductory Psychology and Problems in Sociology, the most promising of the typical freshman courses, were full of statistics and research results to be remembered because the students were held "responsible" for them on the exams. These were the courses that attracted students who were interested in gaining insights into people and society. They found themselves instead under the heavy-handed tutelage of professors for whom it was a matter of honor to avoid the phenomenon of understanding in favor of the intricacies of experimental design.

If these characterizations sound glib, if you think these are cheap shots, spend a few years talking with college freshmen.

Many students were eager to strike a bargain, to make a utilitarian compromise, if only they could identify the utilities. They came to me wanting to hear good reasons for putting up with the boredom and the academic exotica. It would all be given meaning, for example, if it was directed toward a career goal. But these students did not, for the most part, want to be experimental psychologists, literary critics, or academic philosophers when they grew up.

Their professors, however, taught with their hearts in graduate seminars. Large numbers of students, searching for the compromise, could fall back only on the notion of the general vocational advantage of an undergraduate degree. Nobody has much faith in that anymore, and any such advantage is uncomfortably vague and remote. The thought of years of graduate school can be simply terrifying to a person struggling to find some meaning in freshman year academics.

A considerable number of students were ready to worry less about the future if they could find quality and excitement in the present. Instead they faced the unkindest cuts of all: the persistence of unnecessary rote as a major mode of learning; the absence of truly open intellectual exchanges because a syllabus had to be "covered" and because the dynamics of grading produced a reserve in both student and teacher; authoritarian structures that elevated into requirements various petty whims of professors who were generally quite distant as people.

Much of American higher education is stifling and oppressive, insulting to the decent expectations of students and its own ideal function of preparing men and women for life in a free society. At the core of the problem is the denial to students of important personal and intellectual freedoms. Students are pressured to think and inquire in narrowly prescribed ways. Important decisions about their intellectual lives are made by others.

There are students—I was one—who accept the surprising limitations and begin their socialization as academics. Large numbers of other students simply endure, increasing their proficiency at getting by with a minimum of effort. Denounced as lazy and morally weak by the professors who produce their behavior, they set the dominant tone on most campuses. A few students become rebels. They adopt one style or another of radical rhetoric, and they try to describe their experience and suggest remedies. Their vocabulary rarely sounds genuine. As opponents of a major social institution, accusers of the prestigious professoriat, they seem unconvincing and sometimes even foolish.

Students may choose from a continuum of roles that runs from the college dropout to the apprentice in an academic discipline or profession. Whatever choices they make from this array, an enormous number of them display a cynicism that is heartbreaking in light of their recent idealism. They talk about a college as a factory, the college degree as a piece of paper or a union card, and they mean it. Large portions of their energy are wasted; they have been blocked, not helped, in their search for a focus for their lives and work.

It is ominous to ponder the implications of the fact that the first adult experiences of large numbers of people with a major institution in our society, an institution ostensibly designed to serve them, results in alienation. It is not a felicitous beginning to adulthood. One can only speculate about the collective social meaning of these experiences. Individually, the students go home for the holidays and fight with the parents whom they love.

9

The Individualized Degree Program

The external characteristics of the IDP are: no classes, no grades, no credits, no tests; independent learning contracts, detailed written evaluations, interdisciplinary learning, and creative projects. With the exception of the written evaluations in place of grading, these externals are not absolute. Classes may be taken, but in general they are the easy way out of a learning problem. More important is the spirit of the IDP: flexibility, love of learning, search for meaning, and most significantly, autonomous work.

—Donna, an IDP student

I went to Buffalo in 1969 hoping to have the opportunity to create or participate in innovative programs that would give students more freedom. It was a time of extensive liberal experimentation in higher education, so my goal was not unrealistic. The period of rapid growth which allowed for widespread innovation was ending, however. The opportunity I sought did in fact arise, and in retrospect I see that I was rather lucky. The fortuitous combination of political and economic factors that made the IDP possible at that moment is instructive and will be described in some detail later on. At this point it is appropriate to introduce both the program and its institutional setting, Buffalo State College.

The State University College of New York at Buffalo is the largest of New York's state colleges, and it is not very different from the dozens of public colleges around the country that expanded during the fifties and sixties to serve the young people of the postwar baby boom. It is an institution that is typical of a large segment of American higher education. I was delighted to find myself there, for a demonstration of the utility of an innovation at Buffalo State would imply its applicability at many other colleges. When I had talked with people around the country about Antioch's First Year Program, they had said simply, "Yes, you might be able to do that at Antioch, but we couldn't do it on our campus."

Buffalo State is a former teachers college, and most of its students still major in the college's traditional specialties of elementary education, exceptional children's education, industrial arts education, and art education. Like many state teachers colleges, it became a multipurpose liberal arts college during the fifties. The faculty and curriculum grew and were reorganized. New programs in the standard liberal arts disciplines were added. Divisions of humanities, social sciences, and natural sciences were replaced by departments of the individual disciplines like philosophy, sociology, and physics. Young professors, often just out of graduate school, were hired to bring these departments up to date in current scholarship. New professional programs evolved from the traditional teacher training curricula. Nutrition and business administration programs, for example, grew out of the old Home Economics Education Division.

The official rhetoric of the college and much of the private rhetoric of faculty members stressed the goal of creating an "excellent liberal arts college" in the standard mold. This idea was prominent in the recruitment and hiring of faculty and administrators. It was also the implicit goal of many of the college's decisions about new programs. Power and money shifted away from the education faculties and toward the new breed of professors oriented toward the disciplines. Buffalo State was still, in terms of its liberal arts credentials, a weak college, and subsequent developments in budgeting have determined that it will remain so. There was, however, a fair amount of posturing with respect to professional and scholarly status, just as there was at Antioch. Every department was full of "top people" in the field, or people who would soon reach those lofty heights.* I discovered, for example, a philosophy professor with whom I had attended graduate school. He acted and was treated as if he were a philosophical scholar of some eminence, although his work, as both a student and professor, had been far from distinguished.

Some Buffalo State faculty continued to believe in the historic function of the college, the preparation of students for teaching careers, even though the newcomers among their colleagues were full of disdain for it. Many others saw the teacher training programs as necessary evils, by their nature inferior to the liberal arts. The college's politics were often, in the sixties and early seventies, defined by this division. During the period of growth, the momen-

*Such puffery seems to be a common academic phenomenon. Caplow and McGee, for example, report in *The Academic Marketplace* that "the chairmen of 51 percent of the departments sampled believed their departments to be among the top five in the country in their disciplines."

tum of events favored the disciplinary professors. Also, their personal styles
were verbal and combative; they tended to intimidate the education professors, many of whom were former public school teachers who worried because
they had not attended prestigious graduate schools. The liberal arts professors
seemed more sophisticated. The education faculties, however, had the influence that accrues to seniority and to large student enrollments. As the growth
of the college came to a halt in the seventies, power flowed back to the
education professors, who were more strongly entrenched. Then budgets
stopped growing, and issues of economic security became more critical to
faculty; professorial rivalries declined. The college's politics came to focus
more on competing union groups and on labor-management issues.

The teaching styles of the education faculty were paternalistic and
friendly. They were interested in the many aspects of a student's personality
that are relevant to the teaching profession. They also thought they knew
exactly what is required in the preparation of a person who is to be a teacher
for the next thirty years or so. It was a bit confusing to the students. On the
one hand they were confronted with sympathy, interest, and concern; on the
other hand they faced rigid requirements and judgments about their competence by professors who made little allowance for individual differences. Although it is almost a matter of professional ethics for education professors to
express a commitment to innovation, most of the experimentation they did in
their own teaching was minor. They almost never betrayed any doubt as to
the nature of the educational task. It would have been totally foreign to their
approach to seek to collaborate with students in the matter of defining the
educational venture. Professors in the teacher-training programs also began
to defend themselves against assaults from the other camp. They imitated their
colleagues in the arts and sciences by a great deal of talk about rigor and high
standards, the main effects of which were to frighten students and impress
other teachers. The theoretical content of education courses increased,
whether or not there were decent theories available. Bizarre examples of these
phenomena are to be found in certain "learning objectives" included in our
chapter on Eve, a student who majored in education. There was a retreat from
the traditional strengths of teacher training, its pragmatism and the use of
practical experience in learning. It came to seem as if an aspiring teacher
would not be allowed to have contact with a living child without becoming a
graduate statistician and a master of every word ever uttered by Piaget.

As teachers, the professors in the arts and sciences had to deal with the dilemmas of undergraduate education that are typical of American colleges and universities. They were committed to high standards and rigor in the disciplinary courses they taught, yet their students were generally uninterested and unprepared for the academic initiation they offered. This mismatch between students and their teachers was more acute in Buffalo than it was at Antioch, for the culture of the students at Buffalo State was more remote from academic culture, and many of them had goals and interests that were decidedly nonacademic.

Liberal arts professors adapted to the situation in various ways. Some avoided trouble and earned gratitude by being easy graders despite their faculty lounge rhetoric of toughness. Others continually experimented, seeking the relevant angle from which to present their subject to students. Still others projected real or simulated attractive personalities, hoping that good relationships with students would compensate for the lack of vitality in the academic work in their classes. Some teachers were hardened into their roles and essentially ignored most of the students, giving low grades and concentrating on the rare student who had an interest in their academic disciplines. The more enlightened professors attempted to make their disciplines relevant to the teaching careers to which many of their students aspired. The issue prompted them to try some interesting new things. But these professors, no less than their colleagues in education, knew that it was *their* problem to decide upon and then enforce a definition of what the students should learn. There was no inclination to include the students in the process of making the critical decisions about their education.

Buffalo State students usually came from the Western New York region, and they lived at home. A large minority, however, came from the New York City–Long Island area. Students generally came to Buffalo State because their grades were too low to permit them to enter the State University Center at Buffalo or because they were attracted to one of the professional programs in education, several of which had good reputations. Frequently they were the first members of their families to attend college. There was also a large program for economically and educationally disadvantaged students, most of whom were black.

Students came to Buffalo State determined to do well, often by turning over a new leaf. They saw higher education as an important opportunity to improve their lives and career prospects. They were generally not political, and their culture was mainstream. Only a few Buffalo State students would even have thought of challenging the principle that it is a professor's right to define the requirements of a course. The student power movement had a short and limited life on that campus. Yet the students were not excessively obedient. Many were streetwise, and they were formidable adversaries for a professor whom they perceived to be unfair, especially in grading.

The situation at Buffalo State was not unusual, but the late sixties and early seventies was an unusual time, a period of high expectations and of criticism. There was a general sense that education at the college was not going well. The faculty tended to think that the problem was the students: they weren't interested enough, or they were unprepared, or they just weren't bright. It was a widely held belief among faculty that improving the institution meant getting better students rather than doing things better or differently with current students. The students, intimidated and feeling themselves at a cultural disadvantage, were inclined to agree. It was painful, for example, to listen to students or their parents talking with a professor or administrator, struggling with their grammar or pronunciation, afraid that their normal language was inferior and that they would be judged accordingly.

The meeting of different subcultures and purposes was rich with poten- tial. There was a freshness and sense of energy about a campus on which there were many first-generation college students. The situation was ripe for a collaboration among the diverse groups on the definition of the nature of education. But there was little movement in that direction. Neither the faculty nor the student culture contained the ideas or symbols that would support the necessary shift of power. The Individualized Degree Program was an attempt to produce change in that direction without utterly denying the values that were current on campus.

It was not hard to identify with the promise of the IDP once it was articulated. After a short orientation program for the first group of IDP stu- dents, I got this letter:

> Dear Dr. Meisler,
>
> I never imagined that after a three-day orientation program I'd be homesick for Buffalo State. Approximately eight hours have passed since I have returned, and my conversation has just begun to moderate.
>
> Truthfully, the introduction to the program has caused me to reach a

feeling of elation I have never experienced before. My mom said that she has never seen a smile remain on my face for such a long time. (Actually I think that if she were given the chance, she'd seek out the IDP herself.)

I'd appreciate it very much if you'd express my thanks to all the instructors who made orientation such a success. I did not get a chance to thank you personally, but if you observed my face then you understand that words would never have expressed my feelings better.

Thank you and take care.

Much warmth,
Cindy

Many of us felt as Cindy did. Our ability to turn that euphoria into education varied considerably. Cindy herself, despite her initial elation, left the IDP after a year. The year was, in many ways, a good one for her, but the learning that occurred could not count toward a college degree. By contrast, Donna, whose words opened this chapter and whose experience we shall describe in detail later, had similar feelings, but was able to use the IDP to get a superb formal education that was marked also by personal growth. The most interesting part of the story of the IDP lies in these differences in the way students and faculty functioned and in the struggle to understand such differences. We turn first, however, to a description of the structures of the Individualized Degree Program and the ideas that they tried to implement.

There were several concepts basic to the IDP that were generally shared by the eight or ten students, faculty, and administrators who created the program. We believed that academic work should be intimately connected with other parts of a student's life, indeed that it should often be suggested or motivated by those other involvements. This seemed to require a system that did not restrict academic study solely to the disciplines. Another idea that was important to us concerned autonomy: students should, as far as possible, be self-determining and free of coercion. Their lives should be governed by their own choices and not by unnecessarily imposed syllabi, deadlines, and examinations. This commitment to autonomy was both moral and pragmatic. We felt that it was the right way to treat students, and also that it would be the best way to help them become effective independent learners. We also believed that people need community, and that this is expressed in the educational realm by the fact that there is a strong social component to a great deal of learning.

The basic academic structure of the IDP was the learning contract, a written document by which a project formally became part of a student's work in college. Each contract was a kind of syllabus, created by the student in consultation with an instructor, for a program of work or study whose goal was learning. The contract stated the reasons for pursuing a project, the goals, methodologies, probable duration, and the criteria by which its success would be judged. There was a general understanding that, within reason, contracts could be revised during the course of a study.

A faculty sponsor or cooperating faculty member was required for each learning contract. The program had a core faculty of six professors who sponsored some contracts and helped students find sponsors for others. We expected that the relationship between cooperating faculty and students would vary greatly, but the cooperating faculty's minimal function was to vouch, at the beginning, for the contract as a valid program of learning and, at the end, for the evaluation of the learning that had been achieved.

The requirements that each contract have a faculty sponsor, that it include a statement of goals and means, and that it be concluded with a written evaluation were critical parts of the IDP's formal structures. In the process of planning the program, we considered educational strategies and institutional politics, sometimes perhaps confusing the two realms. Educationally, we thought that faculty sponsors would be helpful and that statements of means and ends and written evaluations would clarify and rationalize issues that were implicit in any learning project. We also believed that the omission of any of these requirements would render the new program unacceptable to the larger institution and its faculty. When we discuss the difficulties experienced by many students, it will appear that these stipulations, which appeared minimal at the time, imposed a high price.

Students in the IDP structured their own time. They might decide to work on many contracts at once, or to pursue one or two projects of greater magnitude. A project could include any activity that would yield learning, from the traditional library research and term paper to involvement in off-campus work in politics, government, business, social agencies, or cultural institutions. A learning contract might deal with a standard portion of the curriculum, approaching it in either unusual or familiar ways. A contract might also be formulated to pursue knowledge that simply did not appear in the standard curriculum.

Neither grades nor credit hours were assigned to a project at its completion. A descriptive evaluation of the student's learning was prepared jointly and signed by both the student and the faculty sponsor. It was filed, along with the contract, in the student's folder for later consideration by a degree committee. Each year the titles of completed contracts were recorded on a transcript without grades or credits. This transcript, along with several pages of excerpts from contracts and evaluations, was a student's formal academic record.

The college's degree requirements, including the requirement that a student major in a subject, applied to IDP students. Since the requirements specified particular courses and a distribution of credit hours among fields, there was a process by which they were reinterpreted for IDP students. A degree committee was formed that included the student, the chairperson of the major department, and a full-time IDP core faculty member. After a number of evaluations were received, the committee defined the extent of the student's progress. The committee considered the goals of the major subject's degree requirements in terms of the learning sought rather than credit hours and required courses. The department chairperson's function was, among other things, to be sure that these interpretations were consistent with his or her department's view of the discipline. Operating by consensus, the degree committee was empowered to decide when the work had achieved the same or equivalent learning goals as those intended by the requirements. A regular student majoring in biology, for example, would be required to take a course in botany. An IDP student in biology might well have a contract evaluation for a project dealing with an environmental issue and another concerning ecology that together attested to an equivalent understanding of botany. The IDP student might, at the same time, be satisfying an elective requirement for the major in the area of environmental biology. Or, to refer to a real case, one of our students majored in English with a strong emphasis on film, an emphasis that was approved by the English Department. His degree committee judged that his work in surveying and contrasting the film traditions of several countries satisfied the purpose of the English Department's requirement that students take a course in comparative literature.

The regulations of the State University system made it virtually impossible for us to give the students the freedom to create new majors. But the college already had on the books several cross-disciplinary majors that could be interpreted to allow a number of students to follow quite personal programs that were essentially nondisciplinary. And in general the requirements of standard majors could be approached with a variety of contracts that gave students the flexibility and room to create personalized education.

The functioning of the degree committee sounds, in theory, as if it would be the most problematic part of the IDP. In fact it proceeded very smoothly, with all members being in agreement on the question of progress toward the degree almost all of the time. By the time a student did enough work to meet with a degree committee, most of the problems of conceiving and pursuing a program had been worked through in the context of individual contracts. The quality and quantity of work, often achieved by means of considerable struggle, spoke for themselves. By then, students almost always had relationships with a number of respected faculty members, and these professors' evaluations of contracts would count for a lot with degree committees.

There was a core faculty of four to six teachers in the IDP for about one hundred students. Most of the core faculty had participated in the planning of the IDP and were deeply committed to it. They assumed some risk in their careers by joining the IDP, for it put them at a distance from their departments, even though decisions of tenure and salary would still be made within those departments. The core faculty served as advisers and counselors, and they also sponsored many learning contracts. They helped students find cooperating faculty for other contracts, and dozens of faculty members did indeed cooperate each semester.

At the beginning of every year, IDP students were divided into groups of about fifteen, and each group met regularly with a core faculty member. We called them "home groups," and we hoped that their members would get to know each other well, share information and experiences, and possibly do academic and social projects together. Each month we had an evening "town meeting" to which everyone was invited to share a meal, discuss problems, have a party, or participate in some type of academic event. There was also an afternoon Weekly Academic Program, in which a lecture or presentation of some kind was given, usually by a faculty member from the college who might be willing to do contracts with our students.

The IDP had other structures, formal and informal, that arose and then disappeared as the needs and energies of people shifted. For a while there were personal growth groups, combining sensitivity training and group therapy, giving students the chance to work on problems of personal and social adjustment. We passed through periods in which we took many trips, visiting museums and nearby cities, going on nature walks, and generally enjoying the chance to be together and get away from campus from time to time. And socially, IDP participants experienced a range of associations from shifting friendship groups to serious love affairs to a crackpot charismatic movement. We had one IDP marriage.

Within the structures of the IDP several hundred students and dozens of professors confronted the issues of autonomy in education. Each individual had a considerable amount of previous experience in settings whose assumptions were quite conventional. Indeed the instructional program of the larger institution, Buffalo State College, was derived from principles that were generally in conflict with the IDP's. Many of the following chapters will describe the experiences of individual students and faculty in the IDP, and they will also record particularly important aspects of the program's history and the institution's response. We move, then, to the natural history of a real-world experiment in making freedom for students a more prominent aspect of an educational system.

10

Debbie

I was sitting in the midst of papers, pencils, typewriter and books. My head was throbbing with the weight of the information that I was cramming into it. But why was I working so hard on this paper? I didn't have to meet a deadline, and I wasn't going to be graded. What was this obsession to write a paper? It suddenly occurred to me, after days of little sleep, skipping meals and forcing thoughts on to paper, that I actually enjoyed what I was doing! No, I didn't really enjoy the minimal sleep and the long hours of studying. But what I noticed was that I was learning, *that my mind was soaking up facts and ideas and that I didn't want to miss anything. I finally realized that this was why the IDP was so important to me.*

—Debbie

It may be most interesting to begin a description of Debbie's experience in the IDP with a list of the special advantages that she did not possess. Many people interested in the program had felt that it would be best to limit the IDP to a special group of students, either the very intelligent or the very highly motivated, those students who "really knew where they were going." Debbie belonged to neither of these fortunate minorities, and yet she was successful as a student in the program.

Debbie is very much like hundreds of other college students. She is bright but not brilliant or unusually talented. She had been a competent student in high school, obedient and not especially inclined toward independence. When she started college, she seemed, in many ways, to be pleading for someone to tell her exactly what to do, what was "expected" of her. She knew how to meet expectations. Debbie had a career goal in mind, becoming a teacher. That goal, however, seemed to imply no action for her in the present except asking about requirements, and she had no strong interests in any of the academic disciplines.

Debbie was from a rather poor working class family. She felt proud of her ability to cope with financial difficulties by hard work and care, but she was also embarrassed by her unfamiliarity with highbrow and academic cultures. She was the first in her family to go to college.

Debbie's progress through the IDP is particularly accessible to us for two reasons. Both were important to the outcome of her work in the program. The first is that she had a great deal of contact with me and the other core faculty; she came to us often to ask for help. The second is that she kept a journal, from which the opening quotation of this chapter is taken. The record in Debbie's journal is particularly eloquent about the difficulties of adjusting to the IDP and about her understanding of the sources of the problem. The struggle she describes was almost universal among IDP students, and her description is worth quoting at length:

> Within the first three weeks of college life it became clear to me that learning through the IDP was going to be much more difficult than I had expected. I realized that I didn't have the self-motivation and self-control needed to organize my time efficiently. Without the pressure of tests or grades it was easy to be lazy and non-productive. I found that I had to unlearn habits of study that, for the past thirteen years, had been based on the classroom experience. . . . After thirteen years of schooling I didn't *know how to learn!* I tried to remember what I was taught about learning in grammar school and in high school. These are the things that are foremost in my memory: a) I was taught that the first and most important characteristic of a classroom is SILENCE. A student must not speak to his classmates. If he wishes to answer or ask a question, he must first raise his hand; however he must not speak without first being called upon by the teacher. Above all, he must always pay attention to the words of the teacher who (of course) is the only one who has anything valuable to contribute. . . . b) I must thank all of my grammar school teachers for teaching me the proper way to sit at a desk. Just think of all the learning I would have missed if I didn't know how to sit up straight with my knees together, hands folded, mouth closed, and eyes facing the teacher! c) During my high school years, when I should have been developing the capacity to learn on my own, a trip to the school library was considered to be a privilege. Although the system was gracious enough to fill my spare time with study halls, library passes were rationed out so strictly that I was lucky if I could visit the library twice a year!

Debbie was always around at the beginning of the IDP. There were several reasons. She was, to begin with, public-spirited. When secondhand rugs and furniture were to be purchased to furnish an IDP lounge, Debbie volunteered to come along to help select them and carry the load. When food was to be bought and prepared for a town meeting, Debbie was there to help. An older daughter of a large family, she was adept at stretching small amounts of money and at dealing with a variety of practical problems.

During the evening Debbie worked as a cleaning lady in an office building. Her time on campus was thus limited. Her response was to become involved in everything, to use every available minute at school. It seemed as if she was almost defiant in her attempt to prove that her need to work at a menial job could be satisfied with no sacrifice in her life as a college student. Not only did Debbie respond to almost every call for volunteers to help with the practical matters of the IDP, but she joined many of the group academic projects that sprang up in the first months of the program.

In retrospect the first wave of group projects seems a little desperate. They were usually the associations of students who didn't know how to use their new freedom and found safety in numbers. A good idea would come along and attract a group of students, many of them joining out of anxiety about their disorganized idleness rather than a genuine interest in the subject. It was difficult and frustrating to try to create meaningful personal learning contracts, and it was a relief to be able to buy into a project that had coworkers. Although the existence of the group was at first a source of comfort, the deficiencies of individuals were often magnified rather than diminished by the group setting. A group's progress was often halted by the failure of one individual to do his or her assigned task. Debbie joined the projects, often doing more than her share. She became one of the more visible students in the IDP. But although the group projects met social needs, they helped little in getting her academic career in college started.

Unlike many other students who found their first months in the IDP difficult and troubled, Debbie was able to ask for help. But it was hard to respond to her requests. She would come to a faculty member with a rather general idea for a project. She would not know what to do with it, how to follow it up. It appeared as if she had done little to pursue the idea and as if she was asking for help too soon. She seemed too ready to smile, shrug her shoulders, and wait for someone to help. Yet it also seemed clear that she would make no further progress on her own. Another core faculty member or I would want to help, but we wouldn't want to do too much. An implicit compromise was reached in which Debbie got some substantive help, usually less than she really wanted, along with a lot of encouragement. It often worked, for Debbie was genuinely laboring at the problem of being independent. She was determined and willing to work hard; what she needed most was enough support, moral and practical, to keep the process going.

Although Debbie often consulted with faculty, without telling anyone she undertook a project that was critically important to her education. The help she gave herself was more important than any help that she could have been given. She deliberately set out on her own remedial program to overcome the disabilities that she'd acquired from her previous schooling. Her project was not a formal one, and it represented no official progress toward a college degree. In conventional terms this was time and effort wasted, but Debbie saw that it was necessary. It took courage, and in the end the gamble paid off.

> I had to begin with the basics. I read a book on reading and study skills, and then I tried to apply the methods to my own work. I took notes on *everything* that I read: the newspaper, novels, short stories, textbooks, etc. I tried to organize my notes in an outline form with the main idea of the reading as the first item in the outline. In this way I "relearned" how to take notes. Although this process seems very simple, it is certainly different from transcribing notes that were dictated to me by the teacher, the way we had done in high school.
>
> The second step in "learning how to learn" involved library research. I made frequent trips to the college and public libraries in order to become familiar with the resources that were available. I began to use the periodical section faithfully, as well as to discover what books were available on the shelves. Eventually the library became a very valuable resource and not an impersonal institution. It was there if I needed it. I began to use it.

A momentous thing was happening in Debbie's life. She was claiming ownership of her education, assuming responsibility for identifying and dismantling the obstacles in the way of her learning. She was moving away from the role of a passive recipient of education packaged for her by teachers, and she was learning to create it for herself. Before long it was hard to remember how dependent she had been.

Debbie's program had begun as a rather routine remedial attack on the familiar problems of study skills, but it took an interesting and important turn. Debbie was trying to be reflective about her own ways of learning. It was, indeed, necessary to learn to read and write and do library research, but

Debbie

Debbie knew, and now stated clearly to herself, that she was neither bookish nor intellectual in a scholarly sense. She found that she learned from a variety of other kinds of experience, and this was to become an important factor in the eventual shape of her education.

> But the library was only one of the many valuable resources that were available to me. I found that I could learn a great deal from the community. Volunteer work at a school was good field training. The theater at Stratford, Ontario, made Shakespeare's plays come to life. The experience at college camp gave me the opportunity to see nature through my own eyes, not just through the words of a textbook. I needed the textbook to teach me the principles and the theories that are involved in certain subjects. But experience is the real teacher, for through experience I learn the *meaning* of all those words—I learn how those principles and theories relate to *my own* life.

Slowly Debbie's self-development plan worked. It became less difficult for her to take an interesting idea and find concrete ways to work out a project based on it. Her requests for help became more specific and manageable, less global. She even became stronger and more secure, working in group projects more frequently now out of strength and confidence rather than weakness and a desire to be liked.

Debbie was, for example, an organizer and central participant in one of the IDP's most interesting academic projects. A new park was to be built in Buffalo, and a design was needed for its playground. My friend Dr. Beverly Paigen, an environmental scientist and educator, was in contact with city officials who were interested in an innovative design. Bev needed help on the project, and Debbie and some other students got to work. They watched kids in playgrounds all over the city. They read books about recreation and design. They studied the site of the new park and talked with people in the neighborhood. They studied census data. They pored over catalogs of materials and worked with alternate budgets. They finally designed a playground and constructed a model. Their design was in fact used, and it was a tremendous success, one of the best playgrounds in the city. It made heroes of the bureaucrats who had contacted Bev. They asked whether students would be available to help with other parks, although Bev could not pursue these projects because she was soon to play a critical role as scientist and advocate in the Love

Canal disaster. When it came time for Bev and Debbie to evaluate the learning contract, Bev wrote, in part:

> Debbie stuck to this project from the beginning and contributed a great deal to it. Her creative ideas and her work with the group accounted for much of the success of our work. Debbie came up with good ideas, put herself in the roles of children, and imagined the things that it would be fun for them to do. She was also very reliable, showed up at meetings consistently, met deadlines, and bolstered the group spirit.

At about the same time that the playground project began, toward the end of the IDP's first year, it became clear that many IDP students were having trouble writing contracts. Art Pitts, a core faculty member, and I decided to run a workshop on writing. Debbie participated, and her progress was astonishing. Her first piece of writing was awful. Cute, stilted, unreal, Debbie's writing cheerfully obeyed every rule that had been set down by a series of bad English teachers. (Years later, when I read her journal, I saw that Debbie had always been able to write well. It was in her writing *at school* that she invoked all the rules she had learned.) Her writing was embarrassingly childish, and one didn't know where to start with criticism or help. But Debbie had become sensitive to her weaknesses and was gaining competence in finding ways to overcome them. Within a few weeks, relying mainly on her own perception of the differences between the writing of various members of the group, Debbie slowly began to find a voice of her own as a writer. She learned to write what she meant, using language that was natural to her, doing so with clarity and simplicity. At the end of the workshop Art Pitts wrote the following about Debbie's work:

> Debbie made the most evident progress of anyone in the group. In her early pieces she revealed considerable uncertainty and did not seem to be able to deal directly with her feelings and ideas. . . . In her final pieces of work Debbie is dealing quite directly with personal concerns and writes about them in ways that did not seem available to her at the beginning of the workshop.

Gradually learning became easier for Debbie. She encountered impasses and crises less frequently, and she handled them more effectively. Her confidence grew. She seemed to be having more fun too, and it was more fun to work with her. Debbie took a leave of absence from school for a while, left

Debbie

Buffalo, and got married. She returned to college and graduated with a teaching certificate and a bachelor's degree. The quality of her work continued to improve.

Like many young teachers, Debbie dreams of starting an innovative school some day in a small community. The changes that occurred in Debbie in her college years encourage one to believe that many things are possible for her. We conclude with two entries from her journal. The first was made at the beginning of her college education; the second came later.

> My feelings and ideas sound so childish. My thoughts are very disoriented and as a result my writing is very disorganized. I realize that I have assigned myself a difficult project, and it will be a long time before the pieces start fitting together. I only hope that in the meantime I will be able to withstand the discouragement.

> I began to notice changes in myself. With the freedom of the IDP came a great amount of responsibility. As I became more and more responsible for my own learning I found a certain strength that had never been a part of me. I began to lose some of my shyness; I became more outspoken. I was able to participate in discussions instead of sitting quietly as I did in high school. At times I felt as though the responsibilities of the IDP were a burden I couldn't handle. But as I grew stronger I found the courage to say what *I* had to say. And I saw that others were listening to me! Then the burden was transformed into a freedom that I had never known in the past, the freedom to be me.

11

Paul and Zoe

Many students dropped out of the IDP with few tangible accomplishments, but almost always with feelings of satisfaction. They often believed that they had confronted important problems and made valuable progress in learning to be independent. The faculty usually agreed with them. There seemed to be no such personal growth or learning to redeem Paul and Zoe's year in the IDP. Upon leaving the program, they expressed mainly anger and shame. Paul and Zoe's time in the IDP was dominated by one of the central aspects of any program that violates important norms of the educational world. Innovations inevitably imply that conventional ways are imperfect. Participants in innovative programs can expect disapproval and hostility from educators committed to standard structures. Paul and Zoe had no resources to cope with these reactions.

I've rarely seen Paul and Zoe apart, either during their year in the IDP or since then. When I talked with them, it felt as if I had entered a scenario which they had planned and discussed at length. They were always together, usually in a hurry, moving quickly across campus with Paul in the lead by about half a step. As friends and classmates in high school, they applied to the IDP with almost identical letters that arrived on the same day. They tried to develop the same or similar learning projects, usually without success. Together they contributed to the life of the IDP with their energy and their enthusiasm for good food and good times. When we got together as a group, they would cook for us. Their food was delicious and made us all feel special. Despite their close relationship, and partly because of it, Paul and Zoe suffered from an isolation and loneliness in college that was heightened by their participation in the IDP. They had trouble with schoolwork and did not get adequate help. They withdrew from the program at the end of the year, again writing almost identical letters.

From the beginning, the core faculty and I were optimistic about Paul and Zoe. We considered them to be among the most likely to succeed in the IDP's first group of students. We met them when they visited the Buffalo State campus as high school seniors. They were from Long Island, and they bubbled over with the excitement of leaving home and anticipating college. Paul and Zoe were enthusiastic, and they asked serious and appropriate questions about the new program. We felt that we'd met our first two good IDP students, and we looked forward to their applications.

The letters of application we received from Paul and Zoe supported our optimism. They expressed an eagerness that matched our own. Their high school records seemed to indicate that they were well-suited to the IDP by aptitude, values, and previous experience. They had been academically successful in high school, honor students whose grades were usually A's. They came from a high school in the affluent suburbs, yet they seemed to have a freshness that was unusual. Outside classes Paul and Zoe did many things. As planners of the IDP, we had, as students later pointed out to us with exasperation, come to think of every human experience as the starting point for a possible learning contract. Paul and Zoe provided a fair amount of material for such fantasies. They were active members of their congregation's Jewish youth group. They listed a long series of school clubs and organizations in which they participated. They did volunteer work in charitable organizations. And they were active in community theater productions, both Zoe and Paul were considering majoring in the technical aspects of theater.

The letters we received from Paul and Zoe now seem a bit strange. They were obviously the products of a joint effort, and they were, perhaps, a little too correct, as if they had come out of a guidance counselor's manual on how to apply to a college's special program. Yet the letters also rang true. Paul and Zoe did indeed seem to be bright, active, and independent people. They were serious about education. Their futures were promising, and we felt fortunate to have them in the program. Our reactions to Paul, Zoe, and to their letters were naive. We wanted to be encouraged, and our eagerness extended the time before we would understand that Paul and Zoe were having serious problems.

When the IDP started, our dealings with Paul and Zoe continued to support our optimism. They were excited about being in college and had good ideas for projects. They were retiring, but their friendship compensated somewhat by giving them at least one relationship upon which they could depend. And sometimes, when the IDP had a business meeting which was followed by a party, we would share a beautiful communal meal that had been prepared under Zoe and Paul's supervision. Every detail bespoke care and dedication. Paul and Zoe were painfully shy, but their work on the group's behalf clearly indicated commitment and a wish to belong. We ate and talked, and some of the other students sang. One evening at the very beginning of the IDP, I sat with Carl Bauer at one of these supper meetings. He was a core faculty member who had been a college teacher and administrator for more than thirty years. He deeply believed that students would do great things with their freedom. We sat together, listened to the students sing, ate the food that Zoe and Paul had prepared for us, and looked around at the other students. He leaned over to me and said, "This is too good to be true."

It was not good for Paul and Zoe. Once the glow of the initial weeks faded, the year in the IDP was a bad one for them. They accomplished little and were miserable. There were, of course, idiosyncratic reasons for this particular failure of the IDP and two of its students, but they also shared problems that were widespread among students in the program. In fact, many of the problems faced by Paul and Zoe were identical to those faced by Debbie. The important lesson to be learned is why she was able to solve them but Paul and Zoe, who were as able and highly motivated, were not.

Let us begin with two projects that were central to the year that Paul and Zoe spent in the IDP. They completed one of the projects but not the other. The reasons, the differences between their experience in the two learning contracts, come close to the heart of the matter.

Paul and Zoe continued their work in community theater. As soon as they got to Buffalo, they found the city's most dynamic group, and they volunteered their services. Since they thought they might want to major in dramatics, it was natural to think that their first learning contract in this area might be built around their volunteer work. A project could involve a nice combination of book learning and participation in community productions. Such a contract could have been an important part of their professional education. It might also have helped them to define a positive relationship, in actuality as well as fantasy, between themselves and the IDP, for they would have experienced a major benefit of the program, the relative ease with which action and academic work could be combined. That benefit might have provided the incentive to struggle more effectively to make some of the adjustments and to work on some of the new skills that were required for success in the IDP.

Paul and Zoe

The obstacle that faced Paul and Zoe in this case was the coolness or actual hostility to the IDP of some of the faculty members in the Arts Division of the college. Although the formal position of that faculty favored learning in a variety of creative settings, it was implemented in a rigid fashion. Field-work came at certain specified times and within the context of particular courses. The sources of the hostility between some of these faculty and the IDP are complex and will be discussed in the chapters that touch upon academic politics. Let it suffice here to say that some professors in many fields, because of both heavy time pressures and disagreements with the program, would not sponsor the projects of IDP students. Fortunately there were others, including several young and energetic professors, who helped with a number of field-based projects that were almost identical to the ones that Paul and Zoe might have done. Most of those learning projects were successful.

The important fact for Paul and Zoe was not that many students were successfully arranging to do similar projects, but rather the possibility that they might encounter a hostile faculty member. They knew that IDP students had been turned down by professors. But it was worse than that. IDP students searching for a sponsor had occasionally been put on the defensive by a professor who attacked them for believing that they could find better ways to learn than attending standard introductory courses. IDP students were not, at least at first, prepared for such discussions. They were seeking help on a project, not an argument with a professor. At best these were unpleasant and difficult experiences for our students. At worst the objections of a professor, a figure of authority, could shake a new student's confidence and produce real damage. The core faculty and I tried to steer students to sympathetic faculty, but we were not always successful. There were also faculty bullies who would express agreement to us and then pick on the students. Some were quite cruel, throwing a proposal into the trash or mocking a student.

Even though Paul and Zoe could almost certainly have found a support-ive professor in speech or theater, they could be given no guarantee of it before they set out in search of such a person. Even the professors who were favorably inclined were busy and might eventually stop taking on IDP stu-dents. And everyone has a bad day from time to time; some of the friendliest professors were occasionally difficult. Paul and Zoe could simply not consider placing themselves in a position in which they might be rejected or criticized by a teacher. Paul and Zoe continued their work in the community theater, but they let the idea of an academic project remain dormant rather than risk facing disapproval. At that point much of the promise that the IDP held for Paul and Zoe was probably forfeited. The core faculty or I might have offered help, but we were slow to recognize the problem.

Paul and Zoe did not have to face the possibility of rejection in their most successful IDP project. During their work in theater projects back in Long Island, they had been introduced to experimental productions for deaf audiences. Buffalo State's Exceptional Education Department has a strong and popular program in the education of children with hearing impairments. The courses are full and they are necessarily small, since the students do intensive work learning sign language. Access to small group experiences presented a special problem to a program like the IDP, which was not organized around classes. In the IDP's first year, therefore, we used some grant money to hire one of the Exceptional Education Department's part-time teachers to offer a workshop for our students. This was actually a combination of logistical necessity and a common type of bribery used by academic departments in relating to programs that had grants. The teacher's name was Kevin McCarthy. By arranging to pay for some of his time, we made a series of valuable experiences available to Zoe and Paul and other IDP students.

Mr. McCarthy was an utterly dedicated and loving teacher. He was generous with his time and his attention. He took a deep interest in the work of every student. There was no possibility that Paul and Zoe would miss the fact that Mr. McCarthy was on their side. They thrived under his supervision, and they did fine work.

It is worth describing one more project, a learning contract begun by Paul in which, uncharacteristically, Zoe was not involved. It was not as frightening to Paul as the potential project in theater, yet it was not as easy as working with Mr. McCarthy. The idea for the contract was an excellent one.

Paul had a close relationship with his grandmother, who had immigrated to America from a small Jewish community in Eastern Europe. He had grown up in the same household with her, and he had listened to her stories of the old country for hours on end. Paul decided to study the larger historical events that had influenced his grandmother's life—the pogroms, the wars, the economic dislocations. He would do so, however, in conjunction with recording, on tape and in writing, the old lady's memories. It would be a significant intellectual task and one that was full of emotional and personal meaning. The project would take Paul back to his roots, and it would also take him to the history texts, where the events described would have resonances in his own life. Perhaps he'd continue to find ways to create academic work with this intimate quality.

Carl Bauer sponsored Paul's project, along with a young professor of history. Carl's intellectual style was abstract and speculative. He had gone to Germany, the land of his ancestors, to study design during the early years of the Nazi era. That had been a formative experience for him, and he was interested in the interplay between politics and social movements, on the one hand, and biography on the other. It would have been natural and enjoyable for him to discuss a range of issues with Paul: the way it feels to be affected by large events over which one has no control; the interaction between one's individualistic values and social ethics; what it is like to live through rapid social change, as both Paul's grandmother and Carl had done. Carl did not, however, have the enthusiasm for working on the practical details of a project that he might have possessed when he was younger. He was a kind and gentle mentor, provocative, amused, and perhaps a bit distant.

Paul was well equipped, in both intellectual and practical ways, to do what was required for the project. He got a good start. One day shortly after he began work on the contract, Paul showed me some transcriptions of his grandmother's story. He also showed me a time line of historical events that he believed had a direct effect on his grandmother's life. He was making substantial progress with only a little instruction. In the end, however, Paul's energy flagged and he dropped the project without completing it. He needed the kind of constant support, direction, and encouragement that he could not get from Carl Bauer or from most professors. He needed Mr. McCarthy.

Paul and Zoe never started enough contracts to fill their time. Having little to do, they left their dormitory rooms less often. They thus removed themselves from the setting in which they might have gotten help. The IDP provided only a very thin ready-made schedule according to which students could structure their time. There were a couple of weekly events, which Paul and Zoe usually attended. Otherwise the time had been left open for students to arrange to meet faculty, work in the library, do fieldwork, etc. Paul and Zoe had time on their hands. This was a constant reminder that things weren't going well. They became demoralized and unhappy.

Paul and Zoe were unable to ask for help. Perhaps they had never needed it before, at least in their schoolwork. They had always been very good students, and they were simply ashamed of being imperfect. They could not make the admission, implicit in any request for help, that there were problems. Such a concession, for them, was laden with moral implications. An observer could see that they needed help badly, but their ways of revealing this need did not provide many openings for a person who wanted to be of assistance. They would appear at IDP gatherings and work hard in the kitchen. They were, of course, idle and scared, but they desperately created the appearance of involvement. Their eyes revealed confusion and pain, yet they were shy and defensive at even the gentlest direct approach. One could rarely talk to Paul or Zoe in the absence of the other, and this made it even harder. Perhaps they had appearances to maintain in each other's presence. It was wrong and unsatisfactory to leave them alone, but it was unproductive to encounter them in the ways that were available. And since there were other students fairly clamoring for one's attention, the core faculty's attempts to help Paul and Zoe became less frequent. Things got worse for them. Although they had each other, Paul and Zoe were terribly lonely during their year in the IDP. The normal interactions among students in the same classes were missing.

Paul and Zoe shared another difficulty with some of the other students who did not do well in the IDP. They never had enough confidence in the program to move away from certain basic questions as to whether it would work. Would the contract system work? Would the absence of grades be terrible impediments when applying for jobs or graduate schools? Would anybody outside our small circle of teachers and students ever really understand the IDP? The questions were, of course, valid, but it was unproductive to keep asking them. Fixating on the questions only made things worse, draining energy away from productive activity and making negative answers to them more likely.

When IDP students were recruited and then during the early weeks of orientation, we discussed these questions at length. It was our intention to be scrupulously clear about the risks a student might be taking by joining the IDP. But the answers, the exact nature of the risk, could only be known in the future; a student had no choice but to accept the uncertainties and get on with it or not join the IDP. The students who did well in the IDP handled these issues early in the game in ways that satisfied them that the risks were worth taking.

Paul and Zoe

Paul, Zoe, and others couldn't stop worrying and found that these questions were still prominent in their minds ten months later.

Paul and Zoe were intimidated by faculty, afraid to ask for help, lonely, and uncertain that the IDP would work. These were serious problems, and they were shared, to greater or lesser extents, by many IDP students. Taken together they are easily sufficient to account for Paul and Zoe's inability to function in the new program. Yet I think there was a more basic problem concerning their participation in the IDP, a problem that exacerbated all the other difficulties they encountered. It explains why Paul and Zoe were helpless in the face of problems that other students, no more able than they, learned to overcome.

Paul and Zoe were taken by surprise in a very basic way. They expected, I think, a special program for good students, not unlike an honors class in high school. Participation in such a program would be a badge of honor, something that would be universally approved by teachers and parents. In such a program the best students would do what was expected of them with much less coercion than usual. This is the meaning of rhetoric about independence and freedom in most educational settings, and it is probably the way Paul and Zoe received the message of the IDP. Relationships with teachers are closer in such programs. Occasions for conflict are minimized, partly because problem students are excluded. As long as one could do the work, as Paul and Zoe always could, there would be no risk of failure. It is in such programs that good students and sympathetic teachers ally themselves to achieve some insulation from the obvious evils and chaos of much of contemporary education. Paul and Zoe had learned to seek out such settings and enjoy them.

Instead, of course, Paul and Zoe found the IDP, a program in which freedom and independence meant that they were not to be told what to do. They might have handled this, but any course of action, any resolution of the basic questions, had a potential for trouble, for placing them in conflict with professors. This is precisely what they had learned to avoid by being good students and joining special programs. They were trapped in a bind from which there was no escape. And although the core faculty and I were rapidly learning how to help students deal with a variety of typical problems that arose in the IDP, we were weakest in this area. Paul and Zoe were not the only ones who might come into conflict with established values. We were all in a bind like theirs, although some of us dealt with it better. The core faculty and I, the very people who could have helped Paul and Zoe, had a stake in underestimating the distance we had created between our program and the rest of the college. We thus had less clarity in this realm than in any other relating to problems that students were having. Being blind to all of this, however, could not prevent these facts from becoming strong themes in the lives of several of us, including Paul and Zoe. It did, however, keep us from understanding Paul and Zoe as well as we might have, although I do not think we could have done enough to make the program work for them.

12

Universal Agreement

I have never met a teacher who did not believe in freedom for students. Elementary schoolteachers believe that freedom is appropriate in college and graduate school, for students will then have the background to use it well. College professors say that it is hopeless to give their students freedom, for it all must begin in kindergarten. If it does not start back there, students will never acquire the necessary habits.

13

Free Students

> Students should not play life, or study it merely, while the community
> supports them at this expensive game, but earnestly live it from the beginning
> to end. How could youths better learn to live than by at once trying the
> experiment of living.
>
> —Henry David Thoreau

Knowledge and wisdom have an authority that is almost moral. It is an authority
that is easily and often ignored by those, including young people, who need it
most. It seems to be in the nature of things, however, that those who ignore it
often escape immediate negative consequences. Regrets may come later.

The natural authority that adheres to knowledge is widely confused with
the power, or the institutional authority, that schools grant to teachers. This
is the power to control a student's behavior by threats of punishment in the
form of bad grades, expulsion, negative letters of recommendation, and potential economic harm. The common educational dogma that justifies all this is
that the authority of knowledge by its very nature entails the power to control,
and that it is a function of knowledgeable teachers to use this power to protect
society from maleducated youths who would otherwise rise to high positions.
In fact, of course, the power to control is antithetical to the valid claims of
knowledge, for at the core of the latter is a rejection of coercion in favor of
reason. And one must pray that there are better protectors of society than
teachers and professors. Confusing the two types of authority is, of course, an
easy and strategic thing for educators to do. There is no argument concerning
their institutional standing, though there might be considerable doubt as to
their knowledge and wisdom.

The result in schools and colleges is the distortion of the relationship
between student and teacher precisely because the proper authority of knowledge, on the one hand, and power on the other, are not kept separate. The
avoidance of punishment is almost a full-time preoccupation for many students, who rarely even reach the question of the real contribution a teacher

might make to their lives. The teachers, lulled by obedience and distracted by considerations of the proper uses of power, are in the business of behavior control rather than education. The confusion persists because faculty members profit from it, enjoying the flattery, admiration, and false tokens of respect that come so easily to powerful elites. The rigor of subjecting their ideas to competition in a free marketplace is lacking in a central realm of their lives, their teaching. The opportunity to use their deepest potentials as teachers is lost, just as the corresponding abilities to learn from elders remain unexercised in students.

It has thus come to seem basically contradictory to speak of a free student. Being a student has *meant* being subject to the institutionalized power of one's teachers. Similar thinking has made it seem contradictory to speak of a liberated woman or an economically and socially equal black person. But we know that sexist and racist frameworks of ideas and attitudes can, with difficulty, be discarded. Such could be the case with freedom and education.

In most matters of learning, especially when we are not in schools, we are free students. Although academic tradition opposes the concept, a great body of the human experience of learning does not. As independent adults we choose to learn many things: new hobbies and recreations; new ways to handle our money; new professions or new aspects of current professions; the tenets of a religion that attracts us; a new language. We seek out information about child rearing, family health, psychological problems, sex, travel, home repair, hobbies, new sports, and physical activities. We read books, buy records and tapes, take courses, talk with friends, watch films and television.

As we do all these things, we retain control over our own learning. We make our own decisions about how to pursue new knowledge and skills, and we make our own judgments about how well we're doing. We are free to reject or abandon, without punishment, courses of study, just as we sometimes choose to adopt an authority as a mentor, usually from afar. These projects can elicit enormous levels of commitment and energy from us, and we often find ourselves experiencing joy in our involvement and growth. In short, we retain our autonomy, and it seems perfectly natural that we do so. We are free students. This probably accounts for the joy we find in the process of learning and the commitment that it commands. Yet it seems just as natural to deny these same freedoms, this same autonomy, to students in our systems of formal education from kindergarten through graduate school.

Talk about the joy of learning as free students is not properly limited to rhapsodizing about toddlers learning to play with their toys. It applies to many adults in significant parts of their lives. It could apply to students in schools and colleges.

Students could be treated like real people. They could study a curriculum composed of subjects that are important to them and the world. In higher education, choosing and pursuing one's life goals could be a central theme, and the choices need not come from an array of possibilities heavily biased in favor of the academic professions. Students could be encouraged in the development of personal independence instead of obedience. They could be involved in trying to discover how they learn best, and they could be getting practice in structuring their own time. Students could also be doing things that are socially useful; they need not be immersed in a narcissistic program of self-development, all of whose meaning lies in the future. Students could, in other words, be valued and value themselves for what they are, not only for what they will become. This is a central point. It is easier to deny freedom to people if one believes that it is only their experience in the future, not in the present, that counts.

It is hard to feel good about oneself when a large portion of one's time is controlled, to no clear purpose, by others. Students feel like victims when they fail, and they are often cynical about their successes, which they know to be empty. Plunged into a series of senseless competitions, large numbers of students routinely cheat because they see no reason to play the game honestly. Formal higher education corrupts and oppresses where it could liberate. Students could be free in schools, as most learners are free outside of schools.

*

Free students make their own judgments about what is interesting, important, and potentially useful to learn. Curriculum is not imposed.

Free students make their own judgments about how they are to learn the subjects they select.

Free students make their own judgments about how they will use the human and material resources for learning that are available. They are not required, for example, to use a particular professor or a text in order to learn a subject. An obvious limitation is their lack of control over the terms according to which some resources might be available. A teacher, for example, may set conditions for his or her participation in a student's work. A library sets conditions for the use of its books. But the student is in charge of the project itself and may reject the conditions and seek other teachers or decide to do without teachers. Books may be bought or borrowed elsewhere.

Free students make their own final judgments about how well they have learned. As members of our society they cannot, of course, eliminate, control, or ignore the various certification or entrance requirements of established institutions. They will, therefore, sometimes choose learning content and methods for their utility in these respects rather than for their intrinsic merit. They will have to take examinations and meet requirements if they want certain jobs, and they must plan accordingly. But the learning process itself will not be full of externally imposed and arbitrary barriers of evaluation whose purposes are primarily to control behavior and exert the authority of a teacher. Our academies are, of course, full of such barriers, but they needn't be.

14

Donna

> ... a prophecy of the end he had been born to serve and had been following through the mists of childhood and boyhood, a symbol of the artist forging anew in his workshop out of the sluggish matter of the earth a new soaring impalpable imperishable being . . . a priest of eternal imagination, transmuting the daily bread of experience into the radiant body of everliving life. . . .
>
> —James Joyce, A Portrait of the Artist as a Young Man

> The novel raised religious questions for me and taught me to search my mind, my heart and my soul more rigorously than I ever had before. The experience was an epiphany in the true Joycean sense of the word: a spiritual manifestation of the truth.
>
> —Donna

The impulse to be a teacher may simply be the desire to tell something to someone, to share. What a teacher needs most is a student, someone to listen and respond. While I was a full-time core faculty member in the IDP, my office was next door to that of Art Pitts, a core faculty colleague from the English Department. Art and I talked a lot, especially about books. We also did learning contracts with Donna from time to time, and when she was talking with one of us, the other was likely to drop in and join the conversation. The three of us relished the opportunity to talk about literature, to share our reactions and especially our enjoyment of books and writers that were new to us. I remember vividly, for example, Donna describing her love of James Joyce and the rewards she got from the hours spent with his books. After Donna graduated and I left Buffalo, I wrote to Art and Donna, or imagined conversations with them, and the two of them remained an integral part of my experience of literature. We formed a small intellectual community in which the urges to teach and learn merged; it grew to be important to tell each other about things. There was a sense of challenge present in our little community, partly because my laziness and Art's were not shared by Donna, who pushed ahead into ever more difficult literature, and partly because we respected each other. But there was no sense of labor. Those conversations were fun, and I think that they will always stand for the three of us as particularly intense experiences of good education. Donna was an extraordinary student, whose intelligence, curiosity, and energy added learning and enjoyment to our lives as we attempted to enrich hers.

Donna is not the first person her age to identify with Joyce's young artist. After one has known her for a while, though, it is clear that the implicit romantic view of self is more justified, less a matter of adolescent fantasy, than is usually the case. There is a spiritual and intellectual quest at the center of Donna's life. Certain questions of philosophy and religion are real to her, and she pursues them vigorously. Donna is also occupied with the challenge of creating; she writes and works in graphics and photography. Although she is a person who seeks out books, teachers, and discussion, Donna periodically leaves such company to walk through the woods and marshes and along beaches, watching birds and enjoying nature quietly. Intellectually Donna runs deep, and she is sometimes solitary. But she also establishes productive and happy relationships with people. She has a strong laugh, even a giggle, and they sometimes surprise and embarrass her as they intrude in unscheduled fashion upon serious business.

The variety of Donna's activities and her sheer energy are striking, but they might seem like mere curiosities in an underachieving world until one senses their unity. Donna isn't simply busy; she is doing something. Although she was a very young woman when I met her, still in her teens, Donna had already begun to define an intellectual and spiritual program for herself. Its quality is high, the result of considerable talent and intelligence. Neither she nor anyone else can state the nature of Donna's quest precisely, but it has to do with a search for meaning and an attempt to define a position in culture from which to be creative and useful. It involves the making of a person who will be properly placed and equipped to live well. Donna's chances of success are good. She is sufficiently self-possessed and audacious to aim high, yet she is modest and aware of what she has not yet learned.

The IDP was an opportunity for Donna to use the time devoted to formal education, along with the resources of a college, to address rather directly the tasks of learning and growth that were basic to her life. A conventional academic program would often have been tangential at best, requiring compromises that would have been distracting from her real tasks. In the IDP she experienced few problems and learned a great deal rather quickly. The IDP also allowed Donna to work sufficiently close to her capacities to be able to identify some of the personal limitations which would not have been approached in normal classes. In a conventional program Donna would simply have been the best student in most courses, exceeding requirements with little effort, and having her time filled with busywork. In the three years it took for Donna to earn a degree in the IDP, she had a very different sort of education.

The study of Joyce is a continuing theme in Donna's life. His works provide the insights, puzzles, and challenges that illuminate, or sometimes becloud Donna's experience. Although there are strong recurrent themes, Donna's path twists and turns. There is always a tension within her among the impulses to create artistically, to study, and to act in the social realm. Her early life was haunted by a family misfortune that strengthened Donna's interest in vocations that serve other people directly. This opposes her strong natural inclinations to the solitude of art and scholarship. And when she was a graduate student at a radical university in England, living among a circle of socialist friends, she developed a commitment to the possibilities of political analysis and action.

When Donna came to college she had already read and been moved by *Portrait.* Joyce had made a claim on her. She was also active as an artist. But an unhappy accident was a prominent factor in the life of Donna's family, and it had affected her deeply. When he was three years old, Donna's younger brother, remembered by his family as having been a brilliant child, fell from a moving automobile and suffered brain damage. Fifteen years later Donna described the accident in detail, as if a family discussion had only recently reviewed the event closely, seeking ways to understand an irrational fact that, for all the harm that occurred, makes no sense. The family's life was changed forever. As the oldest child Donna was particularly close to her parents and perhaps wise beyond her years. Part of the burden of care and worry fell on her. It nurtured within her a concern for handicapped people and a desire to help them. In her teens she volunteered to work with brain-damaged and emotionally disturbed children.

Donna came to Buffalo State because of the IDP. She was pleased to find that the college also had an art education program. She was seriously considering a career in that field, and she had a special interest in art therapy. She had found that her artistic skills could be helpful in her volunteer work. She saw art and music as media to help communicate with and stimulate handicapped children. When Donna applied to the IDP she wrote:

> Through my work with these children I have been particularly impressed by their affection for their teachers and their love of art and music. For this reason I hope that during the coming years I may discover methods for helping these children through artistic expression.

Influenced by her father, who is a commercial artist, Donna used her art in other settings. She had designed her school's yearbook cover, classroom murals, sets for church plays, and posters and brochures for charitable events. She won awards for some of this work. All the while, her love of literature and particularly the works of Joyce remained in the background.

Donna anticipated that being in college and the IDP would help her sort things out and become clearer about herself and her interests:

> The IDP will provide me with an opportunity to broaden my scope through experimentation and exploration, and ultimately it will enable me to determine a point of focus. . . . The unstructured flexible nature of the curriculum will enable me to study more thoroughly the areas in which I have the greatest interest. I will be able to accomplish a great deal more, more quickly than I normally would. Most importantly it will provide me with the responsibility and challenge to define my educational program to fit these goals.

The IDP's educational philosophy seemed consistent with her own experience:

> I have always loved school and consistently done well, but in retrospect the learnings with the greatest impact and sense of discovery were those which I designed for myself. In elementary school these took the form of projects which I prepared either for an assignment or merely for my own entertainment. One of the most influential of these projects was undertaken at age ten, when I constructed a simple camera from a shoebox; with the aid of my father I was able to develop and print black and white photographs.

Donna's tone of strength and self-confidence was unusual, but those words could have been written by almost any IDP student. They are not very different from what Paul and Zoe wrote. Yet Donna was very different, and so was her experience in the IDP. Her intelligence certainly helped. Things did come easily to Donna. But there were many very bright students who had a great deal of trouble in the IDP and students of average intelligence who did quite well. Donna would probably say that the main factor was her "love of learning." Here is a statement of Donna's view of herself, a statement that would seem clichéd and self-serving were it not so obviously true:

> . . . it was my parents who exerted the greatest influence on my intellectual development. Neither of them attained any degree beyond a high school diploma, yet both of them nurtured in me something of far greater value than the knowledge a college degree could have afforded them. They gave me a love of learning and questioning, a sense of discovery in the most commonplace situations, and a love of music. From my mother, born in Scotland, I inherited a love of Celtic culture, an influence which certainly enhanced my responsiveness to the literature of James Joyce. From my father, an artist, I inherited not only my ability to draw and to appreciate art, but also a sensitivity to likenesses in the variety of human experiences—the essence of creative thought.

From my point of view, a critical reason for Donna's success in the IDP was her unusual seriousness about herself. She thought that she and her search for learning were important. She had confidence that, even if she were just beginning to study something, her understanding would reach a level of real significance, and she was right. Donna was not without the crises and confusions that mark most people's college years. She had the usual problems of interpersonal relations, compounded by the fact that many people, especially some young men, are puzzled by strong and intelligent young women. Her academic and life goals went in and out of focus. She had a painful and extended crisis as she moved away from her family's religion. Yet underneath it all Donna knew that her education was worthwhile, that there was a promise of growth that would justify a strong confrontation with her doubts and problems. She had a sense of being valuable.

Donna followed her program. The focus of her first year was on projects in psychology and education that helped her look into issues relating to professions serving handicapped people. She also did a contract in drawing and anatomy, and projects in ceramics and photography. As a student of literature and a person with religious commitments, she did work in the Old and New Testaments. And Donna found a young English professor, Dr. Carole

Brown, whose scholarly specialty was the work of James Joyce. From that point on Donna would always be working on at least one major project on Joyce.

The study of Joyce gradually came to dominate Donna's intellectual life. Her interest in working with handicapped people gave way to an ambition for an academic career as a professor of literature. This may have been a result of being away from home and gaining some distance from her family's involvement with her brother. Donna came to think of her life as an artist in relationship to her work on Joyce. Perhaps she could do artistic work that bore on her scholarship. A couple of years later, looking ahead to a Ph.D., Donna wrote the following on an application for a fellowship:

> Although at the present time I do not know what the specific subject of my doctoral dissertation will be, I know that it will deal with the later works of James Joyce, either *Ulysses* or *Finnegans Wake*. I am most interested in imagery and its rhythmic and structural patterns, and I plan to create a visual interpretation to complement my thesis. . . .
>
> I believe that effectively utilized, visual interpretation will prove a valuable means of dispelling the elitism that unfortunately dominates a considerable amount of Joyce scholarship.

It was clear from the beginning that Donna's aspirations were realistic. She had the makings of a scholar. All of her work was of high quality. At the conclusion of the evaluation of a learning contract, a faculty member would try to provide a summary statement reflecting the quality of the student's work. Here are some excerpts from Donna's contract evaluations.

> Through her ceramic and sculptural work, Donna has shown me that she has a good understanding of techniques in shaping clay and in glazing and has produced a collection of vastly different compositions, all showing an extremely good sense of design.

> Donna showed the ability to work independently on a long-term, involved project in anatomy. She was able to set long-range and daily goals and to plan daily and weekly tasks to meet the goals. She displayed the initiative, motivation and fortitude to carry out the project. Donna was able to read advanced materials and apply the learning without outside help. She used the library effectively as a resource. Her final report demonstrated her ability to synthesize the knowledge she gained into a well-organized report. Her journal demonstrated an ability to keep accurate, detailed daily and weekly records of accomplishments.

Donna's written and performance level of activity was excellent. She required very little real direction and worked independently with resourcefulness. She surveyed a wide selection of readings in the areas of learning, motivation and experimental methodology, and evidenced through written assignments and conferences a good understanding and interpretation of the material covered.

Donna is an insightful critic of Shakespeare's drama and was able to discern with perception the complex patterns and issues raised by Shakespeare's most mature plays. She was particularly good in picking up the larger patterns suggested in the comedies and later in the romances. Her understanding of the most recent trends in criticism, i.e., the archetypal and psychoanalytical schools, helped her to understand many of the difficult problems in characterization, and led her to draw conclusions which I found valuable. All in all, her contribution was most impressive.

As a core faculty member, I got to know Donna when she joined a group of students working with me on a project studying the world's food supply. Grain reserves had dropped, and the threat of extraordinary famine was substantial that year. Our diverse group of six or seven people met every day for several weeks. Each of us read and reported on an article or chapter of a book. Every day we distributed a written summary of what we had learned. Our intention was to produce a multimedia presentation that would allow us to share our findings with others. The presentation was in fact completed and offered to a chemistry class at the college and to a number of high school classes.

Before our work had progressed very far, we began to accumulate a great deal of information. We started a filing system, but it worked only moderately well. The natural division of labor that develops in any group saved us from being completely overwhelmed. In our case Donna became the brains and information expert of the operation. She was better able than any of us to remember, connect, and sort through the information we were gathering. It was common for us to hear a new fact in one student's report and then to remember that we had dealt with a related fact a week or so earlier. We'd try to be specific, and then we'd turn to Donna. She'd think for a moment and then recall the fact and the source. The rest of us, of course, came to rely on her. Her command of the facts was so good that she easily compiled, working with Debbie, a booklet listing about eighty-five facts that were critical to understanding the world food supply problem. The booklet was distributed to the audiences at our presentation.

Toward the end of the project, Donna and I had a long talk about her schoolwork. She was concerned that she did not seem to be extending herself fully, that there was a lack of challenge in her life. Things were coming too easily to her. After the conversation I realized that I had not been able to formulate something that had been bothering me about Donna's work, and that it was connected to her complaint. I wrote a letter to her:

> Here's what I think the real problem is: it's not that the things you do are too easy or too conventional, it's that they are too clear-cut. You almost always buy into a venture whose nature is already well defined. . . . You don't allow yourself to have to deal with the question of what to do next. This is not usually noticed because the tasks you do undertake are so difficult. . . .
>
> You'll be at Buffalo State for another year, and you should have some flexibility in what you do. I hope that you'll have a chance to try some really murky, ill-defined projects, projects in which you really have to apply your intelligence to making judgments about what directions to take. I think that kind of thing will be hard and uncomfortable for you, but you should learn a lot. . . .

Donna agreed, and she did, in her final year in Buffalo, try to deal with the more basic questions involved in defining a study.

Donna's three years of college went smoothly. Her seriousness, sense of humor, geniality, and the high quality of her work drew her into close relationships with a number of professors, all of whom were eager to work with her on second and third learning contracts, and to recommend her to colleagues. Donna's education was continuous, for she formulated projects that could be done at home during holidays and vacations. In New York on vacation, for example, she would go to dance concerts and films as part of a study of choreography she was doing on campus. At the end of three years her degree committee had no trouble in certifying her for graduation. She had an impressive range of achievements that easily satisfied the college's general education requirements. Her knowledge of the history of literature compared very favorably with the standard graduate of the English Department, and her work in Joyce was extraordinary. Although students majoring in English had to fulfill a particular requirement by choosing one of three courses, Donna had done projects in all three areas. She saw no point in leaving unnecessary gaps.

With glowing letters of recommendation, but without a conventional transcript that included grades, Donna was accepted for graduate study at Berkeley, the University of Toronto, and the University of Essex, the latter two being among the best places in the world to study Joyce. She won an honorable mention in the Danforth Fellowship competition, the only Buffalo State student ever to do so.

Donna pondered the choice of graduate schools for some time. One of her older female professors, somewhat lacking in the spirit of the new feminism, told her that the choice between Toronto and Essex came down to the question of whether she wanted to marry a Canadian or an Englishman. In the end Donna decided to go to Essex, not for matrimonial reasons, but to study with a particular Joyce scholar and to seek out the adventure and learning to be found farther from home.

Donna's early letters from Essex were full of new friends (students from all over the world), travel, politics, and theories of criticism and culture. She stayed for two years, and as the time passed, a conflict between her politics and her teachers came to dominate her experience. Donna's literary mentors found political thought both soft and dogmatic. I feel sure they stereotyped her; at least it is hard for me to imagine Donna applying any idea or theory thoughtlessly or inappropriately. In any case, her master's thesis, on Joyce and Ellison, was criticized and its acceptance was delayed. Donna was required to make revisions on grounds that she thought were trivial. A period of growth and stimulation thus ended painfully, with considerable embarrassment.

Donna is living in New York, working in the managing editor's office of a major publishing company. She participated in a long and successful struggle to organize the firm's workers into a union. Several of her photographs have been used on book covers, despite the company's custom of favoring free-lance photographers rather than members of its own staff. She has traveled to Northern Ireland and had photographs from these trips published in periodicals and included in a television film.

In the evening Donna works with an organization distributing and supporting political films. She is taking courses in languages and film. She reads, writes, takes pictures, enjoys the city. Stung by her first bad experience in

Donna

academia, she may nevertheless go back to school as a full-time student before long. The constants in Donna's life are evident in her letters and the occasional visits we have: her strong intelligence, supply of energy, good humor, and commitment. One assumes they will continue to serve her well. I will be surprised if she fails to do anything she sets out to do.

15

The Administration Building

I started work at Buffalo State College shortly before construction began on its new administration building. The move from the old administration building to the new one, when it finally came after many delays, was an event of major significance in the lives of the people who ran the college. The simple change of location somehow had the power to reveal central professional values of the participants. Years of intrigue went into settling the critical questions about office space: proximity to the president; square footage for each administrative rank; private lavatories; location with respect to one's rivals; room for growth; a room with a view; carpets; distance from students. In these matters naked egos were on the line. There was an orgy of rationalization. Each vice president had endless reasons for needing, by virtue of undeniable administrative responsibilities, the largest suite of offices closest to the president. Each dean and director had analogous reasons that required being next door to a particular vice president.

In a stunning application of administrative science, the deans, who all had nice offices in the old administration building, were not permitted even to move into the new one. Several deans were bitter for years. I had advance notice of the development from the assistant to the president, a retired Air Force colonel whose heart was still in uniform. Coming out from behind the model airplane and short wave radio on his desk, he confided to me that the president and vice presidents had determined that the deans were really field officers. They should be billeted, therefore, among their professorial troops, in the science building, the art building, and the other instructional battle-grounds around campus.

When I was called into my vice president's office to receive my new office assignment, he treated it as a moment of high drama. My office, it turned out, would be on the top floor along with the big shots, but it would also be as far from the president's office as one could get and also pretty far from the vice president's own office. The vice president had the blueprints spread out on his desk. He explained the building's layout and who would be working on each floor. Then he showed me each feature of my office, emphasizing the status symbols that were available to me. He pointed out the space that could be used for an added secretary or assistant, if I were to acquire new staff. He suggested how the current secretary might be situated so as to make me least accessible to visitors. I was, however, going to share an office suite with someone else; this was lamentable but absolutely necessary. He explained how furniture and decorations were to be purchased and approved, and advised me to allow my secretary to have just the right amount of influence, certainly not too much, in the process. There was an air of ritual and of great generosity in the way my boss spoke to me that day, and I believe he was a little disappointed that I couldn't think of more questions. I also think I failed to be sufficiently grateful for the advantages he had conferred on me.

The administrative and psychic turmoil continued for several years after the building was first occupied. Any institutional problem of significance was met with an administrative reorganization whose main effect was a change in offices. There were constant crises of territorial protection and invasion followed by the moving men who wheeled desks and filing cabinets through the halls. The moves were concluded when the painters appeared to do the walls again, for the halls were narrow, and the walls were inevitably scraped and marked during a move.

The hiring of a new administrator, of course, also entailed a shuffle. Any candidate worthy of employment would get the picture during a job interview and bargain for some good space as a condition of taking the position. The space always came from someone whose administrative star was low, but the new person almost inevitably lost some of it before too long. A really smart young administrator would make moderate demands and thus limit the embarrassment at the end of the honeymoon period.

The story would be incomplete without mention of the worst office in the building. The College Senate was gaining power in those days. As a gesture of political respect, the faculty member who was elected its president was given an office in the administration building. One president of the senate was qualified for the job because he belonged to one faction but was perceived by the other factions as weak enough to manipulate. Some administrator would have to share an office suite with this guy. It was intolerable, and I have known people to threaten to resign if assigned to that office. The threat carried little weight, however, for anyone who could be a candidate for occupying that office was so weak that he or she would probably soon be reorganized back into the faculty.

Each shuffle of offices was accomplished with great satisfaction among the president and vice presidents, who would never dream of delegating decisions on these matters to anyone below them in the hierarchy. There was a sense that every problem of education would somehow be solved if only the right people were switched into the right offices on the upper floors. The faculty scrutinized the moves carefully, understanding that assignment to offices was a sensitive barometer indicating favor and disfavor at the highest levels. I don't know what it means, but within a couple of years the roof of the new building sprang a leak that was difficult to fix. The Office of Academic Affairs labored for some time under huge sheets of plastic collecting large quantities of water.

*

Power in institutions of higher education is concentrated in the hands of self-protective career bureaucracies of administrators and professors. All of these people learn to talk lovingly about students, but the most successful of them are consummate self-promoters, and their interests rarely coincide with those of students. Administrative efficiency, grantsmanship, and good public relations are highly rewarded. Neatness counts, both in appearance and thought. It matters little that many of the best educational practices have a messiness, an individual quality, that is not respected by the dominant administrative or intellectual styles. The bureaucracy runs on rules, and it often seems as if education consists of exceptions.

More basically, the institutions of higher education run on hierarchical principles. Formal power is concentrated at the top. Students are, despite public relations rhetoric, at the bottom. Education that gives students more control over their lives is felt by most teachers and administrators to be deeply disturbing and threatening because it requires the sharing of power with students. It challenges the spirit, if not the detailed regulations, of the bureaucracy that is their professional home. Such education looks and feels subversive to the career educational administrators who have most of the power.

The nature of campus relationships is symbolized by and designed into the new administration buildings that have risen over many campuses. They are often the scene of their own semiannual comedies like the Buffalo State shuffle. The standard design places the president and vice presidents in offices with good views on the top floor, far from the "flow of student traffic." The registrar, bursar, and admissions offices are on the ground floor, easily accessible to students. The computer is in its own special wing, where security can be tightened up and doors locked to student demonstrators just in case the sixties return. In other buildings, professors who rise to chairmanships move from offices entered from the hall into departmental offices, access to which is through an outer office staffed by secretaries. Rank in the system is directly proportional to physical distance from students.

These practical arrangements make sense in many ways. But when one lives with college professors and administrators for years, it becomes clear that something is at work that transcends considerations of logistics and efficiency. Members of these institutions derive prestige and status from their physical distance and, when one looks carefully, their social distance from students. Of course there are critical public rituals during which the most powerful of the administrators don denim and sit on the floor with students. Yet when one knows them, one sees that they often do not really *like* students. They devote a great deal of energy to arranging their daily lives so as to deal with each other and to minimize their contacts with students, the alleged beneficiaries of their actions. When a colleague is praised as "good with students," the compliment is often double-edged; there is an implication that such a person, although humane and possibly amusing, may not be equal to the intellectual and social demands of high office.

Students get the picture. Vice presidents, deans, and other administrators tell them that their doors will always be open, and then they hide those doors in the remote reaches of buildings and set out secretaries to guard them. Timid students often live with problems that could be solved by seeking out an administrator. Their tentative requests for help usually turn out to be futile and even demeaning. Those who are less timid almost never receive the help or even the sympathetic ear that they seek. They speak of their encounters in bitter terms, terms that sound harsh and radical unless one is familiar with the educators with whom they have dealt.

16

Ken

Communal love and strength—that's IDP. . . . I am sorry that the IDP didn't
work for me. I wish to thank everyone for trying to help. Thank you.

—Ken

Ken stayed in the IDP for a semester. The faculty and students who knew him
were sad and surprised to see him leave. Ken felt bad about dropping out of
the program, but he had to do so. He was serious about his education, and
he had to follow his best judgment. He could not see how the IDP would be
able to help him. The faculty was not successful in assisting Ken in using the
opportunities that existed. Our failure, ironically, was due in part to the fact
that we were too impressed with Ken's strengths, his talent, and the absence
of some of the typical problems of IDP students. We therefore underestimated
the severity of his difficulties.

Ken is a small young man with long hair and a shy smile. At the time he
joined the IDP he wore a bell on a strip of leather around his neck, although
the days of the flower children were already several years past. The bell did
not seem wrong. It rang softly as Ken moved. His voice was soft too, sometimes barely audible as his shyness almost smothered his speech. Ken usually
carried a sketch pad with him. He was liable to dash off a drawing or caricature
at any moment. His talent is enormous. His drawings combine considerable
technical skill with a keen intelligence and a fine sense of humor. Ken was
well-disciplined too; he seemed to be able to structure and use his time well.

Ken appeared to be an ideal IDP student. He seemed ready to use the
program's freedom. He was not simply a talented boy who was interested in
art. He was on his way to being a creator who had staked out a meaningful
artistic position from which to work and grow. He also seemed already to
possess much of what the regular college program would have given him. Ken
had many basic skills, so there would be little point in running him through
a series of introductory courses. Just give him his freedom, we thought, and
stand back. It did not, however, work out that way.

Ken's most obvious difficulty in the IDP was one he shared with many of our students. He worried that he might be missing something by not taking regular courses. Ken and the others who felt this way had often been desperately unhappy in conventional classrooms. Most art teachers, for example, would admire Ken's talents, but they would be unable or unwilling to alter the curriculum to produce a course of study that would truly be helpful to him. Ken had experienced such education and rebelled, and this was one reason he joined the IDP.

Rebel or not, it is not easy to set aside the feelings and ideas that are inculcated by a system in which one has grown up. Facing the uncertainties of a new program, a student wonders whether conventional education might, this one time, actually work. Many IDP students had, like Ken, developed extensive critiques, deeply felt and based on experience, of conventional schooling. Yet IDP students and faculty, time after time, found that we had internalized the feelings and reactions that the system had taught. We were well-trained, and we undercut our own efforts at change. Confronting freedom meant deciding how to use one's time, and one couldn't be sure one was right. Everyone else was *busy,* going to classes, taking tests. Perhaps we were wrong in our previous conclusion that much of that activity was wasteful and silly. Perhaps all those people really knew something that had escaped us.

There was a limited amount of help that the IDP faculty could have given Ken. Each student must come to a personal decision on whether to gamble on participation in an innovative program. Intervention with arguments against convention soon becomes a matter of propagandizing students and distorting their decision-making processes. We were determined to be careful not to overstep those bounds. Yet there was some help Ken could have received. We could have offered more gentle encouragement, and more importantly, we could have helped him explore in much greater detail his possibilities for using the IDP. A concrete vision of those uses might have offset the promises, many of them illusory and known to be so, of the regular program.

We did not offer Ken more help for many reasons. We were busy. Ken was quiet and shy. Other students were in more obvious distress. But most of all, Ken's talents and work were so impressive that we tended to romanticize him. Our mistakes in that direction, with Ken and a few other students, were almost certainly systematic and more widespread than we knew. We had created a program based upon the premise that the students were equipped to achieve much more, on their own, than they are usually given credit for. We were under pressure, scared, eager for the program to succeed. It did not help the IDP or anyone in it, but we did tend to exaggerate the strengths of students. We created images of them that were less troubled, more immediately competent than they really were. Or perhaps, like Ken, they had competence but not confidence. We also probably minimized the doubts about the IDP that all of us had. One had to function.

Ken left the IDP and wrote:

> I am leaving the program for want of a more structured organized program. I feel that the motivation I need is in the classes, at the moment, so I must leave. . . . The security of classes, knowing I have the facilities and advisement in my field of study and exposure to things I could not find on my own —these are the things missing from IDP.

At first Ken was happy in regular classes, relieved to be doing things the right way again. After a couple of semesters he dropped out of school. He found what he knew all along, that the advisement would generally counsel conformity, that the exposure would often be to new things that were not timely, that the facilities he sought often came with a price tag that mandated how they were to be used, that his special gifts were not well served by the standard academic program. Its promise, once again, proved to be fraudulent, yet we had not been able to provide an alternative.

17

Cause School, NEIA, and the IDP

My mind is a blank. What do I have to say about Cause School today? The children looked beautiful at Tifft Farm holding their flowering reed grass high in the air, running up mounds against clouds from which the sun was peeping. They explore, they enjoy new discoveries, they run, laugh and fight over petty things. They are so alive and interested in living—maybe that's what I find so beautiful.

—Neia

My children, Josh and Danny, reached school age during our stay in Buffalo. I spent the first years of Josh's life trying not to think about finding a school for him that would be reasonably consistent with my values. I believed that the necessary compromises would be unhappy ones. Less pessimistic and more adventurous, our friend Bev Paigen, the person who worked with Debbie and the others on the playground project, learned about Cause School, and the problem was solved until we left Buffalo. Named for an almost defunct civil rights organization, Cause, as we came to call it, was located in the basement of a church's community building in a black section of the city. There was a handful of students, black kids from the neighborhood and white kids like ours and the Paigens', from the liberal upper middle class. Everyone paid tuition, although poor families arranged to pay less.

When you had spent a few minutes in Cause's crowded, stuffy, run-down, apparently disorganized classroom, you knew that something extraordinarily good was happening there. Life in that room was obviously full of growth and learning; the atmosphere was one of fun, respect, and love. Book learning was in evidence, but so was concern with social and emotional learning. There were art, dramatics, and music. There was evidence that the cultural differences between white and black kids were possible focal points for learning, that they were explored, valued, and understood at levels appropriate for the kids. Cause students played a lot too, and they and the teachers often piled into a van to go to playgrounds (especially the "Paigen Playground" which was designed by the IDP students), parks, markets, museums, construction sites, stores, the roofs of tall buildings, river banks, and zoos. In many ways Cause School was the realization for me of an educational fantasy, whose existence in the real world I doubted in my weaker moments. I was elated to discover Cause, and my later disappointments were only minor. Josh had several glorious years at Cause. Danny's time was not as good, mainly because there were problems for him connected with having his older brother in the same school.

Neia: (This passage and the others in this chapter are taken from the journals and academic papers Neia—prounced Neeyä—wrote while working at Cause School as an IDP student.)
I think I want to work with mentally retarded kids, kids who don't have the mental capacity to scheme and plot and organize to make your life difficult.

The genius behind Cause was Win Evers, its founder and head teacher. She is a tough idealistic white liberal from the South, where a liberal's mettle is tested. Her commitments have survived and been proved genuine by a series of unsympathetic environments. Win is one of those rare people who persist in unrealistic ventures until people and conditions bend to her vision. She is also an especially talented teacher. She can create a classroom in which freedom is the dominant theme and in which people's private needs, including her own, are respected. Win has a temper, and kids learn that she can lose it, just as they may sometimes get angry. But it is absolutely clear to them that Win loves and respects them.

Neia:
Patrick is a second grador. He hasn't "learned" long division or multiplication with carrying yet. His eye caught a new number game I brought down from the main resource room today, and he wanted to play it. He worked his way through long division and multiplication doggedly. He'd say "Wait a minute, let me think" and walk away, think, and come back and tell me the answer to such problems as 12×4, $72 \div 9$, 6×13, etc. The only one he had problems with, the only one he let me tell him the answer to, was $48 \div 6$. Here

is another case of a child having the chance to do advanced work. . . . Patrick didn't want to know the "way" to do these problems. He, a second grader, figured them out in his head. The next step to take would be to try to find out how Patrick does them in his head and maybe show him a faster way to do it.

Win had a protégé named Keith Gmerek. When Keith came to help Win at Cause, he was a neighborhood kid in his teens and had just dropped out of college. Win took people in off the street. Keith had a natural grace with children. He and Win communicated easily. It soon became clear to Keith that there was a great deal to be learned working with Win. They became partners and friends. Keith stayed on for a decade.

Neia:
In discussing the schools I have studied, I have left Cause School for last. Cause School is the most successful alternative school I have seen. By successful I mean that it has a productive, warm, and positive atmosphere. A number of facets contribute to its success: the teachers have a true interest in the needs of the students; flexibility is evident but teachers have a degree of control to assure the stability of the school; children come from a wide range of backgrounds and are allowed to interact honestly with each other; parents have faith in the teachers, leaving final control to them, and teachers have a true respect for the parents' concerns about their children's educations; teachers make an effort to maintain a good relationship with the surrounding community; teachers have an interest in the well-being of the school, and they frequently discuss conflicts and solutions, and also the joys and frustrations they experience with the children and parents with whom they come into contact; the school remains small so the family feeling is not destroyed.

I think a great deal of the success of Cause School comes from the fact that Win Evers, a teacher, has not been afraid to take an authority role when no one else would. All schools need some sort of central figure to provide some consistency in programming. Win is, luckily, very practical and honest in her dealings with adults and children. She has had much experience in teaching and has many interesting ideas about the ways things can be taught. She takes suggestions and criticism well but is able to take complete control of a situation if necessary.

After volunteer teaching part time, I arranged to student-teach at Cause. I continue to visit almost every week. I learn so much not only about good teaching methods in an alternative school but about the excitement one can have in seeing a school grow and change in a positive manner. Win and Keith put much energy into the school, as do a small core of parents. They are realistic about other people and realize that they can't be counted upon to do everything. They speak up honestly if angry about something. Those that have been the mainstays of Cause School are reliable, sensible, honest, and full of energy and excitement about life. They have inspired many children and myself to be that way also.

Cause was almost always in the midst of some crisis. It might involve money, organization, enrollment, facilities, or the spirit. After a while one learned not to panic, to understand that crises were part of the school's way of life. They were a means of focusing and mobilizing energy.

Another factor in the Cause situation in the era in which I knew it was the possibility of Win's leaving. She thought about moving on to other activities or careers, and one of her goals was to see things develop so that Keith and other young teachers could carry on without her. I am sure that Win will indeed move on, but I don't think she was ready to do so in the early seventies, the time about which I'm writing. She did, however, decrease her involvement in Cause for a while, and this coincided with a crisis which the school almost did not survive.

Win drew a tiny salary from Cause, and she was under considerable financial pressure because her daughter had just begun college. As a licensed Buffalo schoolteacher, she could earn much more in a public school. She decided to take a job in one of the city's more innovative schools. She agreed to continue to handle the administration of Cause School, and to assist and advise Keith before and after the school day. As it turned out, Cause's enrollment was way down, influenced by a silly accidental factor, as can happen with such small operations. The parent who chaired the school's board was taking her child out of the school, and she was convinced that Cause had no choice but to close in the face of the current crop of crises, whatever they were. A rumor got around in the limited community of interested families that Cause had closed, and parents registered their children in other schools.

Neia:
I'm having a problem figuring out how to stop the class from getting chaotic. Win was out of the room for a short period. Richie started making jokes, getting the boys all hyper. Soon the girls were involved, and the room was getting crazier and crazier. I told Richie to find something quiet to do. He said he'd sit and think. That didn't last too long. Pretty soon the kids were crazy again.

Solutions: 1) Tell Richie to leave the situation if he can't do something quietly (go to the library corner or out of the room); 2) Have a list of quiet activities that Richie has devised himself (he likes factoring, puzzles, and games).

I tried solution 1 later in the day. Richie started toward the library corner and then begged me to let him stay at his desk—he'd be quiet. I asked him what he was going to do. He said read comics. That was acceptable to me.

During a time in the day when the kids were especially crazy, Hannah came up to me and said Michael hit her with something. I was at my wits' end, and I pounced on Michael in anger. He was indignant, rightfully so, that I'd yelled only at him.

Solution: If I do the wrong thing, I should explain it to the child. "I was mad, at my wits' end, and you were the one most recently complained about."

One Friday evening early in the fall semester, Win and Keith called us and the Paigens. They didn't see how the school could continue and had virtually made the decision to close it down within the week. This was not an ordinary Cause crisis, and it felt like the beginning of the nightmare that we had feared since our kids had first started at the school. We felt there were no alternatives to Cause that would be anywhere near as good for our children. Independently the two sets of parents told Win and Keith to sit tight; we'd be down at Win's house in the country in an hour. Two weekend trips were put in abeyance.

We found Keith despondent. The small group of kids, most of whom he'd known and cared about for several years, was too diverse for him to teach well. The younger kids required a lot of attention, and Keith was near tears as he described the effects on the older kids of idleness and lack of stimulation, the

106

results of his limited time with them. Cause's finances were, moreover, less tenable than usual, and Keith could barely survive on what he was paid. Also Keith, who had never taught alone before, was feeling isolated and lonely in Win's absence.

Frightened at the thought that this might indeed be Cause's last crisis, the Paigens and Meislers encouraged Win and Keith, and together we formulated an emergency program to try to help. We agreed to get commitments of additional money from the affluent families and to collect the extra funds each month, which was easy, for we *were* most of the affluent families. We would also provide immediate help in the classroom ourselves and would search actively for a more permanent solution to providing help for Keith.

My mind turned to a number of the students in the IDP. They had chosen open style education for themselves; Cause and the IDP were kindred programs. Some of the students also hoped to become teachers in open classrooms. I said that I thought we could find IDP students to work at Cause as volunteers and that they'd probably learn a great deal from the experience.

As I thought about it, I became persuaded that a volunteer arrangement would be more than a solution to Cause's problem. The IDP students I was thinking of read the books of Neill, Goodman, Holt, Kozol, Kohl, and Herndon. They derived inspiration from the ideas and lives of advocates of open education. Yet Buffalo State was a teachers college in the contemporary fashion, and with few exceptions the professors, the curricula, the guiding principles, and the requirements of professional education came from another world, an entirely different frame of reference. The training of teachers at Buffalo State was technical in the extreme, almost clinical. It was as if the college was some kind of fifth-rate medical school in which a humane concept like teaching, not to mention loving, was much less important than ideas of testing, diagnosing, prescribing. The education faculty's commitment to professionalism mandated distance between teachers and students, while the best of our prospective teachers were motivated by a desire for closeness. As the students received their professional training, most of their professors urged a false dichotomy upon them, a dichotomy between competence and an allegedly romantic child-centered ideology. The implicit assumption was that students would have to abandon their commitment to openness and child centered education as the price of buying training to be competent. The assumption was hidden, of course, behind approving rhetoric about open education that was so watered-down and qualified as to be meaningless: coercive education with a smile. These contradictions occasionally surfaced with great drama in a student's experience, as we shall see in a later chapter about Eve. Working at Cause school could be a powerful antidote to the college's assault on our students' idealism.

Neia:
It's funny how kids basically believe you. Even though I yelled at Michael yesterday, he knows I care. Today he came back from art early and tearfully told me that he didn't know what to do about Dean and Richie. They keep trying to get him to fight, and he doesn't want to because he might hurt them, and their parents would get mad and sue him or something. He was honestly trying to resolve a conflict. He wanted to fight to prove that he was strong, but he didn't want to hurt Richie and Dean, who are smaller than he is. It surprised me that Michael came to me to talk about this problem. I didn't give any definite answers. I told him I realized it was very hard. The hardest but maybe the best thing to do would have been to ignore them, to realize that they just wanted to get him mad. Yet I knew he didn't want them to think he was a sissy. I mostly listened to Michael and told him he'd have to make a choice between his alternatives.

Perhaps I should have asked why they were provoking him to fight, gotten Michael to think about that. Maybe Richie and Dean should have gotten in on it. We could have talked about it together, figured out an acceptable way to see who was strongest—
Wrestling (Pete the volunteer knows how to do it properly)
Arm wrestling
Boxing
Boys do fight. I don't know if I'd feel right telling them never to do it. Yet if there were a fight, I'd stop it immediately and have the boys talk about it.

On Monday morning I put a note about Cause's need for volunteers in the IDP mailboxes. I knew there would be interest, but I was apprehensive. The semester was more than a month old, and students had already made substantial commitments of their time to other activities. Volunteers would also have to be devoted and consistent. IDP students sometimes were not. If they could not be counted upon to follow through on their plans, they might be more trouble than help for Cause.

A number of students responded to my note. I told them about Cause and its importance to me, my family, and the other families. I described the school's problems and said that I thought a few volunteers might make a difference. I talked about the kind of teacher Win was and Keith was becoming, and about what I thought might be learned by a student working with them. My sense of opportunity grew and with it a feeling of elation. A supremely competent teacher, Win had never been persuaded by an education professor to abandon her belief in freedom or her directly expressed love for her students. Nor would Keith ever be tempted by any such compromise. If our students worked at Cause, the false dichotomy would be removed for them from the realm of abstract argument, in which the professors have all the advantages, to the realm of empirical observation. The students would simply see that a certain sort of education was in fact possible.

Neia:
I'm finally starting to feel that the kids recognize me—both as a teacher and a person. They remember my name, ask me for help (they are discovering that Win is not the only teacher in the room), follow my commands. I must be careful not to bite off more than I can chew. I am doing quite a bit in the classroom. I should work on what I have done before I get into new areas of study. Win is starting creative writing next week. I feel like I should do it, but then I'm doing art, cooking, science, miscellaneous reading, and spelling, plus the possibility of a math group, guitar lessons, and values clarification in the afternoon. That's plenty.

I sent the students over to Cause to see Keith. They talked about their academic work, interests, ambitions, skills, and talents. Together they found ways in which the IDP students could help Keith and at the same time get experience that promised to produce valuable learning. These students, including Neia, began work at Cause, and their joint weekly contribution amounted to more than the equivalent of another full-time teacher in the classroom. On campus they wrote contracts, for which they found cooperating faculty, that allowed them to make their work at Cause part of their academic programs. Neia began an extensive contract on alternative schools. She used her vacations to visit schools throughout the East and Midwest, and later she volunteered in several other schools in Buffalo.

The IDP students came to feel that the survival of Cause was important. They saw that they were making a real contribution to education in Buffalo. They made a commitment and never wavered from it. They consistently prepared for their work at Cause, came on time, did what they said they would do. I often saw Neia on dark Buffalo mornings waiting in the bitter cold for a bus that would get her to Cause before 8 A.M. They were not "mere students," as our culture encourages us to think of them, people who are preparing, attending to their self-development, but not dealing with significant social realities. They were extremely important to Cause School kids, to their families, to Win and Keith, and to anyone who valued educational diversity in that city. I saw Keith recently, and he referred to "the time the IDP kids saved Cause School." They did.

Neia:
I think that the nicest thing today was catching Nicole while she was heckling the boys doing woodwork and asking her if she wanted to read a story. We went into Keith's room (where she was supposed to be) and curled up in a corner to read The Animal Family *by Randall Jarrell. Hyper, fidgety Nicole was laughing delightedly at the poetic, beautiful language Jarrell uses to describe the growing friendship between a lonely hunter and a mermaid. It was just a small piece of the day—only twenty minutes or so—but Nicole got up from the session so calm, so serene, so at peace with life. Days can be so crazy, so full of yelling at kids to stop bugging each other unnecessarily ("Michael, you don't have to kick Nicole on your way to get your math book," "Seaghan, the room is not a place to zoom around like that, that's for outside."), it's nice to see some calming too. I didn't think Nicole had it in her.*

Within weeks Win left her public school to rejoin Cause as a full-time teacher, and so our students had the opportunity to work directly with her. She was encouraged in this move by progress that was being made by Ken Paigen and some other parents, who were developing a proposal that Cause be assimilated into the public school system as a fairly autonomous unit. If that worked out, Win could be paid a decent salary, Cause students would not have to pay tuition, and the school would have better facilities and supplies. One worried a little about whether Cause could maintain its identity as part of the public school system, but it seemed that things would be all right, at least as long as Win was at Cause. There was little doubt in our minds that the massive bureaucracy would be badly outclassed in a head-on confrontation with Win.

Neia:

Today I taught group 3's work (a third/fourth grade group) to group 2 (a second grade group) by mistake. I was supposed to teach the commutative law rather than the "more advanced concept" of the union of sets. Group 2 understood the union of sets. I did not give them written problems, but they could give me the union of sets verbally. So I gave them advanced work by mistake, yet they were ready to learn it.

Cause did indeed become a public school. Shortly thereafter, incidentally, it became a political asset to the school system. When court-ordered integration came to Buffalo, Cause, though small, was one of the city's few genuinely integrated schools, a result of Win's tough, energetic, and stubborn dedication to keeping the school from drifting into a haven used only by the liberal white middle class. Win always worked hard to recruit black kids, teach to their needs, and keep their parents involved in the school. Like all teachers, Win was a political model for the young people who got training by working with her. Unlike most teachers, she was not a model of apathy but of action and commitment to positive values.

Neia:

I was concerned because of the many cute, fun ideas I saw at the Campus School Activity Center during the seminar today. I spoke to Win of feeling guilty about not doing neato things like that. She said it never ceases to amaze her how some teachers don't realize that kids can like simple reading, spelling, and arithmetic. Cause School kids really enjoy getting spelling words and math problems. They like knowing they're working, they're learning . . . If you have to trick them into trying something with a game or a gimmick, then they don't want to learn it in the first place. That's where many open classrooms today go wrong. Supposedly child centered, oriented toward having the child be self-directed, the classrooms in reality are very teacher directed. Little learning centers with specific tasks often exist so the teacher can check off, "Yes, he did math, yes, he did reading, yes, he did science," with great satisfaction. If the subjects were taught in a much more straightforward way, perhaps the kids too could get some satisfaction by knowing they were learning, by having some input into how and what they were going to learn.

18

Neia and I Exchange Evaluations

*EVALUATION—NEIA LIVELY'S CONTRACT
ON ALTERNATIVE EDUCATION*

Dear Neia:

About a year ago you read my sketches of some of the successful IDP students, and you went into your predictable reaction of self-questioning: Why can't I have his devotion to a subject matter? Why can't I have her scholarly skills? Etc. Self-confidence is not your strongest suit, and it may never be. But I think you're changing some. As you kept your log of student teaching experiences, the fears and worries consistently gave way to real questions about education. I think you are becoming a very fine teacher and a very fine student. I hope you stop every once in a while, take stock, and let the evidence for these facts penetrate enough to moderate your feelings of inadequacy.

You have learned a great deal in the contract on alternative education, but one very important thing has been left out of your writing about it. During the shaky period of last year at Cause School, when the school's continued existence was in doubt from day to day, you helped it to pull through. It is now strong and healthy, but in those days it was not. Keith was the only teacher, and I remember going to Win's house one Friday evening. Tears came to Keith's eyes as he talked about how the older kids were neglected and bored because the younger ones consumed so much of his time and attention. Keith simply was not going to be able to keep going. You arranged to work at Cause almost full time, as I remember. It was a great opportunity for you to learn, but it also must have been very frightening. You made an enormous contribution to the survival of the school. As a teacher in the IDP I have hoped that students could make real contributions to the world, and you did. As a Cause School parent I am grateful for the help you gave the school, and for the fact that I did not have to make the choice of where to send Josh and Danny after Cause collapsed. It would have been a bad day in our family.

Most of us who are interested in alternative schools are attracted to them by ideas of increased freedom for students and student centered school structures. Your work was interesting in that you looked at alternatives that have developed, at least partially, to meet other needs, like the wishes of suburban parents or the needs of a school system's administrators to segregate misbehaving students. Like establishment education, alternative education responds to the imperatives of many people and systems, and I think your work has been especially good in dealing with these facts.

On the issue of freedom for students, your work has really gone to the heart of most of the questions. The contrast between Central Community School and Cause School seems to touch upon everything that is important. It looks like this to me: a classroom or school should be organized around the concept of maximum freedom for everyone, minimum infringement on each other's rights and freedoms. CCS was doctrinaire, based on a romantic notion of what children will do if given freedom. The rights and personalities of the teachers didn't count. They were oppressed, and their behavior poisoned the environment, just as the resentful, angry reactions of students poison the air in most schools. They could not be constructive, helpful, or stimulating in relation to the children because they were stifled. It doesn't make for much of a school, because both teachers and students are significant in a school, and a free school requires that both groups be free. (A lot of the values and attitudes of the CCS kids were problems, but in another setting they would have been dealt with better. Now that some of these kids are going to Cause, they are much less disruptive.)

The personalities of the teachers at Cause School count. I am not crazy about everything they do. Much of their academic work seems to me to be designed to make the teachers happy, but this may reflect an unrealistic view of children that I have. Nevertheless, the Cause School teachers are very sensitive to issues of children's freedom, and they are also concerned about their own rights and freedom. Since they look after themselves, unlike the CCS teachers, life is interesting for them. Remarkably talented to begin with, they grow into the best teachers they can be, and it is a very good school.

As I read your paper and log, it became clear to me that you are rather far along in this same process, especially considering the fact that you are only now graduating from college. To me the die seems cast. You will be less exuberant and more organized. But in your own way, you will function as a teacher as Win Evers does. As you know, this is the highest praise I can muster.

Another impression I had when reading your materials: schools whose primary value is freedom are truly marginal in our society. Massive quantities of dollars are poured into oppressive schools. Those of us who wish to create another kind of education must scramble for a few crumbs. We hear the cries of poverty—scarce resources—all the time, and then we are evaluated to death. Meanwhile millions go into regular schools, and Johnny Regular School can't read. The cards are stacked. I hope you find a way to remember this but to continue playing.

Stay in touch; our new address is . . .

Love,
Dick

AN EVALUATION OF DICK'S EVALUATION OF NEIA LIVELY'S CONTRACT ON ALTERNATIVE EDUCATION

Dear Dick:

I want to express some further feelings about your evaluation of my contract. You have been very honest in discussing your impressions of the changes that have taken place in my personality as a result of the contract and of the characteristics that will never change. Your comments have helped me to look at myself and see the way that I really am. I don't like all what I see (the lack of exuberance, for example) but it is what I am, and the sooner I realize this fact the sooner I'll be able to build up a fuller self from all that I am.

Your uncanny way of putting into words what I feel about myself is surprising, but what really impressed me was the energy you put into the evaluation. I have never had a teacher look at my work and so completely try to explain what it meant to him as well as describing the learning he saw the student gain. You put part of yourself into the evaluation, as evidenced by your comments about schools, and you truly tried to see what the contract did for me.

To me, this evaluation is the essence of IDP. I will cherish it as a token of what learning can be in a situation where someone really cares that I have learned.

115

Thank you. If everything else had gone bad (which it did not), I would say that this evaluation made attending four years of college worth it. I could have done the learning on my own—it was the interactions with teachers that made the difference.

Love,
Neia

19

Eve

*A group of IDP students has decided that there are a number of problems
facing our Individualized Degree Program that must be resolved for this
program to continue effectively or even continue at all.*

—The Squeaky Wheel

Eve organized the only student rebellion in the history of the IDP. She is
charismatic and determined, brave in confrontations with authority, a formidable opponent. Eve was also one of the IDP's most energetic and successful
students, whose education brought her to a position of political radicalism that
was far from her liberal beginnings. Both parts of Eve's story, her period of
opposition to the IDP and her ways of using it, are worth telling.

Eve entered college an unabashed liberal. She wanted to change the
world by working within established structures. Eve believed that the key to
the future was the next generation. She intended to devote her life to children
and education. Her letter of application to the IDP included these paragraphs:

> There is so much work to be done in this world, and I'm anxious to work
> in many aspects of its development. I want everyone to develop into the
> most beautiful person they can be; which means equality for the races,
> liberation for women, a good governmental system, a clean natural world
> and enough love for everyone to have some.
>
> My goal in life is a simple and definite one, for I believe children are
> our doors to the future and it is to their education that I plan to devote my
> life. I want to share my knowledge and dreams with children, especially in
> the Black inner city where dreams are stifled so easily. For the past year and
> a half I have tutored young Black children every weekend in downtown
> Buffalo and found the greatest challenges and rewards in my life. . . .
>
> Your new program seems to hold a wonderful opportunity for me to
> open my mind and learn the most during my college experience, and maybe
> even be better prepared and better qualified to enter into teaching and social
> work in our cities.

Unlike many young people who are breathless and visionary, Eve was as much action as dream. She wasted no time. Her actions and seriousness commanded respect.

During the first weeks of the IDP, most students labored to develop ideas for learning contracts. They tested us and the program, attracted by its freedom yet suspicious that it would be withdrawn by some hidden provision. Some feared that their real interest, once revealed, might be rejected. Some still couldn't find their real interests. Others wrestled primarily with problems of organizing their time and energies in the absence of an imposed schedule. In favorable cases students dealt with the question of how to write a learning contract, usually producing sterile and stilted documents. Like Donna, Eve was an exception. She would have none of this agonizing. Eve started two major projects immediately, easily writing learning contracts to formalize her work. They described her long-range plans in order to set each project in perspective, and they then listed detailed and realistic programs of work.

The first project was Readings in Open Education and Black Literature, a combination of subjects that reflected Eve's interests and activities. She included in her contract a poem that she had written about driving through the ghetto, the last stanza of which was

> His hands were small and black as night,
> His body full of youth,
> And in that face I saw the light
> Of God's eternal truth.

Nobody who knew Eve could doubt that those lines expressed something powerful that lived within her. The contract went on to include a schedule of readings. Each week Eve was to read a book on open education and another dealing with some aspect of black culture.

As director of the IDP I was spending my time trying to help students cope with the problems of adjusting to the new system. It was an enormous relief to see Eve getting such a good start, and I wrote her a note:

I was just reading your contract on Open Education and Black Literature again, and I thought I'd tell you again that I think it's excellent. Your willingness to do a thorough job in writing up the contract will make things easier for us in explaining and interpreting your work to people outside the program. Also, your willingness to put your philosophy and feelings into the contract is helpful in making it a document that will be meaningful to others.

Eve's second contract related to her participation in the Buffalo Tutorial Program. She had been a volunteer tutor for several years. Her contract began with her view of that experience:

> . . . we tutors have found that the interpersonal exchanges between child and tutor are the most beneficial outcome of the program. It is a very beautiful experience to see how a white suburban student and a young underprivileged Black child can grow to understand each other week by week. . . .

At end of each year a tutor was selected to organize and run the program for the following year. Eve had been chosen for that position, but things had changed drastically over the summer. Most of the tutors had gone off to college, and the program had lost its financial support and its rooms in a Jewish center. If the program was to continue, Eve would have to rebuild it. She set out to do so.

It was clear that Eve had undertaken a large and complex task. She would have to deal with community organizations, understanding their relationships and functions. She would have to negotiate for money and facilities, establish and nurture relationships with supporting organizations, and then recruit, train, assign, and schedule tutors. It would also be necessary for her to prepare a budget, purchase materials, and cope with the common crises that arise in any program.

Eve's learning contract said that she would study community organizations and administration, both standard subjects in the Buffalo State curriculum. She'd examine her experiences, do some readings in the area, and have discussions with her faculty supervisor. I am sure that the tutorial project was a crucial and positive step in Eve's education. I do not know, however, whether the terms in which the learning contract were formulated were real to Eve. For years, before and during the IDP, I participated in subterfuges in which unusual but clearly educational experiences were described in conventional academic terms. The descriptions often didn't function in the lives of the students except to provide a respectable academic cover for learning that didn't fit easily into standard categories. Although I have no doubt as to the value of the project, Eve's contract may have been one of those covering documents. I make the point here merely to describe a common phenomenon that was, regrettably, still occasionally necessary in the IDP.

Before the end of the first semester Eve had started a couple of other contracts. A project in dramatics was based on her first experience as an actress, playing the lead in a children's theater production of *Alice in Wonderland*. By taking a noncredit course in automotive mechanics and expanding her work under the sponsorship of a professor in the Industrial Arts Division of the college, she did a learning contract in that area. Eve's style was energetic and eclectic. It was clear to her and those who knew her that she learned in many settings. The IDP was basically receptive to the variety of learning activities in Eve's life, and she was competent at meeting the program's minimum requirements, finding faculty sponsors and writing contracts.

Eve was one of several students who started quickly and successfully in the IDP. Certainly nobody had a more productive first semester than she, and I and some of the other core faculty tried to make a point of telling her so. Yet she became less happy with the program. She talked of dropping out, and that frightened me. If Eve couldn't be happy in the program, what about all the other students whose early experiences seemed so much less satisfactory? She asked questions about whether the IDP would work, questions similar to those of Ellen and Ronda. She didn't seem to believe my answers. Her questions became challenges, and feelings of tension and anger grew between Eve and me. We were no longer on the same side. This happened slowly, and it surprised me. In retrospect the reasons are clear. While she avoided the common problems of getting started in the IDP, she experienced some of the more subtle difficulties of the program. She also became involved through one of her teachers in some academic rivalries and the interactions of professional egos, and that could not help but make things worse.

It is easiest to begin with two problems that Eve shared with many IDP students. First of all she was lonely, and hers was a loneliness made more acute by her hard work and drive to achieve. She accomplished a great deal, but that wasn't enough. Something was missing in the personal dimension. In response to a midyear questionnaire, she wrote:

> I have spent some of the most rewarding and frustrating days of my life this
> past semester in the IDP. I am remaining in the program because I enjoy

learning in the way the IDP enables me to—however, I feel there is a great deal of room for improvement and revision in the program. Isolation is the worst handicap of the program, and I feel the major problem to resolve next semester must be developing better communication between the students and faculty through joint meetings.

Eve was certainly identifying a structural characteristic, felt as a problem by many students, of a program that emphasized individualized work. Her loneliness was also a consequence of a personal program of pursuing independence, a quest that is not uncommon among people who are just starting college. Autonomy is a central issue in many of their lives. And Eve pursued it, as she did everything, with a bit of extra energy and determination. A few months later Eve looked back and wrote the following:

I came to school this year looking for independence and maturity, but as the year progressed I realized that I had lost Eve in this masquerade of college. I wanted security in who I was as a person, but had not yet discovered just who this person was. . . .

Today I no longer want total independence. I know now that love and freedom are much greater for a person to cherish, for no matter how much independence I have, if I can't feel free and feel the love of life around me, I am a machine and not a breathing person. . . .

I think that Eve was saying that some of her loneliness came from a pursuit of achievement and autonomy that was too fervent, for it tended to cause her to neglect self-knowledge and relationships with others.

IDP students experienced another problem that was the result of the program's academic design. This too was particularly acute for Eve, heightened as it was by some strained relationships between one of Eve's professors and some of the faculty in the IDP, and Eve took sides. To describe this part of Eve's experience, it is probably easiest to digress briefly to comment on the IDP's system of degree committees and on interdisciplinary work in the program.

*

Simply stated, learning in the conventional system is measured before it happens. In the IDP it was measured afterward. Conventional courses are always assigned a specific number of credits before a student registers. Thus, as long as they do not fail their courses, students in a regular college program can know at the start of a semester exactly how many credits they will get and how they will stand with respect to graduation requirements when the semester is over. By contrast, learning in the IDP was to be measured after several contracts were completed. This was to be the work of the degree committee. A student did not contract to earn a specific number of credits, but to work and learn. The magnitude of the accomplishment was to be determined later.

There was considerable educational realism in the IDP arrangement, for all learning projects, including conventional courses, are unpredictable and full of both pleasant and unpleasant surprises. The standard three- or five-credit course is a fiction that goes unquestioned because it is so important to the system* and also because it provides significant safeguards for students. The IDP arrangement was designed to focus attention on the student's project and its own logic, without distraction from the seductive question of whether enough or too little work had been done to warrant a given number of credits. A learning contract might count for a little or for a great deal, and one couldn't really know until later. We hoped, of course, that the system would work to the advantage of students, allowing them to make rapid progress toward a degree. But IDP students had no guarantee that this arrangement would work in their favor. Not only were they unprotected by the conventional structures of the academic world, but the first group of IDP students, Eve included, could derive no comfort from the successful experiences of students who had gone before them. Ironically, although Eve's experience would provide just such assurance to later students, the issue of faith in the eventual fairness of the IDP became a central issue for Eve as it had, in slightly different form, for Ellen and Ronda.

In order to function, IDP students had to believe that the degree committee would eventually treat their work fairly. Alternatively they could suspend belief and try not to think about it. One student (Barbara, who is mentioned in the chapter about Carl, a core faculty member) was even convinced, wrongly as it turned out, that the system could not possibly work for her, yet she fatalistically resolved to go down to defeat along the path she had chosen. In general we could only speak bravely, emphasizing the fact that the student and an IDP core faculty member would constitute two-thirds of the degree committee. It was also probable that the third member, either the department chair-

*One of the other important functions of credit hours is, for example, to provide quantitative measures of faculty effort, thus allowing administrators to avoid difficult questions of quality.

person or someone appointed by the chairperson, would be a professor with whom the student had worked. Beyond this we could provide no comfort. Answers to these questions necessarily lay in the future.

There was an element of the self-fulfilling prophecy built into our situation. If you could believe in the IDP's structures, you were more likely to behave in ways that would increase the chances that they would work well for you. In this matter, as in others we met during the course of the IDP, confidence and morale turned out to be critical determinants of success, especially at the outset when there was little else to go on. This is probably a theme in the natural history of educational innovations.

Eve got worried early in the game, and events and people encouraged her to become more nervous. The difficult question of interdisciplinary studies came up. One of the central goals of the IDP, and one that was clearly relevant to Eve's education, was to make it easier for students to do interdisciplinary work. Eve's first contract, for example, dealt with both literature and educational theory. Although we had a fairly clear institutional mandate to do this, the core faculty and I worried that such work would raise political problems for the IDP. The disciplines are jealously guarded territories that are thought to belong to particular academic departments. A professor in one department who deals with subjects in another department's discipline is liable to get into trouble. The internal politics of our colleges and universities are marked by bitter and wasteful conflicts over academic border violations. My own career involved painful arguments with colleagues over the question of whether I was really doing philosophy or something else, the idea usually being that I was doing something else that would be better done someplace else. Core faculty members, because they had temporarily left their departments to assume unusual nondisciplinary responsibilities, were particularly sensitive to these questions. Their decisions to work in the IDP were seen as frivolous, sometimes treasonous, by departmental colleagues, and there was therefore considerable professional risk involved.

We tried to limit the IDP's vulnerability in the area of interdisciplinary study by urging, though not requiring, that students seek special sanction for interdisciplinary contracts. We would be safest, for example, if we had the collaboration, or at least the appearance of collaboration, of professors in the different departments whose disciplines were represented in a project. This participation was sometimes only formal, amounting to a signature on both the contract and evaluation attesting to the professor's judgment that the other people involved in the project were qualified to do a respectable job in the area. Many professors were, with good reason, willing to vouch for others in this way. And although this was mainly a political maneuver, there were sometimes educational benefits in the form of suggestions and ideas that emerged from the conversations in which these arrangements were made. Our caution, indeed our anxiety, concerning interdisciplinary work, contributed heavily to Eve's loss of confidence in the IDP.

*

Mark Penta, the core faculty member from the Education Division, talked with Eve about the potential dangers of interdisciplinary contracts. Although it was undoubtedly realistic and proper for Mark to raise the issue with Eve, his warning may have been too strong. Perhaps he was harsh. In any case, it offended Frank Diulus, the faculty member with whom Eve was doing her first two major contracts.

Frank was a young professor of education, new at the college, bright, liberal, and oriented toward students. He was a natural ally of the IDP and was, in fact, extremely helpful to Eve and several other students. He was angered by Mark's warning to Eve, believing that it might mean that we doubted his qualifications to work with Eve in the fields they had chosen. Frank also became suspicious of our real commitment to interdisciplinary study and our professed ideals concerning student centered education. He came to believe that we had created another phony liberal program that looked attractive, benefited the faculty and administrators involved, but in the end would rip off the students in some unspecified way. Frank was attracted to the role of true defender of the faith and of the interests of students. He also played the martyr with Eve, stressing the enormous amount of time he was devoting to her education even in the absence of extra pay.

Persuaded that the degree committee would not adequately recognize the value of Eve's work, Frank championed the student cause in a series of ritualistic confrontations with me and Mark. He was hostile, combative, and sported an air of moral superiority—probably, I am sad to say, not unlike the one with which we may have approached colleagues on other occasions. Eve and Frank had constructed an elaborate case against Mark, me, and the IDP. It was somehow more attractive to attribute Eve's problem to our bad will than to the uncertainties, political problems, and imperfections of a new program in an unsympathetic setting. We had long talks. The tensions eased slightly, but nothing could be resolved until Eve's degree committee met, and it made no sense for the committee to meet until Eve had completed several contracts. That was at least a few months in the future. Eve's would probably be the first degree committee to be convened, and it was important for us to be able to present a strong case substantiated by a good bit of academic work.

Before long posters appeared in the IDP work areas and meeting rooms saying "Help *The Squeaky Wheel* Get Rolling." *The Squeaky Wheel,* an IDP newsletter published by students, came out a few days later, introducing itself as follows:

> A group of IDP students has decided that there are a number of problems facing our Individualized Degree Program that must be resolved for this program to continue effectively or even continue at all. We feel that it is the students who must unite to work out solutions to our problems and strengthen our bonds of communication and interaction. Those of us in this program are independent, free-thinking people, but we must not let this isolate ourselves from each other and develop apathy towards the IDP. We involved ourselves in a unique educational experience, hoping that it was a positive alternative to the traditional college education. Our program gives us freedom, but no one is free without responsibility to the program and ourselves.

Eve was the organizer of *The Squeaky Wheel* and had written most of the first issue.

The Squeaky Wheel included a questionnaire for students to complete. Although it nominally sought both favorable and critical responses, it was clearly written to elicit statements of dissatisfaction. Questions 11 and 12 were almost a direct plea for affirmations of Eve's anxieties about the fair recognition of her work. Question 12 could be answered by nobody, for no degree committee had met. The reference to credits in both questions was confusing, for credits would not be used to measure progress. The questionnaire:

1. Are you satisfied with your work last semester?
2. Are you satisfied with your progress this semester?
3. Do you think that the program and/or yourself have taken progressive steps toward improving the IDP?
4. Are you satisfied with the way IDP is moving?
5. Do you have personal dissatisfaction with last semester's work?

6. Do you have personal dissatisfaction with this semester's work?
7. Do you favor the contract system?
8. Do you think there is a community spirit in the IDP?
9. Do you think a community spirit is necessary for the IDP to be a success?
10. Are you having problems with contract evaluations?
11. Are you discontent with not knowing how much credit you are getting for what contracts?
12. Do you feel comfortable about how much credit you will receive from your evaluations?
13. Do you support the idea of having to pay for summer tuition before any summer contracts are OK'd?
14. Would you like more information about campus and community resources?
15. Are you having trouble finding the right cooperating faculty that have time to work with you?

Please write any additional criticism FOR and AGAINST the program.

The results of the questionnaire were not especially strong one way or the other. The second issue of *The Squeaky Wheel,* unsigned but not written by Eve, featured "A Call to Action" that was rather impressionistic and did not report the results of the survey in detail:

> As a result of the survey, I have found there is some dissatisfaction with the program. There is a tendency to pass on the responsibility for the difficulties we face to someone else. . . .
>
> Talking with students I have found there has been a need for some type of structure. Some have requested a return to home groups, while others expressed a need for weekly workshops. If you have other needs in the way of structure, we would like to hear about it.
>
> There have been complaints about noncooperating faculty, unavailability of the core faculty, a question of their competence, a lack of guidance from them. There has been criticism about the vagueness of the administration's policies. If there is something you want from the faculty and you are not getting it, let us make demands, set standards as to what we expect from them.

The founders of *The Squeaky Wheel* demanded office space, typewriters, and supplies, most of which were available out of the resources the IDP could call upon. *The Squeaky Wheel* generated a good bit of enthusiasm. The original group grew, the office was set up, and plans were made for regular publication. The newsletter came out for some time, although its militancy

Eve

vanished almost immediately. The articles reflected the interests of the students who were active: satire, politics, nutrition, film. It had periodic crises around the group's failure to share responsibilities equitably. Its relationship to me changed sufficiently so that I was called upon to try to help solve the group's organizational problems. When it was published, *The Squeaky Wheel* was almost always the work of one or two individuals who were very active for a short time. The project had considerable vitality, but its initial opposition to the IDP status quo rapidly became a minor part of its life. It was clear that *The Squeaky Wheel* had no program of reform, although it had initially hinted at my replacement as director, changes in the core faculty, and a change in the contract system. Eve dropped out of the group after a few weeks, returning to work on her learning contracts.

Eve finished out the year, working hard, learning a great deal, complaining about the IDP, and agonizing over the decision to remain in it or return to the conventional program. At the end of the year her degree committee met. It was composed of Eve, Mark Penta, and Barbara Frey, the chairperson of one of the departments in the Education Division. Barbara was an influential figure on the faculty and was later, as vice president of the college, to play an important role in the last chapter of the IDP's history. Barbara's presence on the committee lent it impeccable credentials from the point of view of faculty politics. It was politically inconceivable that the committee's judgments, with Barbara participating, would ever be questioned by unsympathetic faculty or administrators.

The degree committee did not cheat Eve out of the recognition her work deserved. It did, in fact, work exactly as we hoped degree committees would work. The quality of Eve's learning spoke for itself, and there was really no occasion for quibbling or disagreement. Eve wrote the following letter to *The Squeaky Wheel:*

Dear *Squeaky Wheel* Staff:
I want to share with you the good news that my Degree Committee has looked at my contracts of this year very favorably and feels I am ready to begin my Elementary Education junior participation at the Niagara Falls Abbott School next fall within IDP and the APACE Program—meaning I can graduate in three years instead of four. I can hardly believe the wonderful results of the committee.
This year has been one of the most difficult of my education and yet

127

I have never learned so much academically and personally about my world
and myself. I believe in the dreams and goals of IDP, however, I wish there
were more core faculty and released time for cooperating faculty to help IDP
students fulfill their educational goals. I plan to remain in the IDP next year
because although the growing pains of such a new program are extreme,
the personal rewards of being part of such an idealistic program are very
great.

IDP demands a lot of those who *dare* to shape their own education
and life and yet in the end the personal satisfaction and rewards *are* much
greater than any given by the conventional system. IDP means hundreds of
individuals working personally together. That in itself is a pretty tremendous
dream but one that I want to work towards becoming a reality. Because I
have seen it this year and have become part of this reality this year.

I am indebted to IDP, the core faculty, Dick Meisler, and especially all
the IDP students and cooperating faculty. . . .

The crisis of Eve's participation in the IDP was over, although her education continued to be marked by drama and conflict. The IDP was never again
to be the focus of Eve's concern, but it was to be a catalyst that accelerated
her further development and also her departure from college.

Eve's decision to participate in the APACE program was made in the
euphoria that followed her degree committee meeting. She was encouraged
to join APACE by Barbara Frey, who had helped develop it. I'm sure that
Barbara was pleased to have a student of Eve's quality in APACE.

APACE was an acronym for A Personalized Approach To Competency-
Based Education. The program was a response to directives from the State
Education Department that teacher training programs specify the skills and
knowledge necessary for a student to obtain teacher certification, rather than
simply require a series of courses. There were several reasons to believe that
APACE would suit Eve's style of learning. She would be working in one of
the area's most innovative and open public schools, and APACE seemed to
believe in combining learning with work. APACE also allowed for accelera-
tion, which fit Eve's plans, and it was vaguely innovative in spirit. We were
all relieved that Eve could enter a program of study that was innovative but
structured, and sanctioned by the college's education faculty and about
which, therefore, there was no question of legitimacy. Although her IDP
crisis had passed, it felt good to see Eve choosing something that was safe.
She would get a respite from some of the uncertainties of the IDP, and she

could do this without leaving the IDP and forfeiting the opportunities it represented.

Our relief and pleasure at Eve's successes caused us to ignore some hard realities. If we had looked closely, we would have seen that APACE was precisely what Eve didn't need, at least if she was to remain on course to a college degree and teacher certification. Despite its rhetoric, it was thoroughly prescriptive, and Eve didn't like being told what to do. To make matters worse, the things that APACE would tell Eve to do were odious to her, for they represented the kind of education she was fighting, both in her own life as a student and in her activities as a young educator. These problems were slightly hidden by liberal rhetoric which none of us had the sense to question. She entered APACE still full of enthusiasm, and she gave up her ambition to be a teacher within a few months.

Eve's learning contract incorporated material from APACE documents. Here are some excerpts:

> The professional year program has emerged as a result of the APACE faculty team's belief that the separation of theory and practice in two or more semesters, with different faculty responsible for each segment, does not provide the continuity nor the best possible learning situation for all preservice teachers. . . .
>
> Just as the elementary school is emphasizing greater response to individual differences among children, so the teacher education program should relate to differences among its learners.
>
> Teachers are expected to demonstrate a great variety of abilities and skills as they work within the school setting. Extensive research has been conducted to define just what knowledge and skills as well as personal characteristics and attitudes are vital to successful teaching. . . .
>
> The APACE faculty team has given considerable attention to identifying competencies which we believe are appropriate for pre-service teachers and within the scope of the program. . . . We have also tried to provide an opportunity to "open" the program to your development of self-selected competencies.

Eve also included materials from APACE that described some of the several hundred competencies that were said to have emerged from research on good teaching. Some of Eve's examples:

> Objective 215: You will be able to suggest five reasons why the self concept of the child should be an area of concern for the elementary school teacher

and be able to support your choices by citing evidence from the learning plans sources.

Objective 230: Given a list of ten questions sequenced for a lesson, you will classify each question as cognitive, memory, convergent, divergent or value. A score of 80% is acceptable.

Objective 372: You will examine at least five sets of mathematics papers completed in your classroom, identify the common error patterns found, and hold conferences with at least three pupils in which their work is discussed.

Objective 365: You will demonstrate the ability to use good form and reasonable speed in both manuscript and cursive writing by writing two paragraphs on the chalkboard. One paragraph will be manuscript and one in cursive writing.

The clash between these materials and Eve's own goals for herself is so dramatic that I can't believe, in retrospect, that we did not try to advise Eve to do something other than APACE:

> . . . [I had] two very personal goals in mind. The first was that this year, as I was becoming a teacher, I would retain the freedom to be me. The second was that I do not want to become a teacher to exercise control over young people, but a resource person and co-discoverer of the vast amount of knowledge there is to learn.

During Eve's first year in the IDP, she had been clarifying her basic values concerning education; she was strongly influenced by the open education movement. APACE required that she act contrary to her educational philosophy, and in so doing it demanded that she abandon herself, her processes of growth and self-discovery. A year later, reflecting on the experience, Eve wrote:

> I found the year terribly disturbing as I experienced the meaning of being a "professional" teacher in the public school system. When I entered college to become a teacher I felt teaching was a means of changing society through freeing the children to find their individual strengths and needs. . . .
>
> The interests of the children and their learning, I felt, should be the first priority during my student teaching, and I made a conscious decision to work in this way. I realized then that this would mean not completing the objectives the APACE team had, without student input, decided were neces- sary for successful student teaching. I felt that the majority of the learning objectives were petty and produced a standardized model of teaching tech- niques and methods which neither challenges students nor developed crea-

tive skills which would aid them in pursuing their own learning. My supervising teachers in the classrooms felt my work with children was creative and
exciting but I challenged the norms of the APACE college faculty. Therefore
I did not complete my APACE objectives and during the course of student
teaching realized that I could not continue working in this environment and
keep my sanity. At this point I decided to stop student teaching and begin
studying the structure of our society and ways in which radical changes can
be brought about.

Eve's involvement in radical politics began during her year in APACE.
She brought to it the same energy and commitment that she had devoted to
liberal projects in education. While she was still trying to cope with APACE
and her work in public school, Eve began working in the most interesting and
lively of the current radical political activities in Buffalo, the movement in
support of the Attica Brothers. Buffalo was the site of the trials of Attica
inmates on charges relating to the rebellion of 1970. The Attica Brothers
Support Movement organized demonstrations to publicize the political nature
of the prosecutions. Eve worked in the organization, met former inmates, and
heard visiting radicals like Angela Davis and William Kunstler. It was an
intense, star-studded course in American radical politics. Eve described one of
her experiences in a letter to the college newspaper:

> As I spoke with a few of the Brothers I realized that I could no longer live
> in my blind world, because these men were my brothers and their lives
> affected mine more than I ever believed.
> That night in my apartment I began to try to imagine the cold isolating
> world of the cell block that these men were fighting so desperately to escape
> from.
> I realized then that I could never really live a free life without becoming
> a part of the revolution to free the Attica Brothers and change the Bureau-
> cratic Government that made them, and will make all of us into political
> prisoners if we don't fight back.

Eve became a Marxist, and she turned to campus issues and organizing.
In the course of these activities she developed a close relationship with a
radical instructor of sociology, and most of her work during her remaining
year in college was done with him. Eve's education in her third year of college,
the year following APACE, was structurally similar to her activities in the first
year. She combined theoretical study with work in the world beyond campus.
Her main practical project was organizing students in opposition to a tuition

increase, an issue that student radicals thought was promising. Her activities also included continued participation in the Attica support movement, a summer residency in an Indian reservation for several weeks, work on a factory assembly line back in Buffalo, and collaboration with a group of people making a videotape documentary about a wildcat strike and the resulting conflict between activist workers and the union bureaucracy. Eve also became deeply involved in the campus politics relating to the college's failure to renew her professor's contract. At the end of the year Eve wrote about the course of her political education, emphasizing some of the experiences that influenced her most:

> Celia had tried to work in a shop on the reservation, but when she earned more than $400 per month she lost her family's food subsidies, and she could not feed her family and pay the rent on $400. She was therefore forced to give up the job which could have supplied her psychologically with some self worth. . . . Like most Sioux mothers, Celia can only watch her children's malnutrition develop and their teeth fall out as her hopes for a better life are killed systematically by the capitalist government of America. The poverty and suffering I saw of a people whose culture and civilization had been destroyed by the merciless hands of the white profit motive followed me home to Buffalo where my experiences were broadened.
>
> Five days after leaving the prairie I was making aerosol cans on an assembly line with ten other women. It was my turn to sell my labor power eight hours a day for $2.10 per hour. It was hard to observe the women since we were only part of the machinery. There was always pressure to keep up with the thousands of cans passing without pause in front of me. Along with the constant clanging of the machines filling my ears was the 90-degree heat which made me feel as if my mind was drained of its ability to think. During lunch as I spoke to the women I worked with I began to understand how powerless working class women feel, and what sociology calls working class consciousness. . . .

I had little contact with Eve during the year. I saw her at Attica demonstrations and read her letters and articles in the college newspaper. She was part of a radical campus in-group. I found the rhetoric of her group shrill and oversimplified, its Marxism automatic and thoughtless. Eve once described someone to me as having "no politics," and I could almost hear her saying the same thing about me. I am sure she considered me a hopelessly confused liberal.

One Friday afternoon on my way home, I met Eve outside the college's administration building. She told me that a group of students was about to occupy the building for the weekend to protest the tuition increases and to hold a teach-in on the subject. "Occupation" was a strong term, for permission and ground rules for the use of the building had been negotiated with the administration. Eve asked me to join the students. There were only one or two faculty members who said that they might participate, and faculty were important.

I was distrustful of Eve, yet her pitch to me was persuasive and not particularly manipulative. I felt that her group's analysis of the tuition issue was doctrinaire. But I shared with them the basic belief that the budget crisis in education was due to a long-standing government priority in favor of weapons. And so, with many liberal misgivings, I decided that I belonged in the building with the students.

The weekend was wonderful. The group sincerely attempted to educate itself politically. Eve and her core of associates were more democratic than their tone and rhetoric had led me to expect. The discussions were good, and the decision making process among the demonstrators was open, a model of rationality compared to any other part of the college I'd observed. Eve and I became closer; we were on the same side again. I felt indebted to her and a bit abashed by my suspicions about her.

At the end of the year Eve decided to leave school and go to Europe. Her friend and teacher had a position at the Free University in Berlin, where Eve hoped to study. Otherwise her plans were vague. She wanted to tie up the loose ends of her academic work in Buffalo by having a degree committee meeting. The committee would provide a definition of the requirements she had not yet fulfilled, so that her situation would be clear if she ever decided to return to complete her degree. Replacing Mark Penta, I joined Eve and Barbara Frey on the degree committee.

Barbara had become academic vice president of the college. As a major spokesperson for the administration, she and Eve had had several confrontations over the college budget during the tuition controversy. It was clear that each believed that the other had lied. I was nervous about the degree committee meeting, for Eve's style was to provoke, and I could not imagine her changing it for the occasion. Also Eve's recent contracts and evaluations were cast in Marxist terms. Often it seemed as if the point of these documents was to assert the right to use ideology in an academic setting, rather than to use it well. The word *Amerika,* used profusely, was an added irritant to me, and I expected Barbara to feel the same way. Yet it was obvious, as it always was with Eve, that she had worked hard, done serious projects, and that she had learned a lot. Just as her sincerity and hard work had given substance to the liberal clichés she used as a freshman, there was real effort and learning behind her current radical language. I was prepared to defend all of Eve's work and had an absolutely clear conscience about it.

I rehearsed my arguments about academic freedom, hoping I wouldn't have to use them. I read the college catalog, collecting dozens of examples in which establishment political or ideological assumptions reposed unnoticed in the standard curriculum. Our potential problem, however, was that Barbara was at the top of the academic hierarchy. If she would not recognize the validity of Eve's learning, either because of anger at Eve or because of her view of the curriculum, there would be no appeal beyond her.

Again the degree committee meeting went very well. Barbara responded positively and with understanding to Eve's work. She ignored a couple of digs that Eve apparently considered obligatory. Barbara was even apologetic for some of the failures of APACE, which had turned out to be a fiasco for other students besides Eve. We agreed on the amount of progress toward the degree that Eve had made. At that point, in all probability, Eve's formal academic life ended.

I last heard from Eve in a letter from Berlin. She was enthusiastic about living in another country. She was working in a day-care center for the children of Turkish workers, she was reading a great deal, and she sounded as if she was in pursuit of education and effective action with her typical energy.

20

Educational Freedom: Adaptive or Maladaptive?

It is my belief . . . that the talents every child has regardless of his official "I.Q.", could stay with him through life, to enrich him and everybody else, if these talents were not regarded as commodities with a value in the success stakes.

The other thing taught from the start is to distrust one's own judgment. Children are taught submission to authority, how to search for other people's opinions and decisions, and how to quote and comply.

—Doris Lessing

Many critics of educational convention, including many of those who start with leftist political analyses, believe that our schools and colleges are closely coordinated with other institutions of our society as, of course, they must be. The job of education delegated to schools, according to this view, is to provide pliant workers, bureaucrats, and consumers who are trained to fit nicely into America's massive organizations of production and control. Schools and colleges are expected to produce people who know how to obey and consume and who will not disrupt things by thinking for themselves and otherwise behaving like individuals. In the best of worlds, this argument goes, students would be free, but it makes no sense to expect freedom to exist in our current institutions of education. The very function of the schools is to oppress students and keep them in training for further oppression. And they are doing their job well. If one is interested in educational freedom, the argument goes, one should see to the revolution or some other means of radically transforming society.

A simpler version of the same position is held by a very large number of parents and teachers, although they see the schools as essentially decent institutions. They are against freedom for students. In its place they advance realism: our sons and daughters are headed for life in a rough world. Most jobs are not intrinsically fulfilling or rewarding. Bosses of all varieties exercise control over us. Demands are made from every direction. We are constantly judged, often unfairly. We are not free. It would be a disservice to our children to educate them as free people. Teachers are right to exercise power, be judgmental, perhaps even be a bit difficult and arbitrary. It is not the mission of education to produce misfits.

The substance of this argument is important, but so are the feelings that commonly go along with it. They dominate the emotional dimension of discussions about education, and they are revealing. Assertions that the world is a hard place and that education must match it are made in the spirit of pride and self-satisfaction. We have survived by strength and cunning, these adults seem to say; let the youngsters do the same. The connection between student suffering and adult enjoyment is too direct to ignore. The rough-world philosophy allows teachers at school and parents at home to enjoy the power of tyrants and to do so with the self-righteous assurance that their victims are being helped. Sometimes there is a note of inappropriate vengeance: "I suffered through these sorts of trials, and it will do you good to experience them too." As if the ability to inflict educational or domestic suffering upon a new generation somehow gives meaning to or redeems the struggles of an older generation. And there is envy: "I never had the chance to grow freely; why should you?" And there is defensiveness: "I didn't have all that freedom, and I turned out just fine. Do you think there's anything wrong with me? What makes you better or more deserving?" Clear statements of these themes are embarrassing and only rarely made. These responses are familiar, however, to anyone who spends time in our educational institutions. There's also a strong note of old-fashioned puritanism in all of this. If something is pleasant, it can't be good for you. One really can't learn by being autonomous, for that is dangerously close to having fun or following one's own wishes.

In our culture these ideas are supported, I believe, by strong feelings of anger at young people, especially at adolescents. They were strengthened and brought to the surface during the 1960s when the discontinuities between the generations were particularly evident. Our real or professed love for our children does not permit us to express such anger directly. We do it through our educational philosophy. We decide that education must be difficult and unpleasant, even punishingly so, and that it should not be controlled by the students themselves. These feelings are strong barriers to the clear consideration of the value of freedom in education. Having recognized this, let us return to the important issue of whether, when viewed in a social context, it makes sense to think of education as even a potential force for liberation. Is educational freedom maladaptive, either socially or individually?

Clarity begins, I believe, with the recognition that rigid imperatives and significant options coexist in our society. Uniformity is encouraged and enforced, diversity is restrained, by powerful forces: an economic system whose highest value is profit; the machinery of mass production that requires obedient workers and predictable consumers; a legal system in which wealth is a main determinant of outcomes; homogenizing bureaucracies we encounter as clients and serve as functionaries; a political system in which a limited ranged of positions is tolerated; powerful mass media that function for much of the time as commercial instruments of mind control. None of this is new. These forces all produce major limitations upon our freedom. Yet in the face of all of these factors, we retain substantial freedoms, and it would be foolish and intellectually dishonest to deny it. Unconventional and unpopular choices are available to individuals in our country in many realms of life. This is not to ignore the fact that many other choices are proscribed or that some apparent freedoms are really illusory. And, of course, even when freedom exists, the social order will find informal and formal ways to penalize people who make the "wrong" choices. But many of the penalties are mild and acceptable to individuals and groups who choose not to conform. Our freedom is flawed, but we are not in a totalitarian situation. To maintain otherwise is simply to be irresponsible.

Consider the issue that is always raised by way of objection to the permissive education of young people: making money. Individuals in our society must, to be sure, order their lives to arrange for their minimal economic well-being. Some of us have few choices in this matter, for we are born into deep poverty and find ourselves trapped by circumstances that allow no significant options. Many of us, however, have some freedom to determine the manner in which we live our economic lives. We may choose among standards of living to which to aspire. We may choose among a variety of means by which to pursue each of the possible economic goals. Every combination of means and goals has its own characteristic advantages and disadvantages. If we settle for less affluence, we pay lower prices in such matters as imposed conformity, loss of control over our own time, and the intrusion of economics into certain human relationships. We may, for example, work for a salary irregularly, adopt nonconforming life-styles, avoid situations in which we have to be submissive to a boss. Deviant paths, of course, involve costs, especially in the realm of financial security. If we opt for an increased chance of enjoying greater material wealth, on the other hand, we may find that the pleasures of the affluent justify the compromises involved in their pursuit. Or we may not. Consciously or unconsciously each of us defines a preferred package of economic, social, and psychological gains and losses. The system does, of course, limit the number and nature of these packages, and a wider range of possibilities is certainly available to the already wealthy. There is less freedom than we might like. Yet there is a job market. We have physical and some economic mobility. The society has a variety of roles to be filled. We do have significant choices.

The economic example describes a basic condition of our lives, and it is also a symbol of the broader situation of the individual in our society. We live in a mixed and complex order that allows for the coexistence of significant freedoms and real limits on individual choice. Many parents, educators, and students tend to ignore these freedoms when they discuss education. They simplistically prefer a model of schooling based on an exaggerated view of the society's constraints on the individual. A major reason for this preference is the enormous potential for value conflict that is implicit in the exercise of freedom. If students are educated to follow standard paths with little consideration of options, their choices will be consonant with the dominant values of their elders. There will be minimal conflict. They will less often choose to be hippies, dropouts, rebels. If they were educated in the use of freedom, they would more likely become people sensitive to the range of choices that are available. If they were to live, while students, as free people, they would not necessarily be involved in a training program for hippies. But the likelihood that they would make "wrong" choices, choices that conflict with the values of teachers and parents, would be dramatically increased by such education.

The tendency of parents, teachers, and many students to see society and proper education as less free than they really are disguises a wish to impose or accept standard values. Why make trouble? "Trouble" means diversity. It means people using their freedom, and the results are not predictably mainstream. The nature of the question is not changed by the fact that it is often asked out of love and concern for the well-being of the young. The answer, of course, is that although painful, the problems associated with diversity and freedom are desirable. They enrich life. And freedom is also something to be valued for itself.

Even if our society were significantly more repressive than it is, would we really want to reproduce that defect in the schools? It would, of course, be folly to attempt to create a school system that was totally disconnected from the rest of society. The schools have only limited promise as a source of major transformation of other institutions and society. It is a valid choice, however, to seek to make education a progressive force, using the space that already exists to extend freedom while still offering students a reasonably realistic preparation for adult life as it is lived.

Educational institutions are in fact experienced by students either as oppressive or liberating. We can, within limits, create institutions in which our young people live as free people; they can grow up knowing freedom and its uses. They will, in such institutions, learn to value freedom and fight for it. Or the institutions can be experienced as oppressive, and young people can learn primarily how to submit to authority, withdraw, and do what they are told. The choice involves issues of politics, social ethics, and individual morality. The choice is mandated by no inexorable force. Although there will be difficulties involved, we can opt for freedom.

21

The Core Faculty: Carl

I was in the hospital recovering from a gall bladder operation when Bob Shoenberg, who was at that time Associate Vice President for Academic Affairs, visited me and tried to persuade me to become involved in the program. When you're lying in a hospital bed listening to the glucose solution drip into your veins and the pump draining your stomach, glug, glug, glug, glug, glug, glug, you start to have a different perception of the world around you than you have when you're outside where it's a little more cheerful. I started thinking, well, what am I doing with myself, what are my goals? And I felt that the IDP might give me an opportunity for a new kind of personal growth, an opportunity that I might not normally have. And I found that it did do that.

—Carl, in remarks to the faculty committee evaluating the IDP

The IDP years did indeed begin as a period of growth and challenge for Carl. His experience in the program gave hints of what he could have accomplished and learned. Those years, however, were also marked by personal trauma and decline, and his energy necessarily shifted away from his professional life to more basic issues of survival and personal happiness.

Carl's potential as an educator may well have been most fully realized in his relationship with Barbara, one of the IDP's first students. Carl and Barbara were kindred spirits, both intelligent, artistic, and high-spirited, with a penchant for irony. They were a funny-looking pair, and the contrast amused them both, as it did the rest of the world. Carl was past sixty, gray and bearded, well over six feet tall and 240 pounds. Barbara was a young seventeen, about four feet ten inches and ninety pounds after a big dinner. Waiting in his office for Barbara one day, Carl wrote a poem, decorated it with drawings, and handed it to her when she arrived. Years later she showed it to me. Carl and Barbara both enjoyed a poem that was corny, idealistic, heartfelt, and slightly mocking of its author:

When I am alone there is only
>   me.
When two others come we are three,
A group, new born—fresh, strong and
>   free.
Humanity is our name. We belong.
We belong to earth and sky; to friend
and foe; to all that wind and sun and
>   water touch; we are the living end—
>   we three. So strong and whole.
>   So stay away you who are only *me*.
>   A part of humanity I prefer to be.

>   for Barbara, to
>   read and smile
>   that secret
>   smile.
>   —Carl.
>   Write your own
>   version—dream
>   your own dream.

These were the things Carl wanted to say to all of his students, but he could only rarely find the right time and medium. Barbara had a sparkle in her eye that matched Carl's, and she was also especially bright. Both qualities made it easier for Carl, and so did the fact that Barbara didn't mind being teased from time to time. After she graduated, she was director, for a while, of a program of art classes for children in an Appalachian slum section of Cincinnati, work which would have pleased Carl and made him terribly proud of her. I visited her, and Barbara told me that she felt that Carl was the first professor, perhaps the first adult, to take her seriously and treat her as an equal.

When Bob Sluenberg, a close colleague and friend, visited Carl in the hospital to try to persuade him to join the core faculty, Carl had already declined an invitation from me. Bob tried again, and in so doing he was really representing me and a number of other young administrators. We had good reason to believe that there would be many students whose lives would be enriched by Carl as Barbara's was, for he had done the same thing for us. Carl had been our boss when he was academic vice president of the college for a few years in the late sixties and early seventies. He was different from the other senior administrators under whom we worked. He was very intelligent, humane, and fun loving, and he had depth. He often rose above the constraints of bureaucratic role to offer us freedom, guidance, support, and even love. He touched us deeply, while to our other superiors we seemed to be means to the achievement of their current ends. Since then, however, Carl had chosen not to continue in administration and had returned to the faculty. Over the years we had watched him become enmeshed in faculty politics, and it seemed a waste of his talents. In the last years of his career we hoped that he'd turn back to the students and give them the sort of thing he had given us and was to give Barbara.

I wanted Carl involved in the program for other reasons too. I knew his participation would be a political asset and that he would be a protector and defender of the whole program. He was a faculty member of the highest status in our college, and I hoped that he would use this position on behalf of the IDP, an innovation that he supported and wished to help. The IDP was, in fact, a very strong expression of Carl's values, and it seemed like a perfect vehicle for him as an educator.

Carl and I went to lunch often, and I would question him about his life as a student and young man. There had been two central formative experiences in Carl's professional life, and these led him to positions that were consonant with the IDP. The first episode was attending art school after he graduated from high school. Carl thought of himself as a designer, and he felt that he'd always been one. Art school gave Carl the freedom to explore the things that were important to him, and he flourished. His previous time in school had been spent fighting requirements, teachers, and other students. He resisted doing things that he didn't want to do. As a student, therefore, he had previously been a rebel and an outcast. The opportunity to do what he really liked had ended a long period of alienation from his own education. From then on he advocated educational freedom.

Carl's second discovery came during World War II in Europe. He found that he had a gift for administration and for working with people. He rose as a staff officer to positions of substantial responsibility. What he did best, administration, had been learned on the job, under the pressure of events and necessity. Although he sometimes kept his more radical educational and political beliefs out of sight for the purpose of working effectively with people who were more conservative, Carl had a deep commitment to the importance both of free choice for students and of nonacademic experience as a source of learning. These were to be key themes of the IDP. But even though the IDP was a strong expression of Carl's central educational values, he was not being modest when he told the faculty committee that he saw the program as an opportunity for personal and professional growth. Significant changes would be required in Carl's behavior with students if he was to be a good core faculty member.

Carl had a paternalistic, even patronizing, style that would not work in the IDP and had ceased to work particularly well in the conventional class-room. Bob and I and our other colleagues accepted it easily and with amuse-ment. Mostly we were beyond the adolescent period that breeds resentment of such things, and Carl daily demonstrated his respect and concern for us in many ways. But it was different with students. Carl tried to stimulate thought with leading questions, a device that was part of an older style of liberal classroom teaching, and it just seemed peculiar to students. Nor did it fit the face-to-face exchanges that would be the norm among IDP students and faculty. There was a teasing, grandfatherly quality to Carl's probing. A few students like Barbara saw the love and playfulness that lay behind it. But these were easy to miss if a student was insecure or defensive. Many students saw Carl as strange and eccentric. During his participation in the IDP, Carl spent many frustrating hours in his office, waiting for students who had been turned off, not knowing how to communicate his concern for them.

Carl was aware of what was happening, for he was intensely reflective and observant in his relationships with people. He and I talked about his work with students. He saw that he'd have to change certain habits in order to be a more effective teacher, both in the IDP and elsewhere. He began to work on it and make progress. But more important things intervened in Carl's life, drew his attention away, and took increasingly large portions of his time and energy.

Carl's wife died during the semester in which we were developing the final plans for the IDP. She had been a strange, fearful, and troubled woman, and one could not escape the belief that she had been a burden. Carl was gregari-ous, for example, but he had had virtually no social life off campus because his wife couldn't handle it. He had abandoned his career as an administrator and gone back to teaching because the pressure of administrative jobs was too great when added to the stress of his life at home. This was a sacrifice for Carl, for he liked those jobs. He thrived on the social interactions that were built into the daily professional life of a vice president of a college, and he was effective as an administrator. Carl's friends on campus said to each other that it was only his extraordinary devotion and care that kept his wife from permanent institutionalization. We expected that the shock and sorrow of her death would give way to relief, liberation, and a period of great energy and productivity in Carl's life.

After a while it became obvious that if Carl's wife had been a burden, he had nonetheless loved her very much and that caring for her had also structured his life. He spent many evenings in the next year at my house, amusing my young children with funny and philosophical drawings, exposing a wellspring of the particular type of love that had not been deeply tapped because he was childless. Carl also had an active social life. Yet he did not seem to become less lonely, and he grew despondent. He gained weight, his blood pressure rose, he became lethargic. Later one saw, in retrospect, that he had been developing a nervous system disease that went unrecognized for some time, masked by his emotional state and by the symptoms of other, less serious medical problems.

Carl continued to function as a member of the core faculty. During the planning process he assumed his share of the tedious tasks, and he was sincere in his assertions that he would have a lot to learn from the IDP. He was also shrewd and decent in his efforts to ensure that his seniority and status would not separate him from the rest of us. He wanted to join the program as a real member of the team, and he did. When he was not completely drained by the emotional turmoil following his wife's death, he was cheerful, enthusiastic, and tended to be one of the more radical voices in our small group as we tried to create a realistic program without losing sight of the basic question of autonomy for students. We knew enough to be scared about the potential for conflict in our institution, and Carl reassured us and encouraged us not to compromise too much before it was necessary.

When the program began, Carl was rather strong. At times he was energetic and could put some of his younger colleagues to shame with his enthusiasm and idealism about education. But he seemed to age before our eyes, and he was never to be the IDP teacher or colleague we had all expected him to be.

Carl remarried happily, left the core faculty after three years, and reentered the realm of administration and college politics as the acting chairman of the Design Department. He had a wife and home life now that were consistent with the professional role he had been forced to give up earlier. His ambitions were rekindled. When the job became vacant, he applied to be academic vice president, a position he had held and could, a decade earlier, have had permanently for the asking. Such jobs were now, however, going to young and upwardly mobile outsiders instead of to respected senior faculty. The institution thought it needed young people who would stop off on their way to better things rather than older people committed to it. Carl was then rejected as chairman by his own department in favor of a younger man. Carl's folksy and humane wisdom was no longer the style. He was respected and liked, but he had lost some of his influence, was no longer the factor in the affairs of the college that he had once been, and was viewed as a nice gentleman who was declining, both physically and mentally. And, in fact, Carl may not have been fully aware of the extent to which he had lost some of his intellectual quickness, although he was still a good bit sharper than most people on campus.

Carl continued to function as a cooperating faculty member and a supporter of the IDP after he had left the core faculty. I and the other younger men who had worked under Carl now tried to repay the kindness and love he had extended to us. Carl had no family, and before he married again, we tried to include him in our own families. When he was hospitalized, we tried to visit him regularly as sons would, not as colleagues. When he married into a large family, we wished to be available to function as his side of the family if we were wanted. It was in this context, specifically in his relationship to me, that Carl made his final unsuccessful attempts to influence the course of the IDP.

I was not, in our small group, the "son" who was closest or most devoted to Carl. Early in our relationship we had had some conflicts, which I think Carl thoroughly enjoyed, but in which we had both spoken too strongly, and Carl was proud. He never expressed to me, as he did to one of the other younger men, for example, the pain he felt at not becoming vice president again.

Although more distant from him emotionally, I was rather like him in values and intellectual style, and I was the one who came to need Carl most, as I and the IDP became more controversial and vulnerable. Carl wanted to help. He believed in me and in the program. He also saw in me, I think, a set of choices that he might have made and for which he certainly felt sympathy. He had become a central member of any establishment he worked in. I could, apparently, only choose to be marginal. The choice between the two ways of living may have been a real issue in his life in an earlier phase. In my first years at Buffalo State, when he was the most powerful faculty member on campus, he had protected me quite successfully, and he wanted to do it again.

*

The college was, in the late sixties and early seventies, always in the midst of a genuine or imagined crisis. In addition to the real turmoil we experienced, a cause of the campus hubbub was the fact that crisis management was still recognized as a glamorous style of administration. It radiated from Washington to the provinces, even to provincial campuses. The college's top administrators, including Carl, would meet for hours on the rumor that students might decide not to attend classes for a day. When the rumors were vivid, they might well meet, protected from capture by locked doors and secrecy, in their secret headquarters in a campus warehouse and garage. (Carl always spoke of the garage with amusement.) After much discussion they would, in the end, decide to wait, see what would happen, and keep their options open. In the extreme they might distribute a mimeographed statement from the president in favor of rational techniques for solving disagreements. It was in this setting—always dramatic and sometimes hysterical—when he was the vice president, that I got to know Carl.

Carl was the most liberal, the calmest, and by far the most intelligent of the advisers trusted by the president of the college. He was sympathetic to the antiwar students. He understood their frustration. He could also see that the fears of the administrators and conservative faculty, though inevitable, were way out of proportion to the real dangers. Carl was, in short, a voice for sanity. He was also shrewd and knew when to intervene and let his voice be heard. It was his influence, for example, that kept the police off campus on several occasions, almost certainly avoiding violence. He was also responsible for the rejection of harsh and provocative disciplinary action against students. The president would say something like, "We have to show them who's running this college." Carl would remain silent, allow the steam to be vented, and twenty minutes later, or perhaps two hours later, resolve the situation with a reasonable suggestion.

In those days Carl and I developed a little game of argumentation. After a long and nervous day, he would sit down in my office and describe some of the more dangerous and ridiculous of the proposals that had been considered recently by the crisis managers. He constructed plausible rationales. I would argue with him. After a while he would say that he agreed with me and in fact, in the meeting, had taken a position like the one I was espousing. He would say that I kept him honest, "raked him over the coals of his own conscience." He had, of course, kept himself honest, and was simply looking for some companionship and fun in a lonely and stressful time. These discussions did, however, draw us closer, and in later years Carl referred to them often and liked to mock me with expressions of fear of my logic.

These issues turned quite serious from time to time. There arose on campus real matters of conscience and politics, even though, like all actors on a small stage, we had an inflated view of the importance of events. Carl and I were drawn together because, when it came to politics, we were part of a small liberal minority among our peers. During the last year of Carl's life, both of us knowing that he might not live long, I sat beside his hospital bed, and we talked about the key events of the antiwar movement at Buffalo State College. Although each of us had, in his way, been among the group of faculty most supportive of the protesting students, we looked back and saw that we had been intimidated by the threats and rhetoric of the Nixon years. We felt that we'd failed, and we weren't cheered by the parallels that Carl saw with the early Nazi years in Germany, which he had observed during a visit as a young man and which he could not forget. I feel certain that Carl's decision not to be more politically aggressive concerning the Vietnam war was one of the major regrets of his life.

Our political beliefs and positions on campus brought Carl and me together in a more practical way. Carl saved my job more than once, for I was a visible liberal and, as an administrator, could be fired more easily than a faculty member. The president, with a directness that was most uncharacteristic of him, once warned me, "Administrators don't have academic freedom." Early in my stay at Buffalo State, for example, when I was in charge of freshman orientation, I hired six faculty members to be academic advisers during a summer orientation program. Most of them had worked in the program before I came to campus, but one who had not was also a political radical. Someone, in a splendid moment of paranoia, caught wind of my action and ordered someone else in the mail room to intercept my letter of appointment to this faculty member. The vice president, whose responsibilities were administrative and not academic at all, had decided that people like this radical professor could not be trusted to advise freshmen on whether to take biology before chemistry. A whole generation of Buffalo State students was imperiled.

The vice president worked on the president, a malleable man whom I describe in another chapter. The president told Carl, my boss, to tell me that I couldn't hire the man. I told Carl that I thought it was a matter of academic freedom, and that I'd resign if I wasn't allowed to hire people without a political test of their beliefs. (I really thought, wrongly as it turned out, that the fellow would be a good freshman adviser, a fact that soon got lost in the controversy.) Carl said, "I thought that's what you'd say," and went off to talk to the president.

The deliberations lasted for a week, during which the vice president said that *he'd* resign if I was kept on. Regrettably he didn't, even though Carl convinced the president that my position was correct. The story has its comic aspects, as did several others which might well have ended with my resignation or dismissal. At the time it was all serious and intense, and it even took some courage for Carl to defend me as he did, for I was badly smeared on a couple of occasions. The mood of the faculty and administration was turning ugly, and I was a minor administrator whose departure would have meant only the slightest inconvenience for the college. I was grateful to him, and Carl himself was pleased by what he had done for me.

*

Carl valued the IDP highly, yet he had seen programs come and go. But as this program came under attack, he saw it as my program, as many of the attackers did, and so it acquired additional importance for Carl. It certainly, for Carl, became an issue of defending me again. He lobbied informally among top administrators, some of whom, especially the president, had relied heavily upon Carl's judgment and sense to pull them through some of the hardest moments of their careers. Carl expected loyalty from them, but he got only politeness. He testified at the open hearings about the IDP, and made strong statements concerning its value. The following is from a tape of one of those meetings:

> I felt that this college needed a kind of an opportunity for students that allowed them to grow as individuals. I felt that our curriculum was rather rigid and that it didn't provide the options for students to be in control of their own educational directions as much as would be good for them. . . . Here [the IDP] was one place you could go and feel free. That is to say you weren't clamped in by the bureaucracy and by the institutional norms that seem to frustrate every good idea that anyone ever has. . . .

Members of the committee wrote him off as an old man trying to be nice to his friends. He served as my representative in a personnel grievance, and we lost. Saving my job and "my program" was the last thing that Carl tried to accomplish on campus before he became too ill to work, but his remaining influence was not equal to the task. He was saddened. He did not reveal his feelings to me; I think he was trying to keep my spirits up. He told Wendel Wickland that it seemed as if everything he had worked for was being destroyed.

Carl died a few months after I left Buffalo, as the remnants of the IDP were being dismantled. There had been happiness in his final years, especially in his marriage and the large family, including grandchildren, he had acquired overnight. There was joy too in his work, in a few relationships with students, especially his relationship with Barbara, and in his sense of shared purpose and friendship with several members of the core faculty. There were also pain and frustration in that period for Carl and for those who loved him. For all of us there was a sense of opportunities lost when illness overtook him too soon.

22

Mark

I was one of the three teachers closest to Mark during his college years. When I went back to look over Mark's contract evaluations and letters of recommendation, I found that all three of us, in almost identical terms, had described him as a courageous student. Intellectual courage is not the quality that instantly springs to mind when describing contemporary American college students. Mark was indeed an unusual person who created a special kind of education for himself. Although he was far from solemn, he had the courage required to face, not to turn away from, important questions about himself and the world.

Mark is the son of a Long Island Jewish family. He is an artist, thinker, clown, craftsman, and designer. He is a 200-pound wrestler who took up tap dancing to fulfill a gym requirement, and talks gleefully about the fact that the teacher judged him lacking in style. His Bicentennial New Year's card featured him posed nude on the classical facade of Buffalo's Albright-Knox Art Gallery. He is a person who devotes sixty or seventy hours each week to his work, bringing considerable talent to it. He writes poetry and tries to open himself to religious experiences. He is a person who is saddened by his father's difficulty in expressing love and who wonders whether he will have the same problem with his children.

Mark wanted formal education. He wanted to know the things that could be learned from teachers and books, but he was also rebellious, unwilling to put up with requirements that seemed senseless. He remained in college because the IDP offered him the opportunity to stop fighting the system for his own time and to use it as he saw fit.

In a sense Mark had been a dropout for several years. In high school, searching for a direction for his life, he found that academic work was not helpful. He was outraged by the paternalism of the school administration and by the dullness of the curriculum. He stopped bringing his books home and did very little schoolwork during his last two years. He survived under the protection of a sympathetic football and wrestling coach who gave him sanctuary for most of the day in the gym, away from many of the school's routines and regulations. Mark's rebellious spirit got along nicely with his bizarre sense of humor. Without the help of his coach, Mark might well have ended his secondary education by doing something crazy and funny that would have gotten him expelled.

In the conventional college program Mark settled into work that was important to him, but he was frustrated in his attempts to pursue it. He became interested in design and woodworking. He was consumed by the desire to design and build furniture. He was always working on one piece of furniture and involved in the process of designing another. Mark took the relevant courses in design and woodworking, and he worked hard at them. His time, however, was substantially occupied with courses taken in order to meet other degree requirements. He continued to follow his high school dropout strategy. The gym was replaced by the wood shop. He did the bare minimum to pass his other courses and spent his remaining time, twenty or thirty hours each week, working with wood. His life was thus divided between two realms, one intensely significant to him and one that meant little. The fragmentation left him frustrated and unhappy. Mark's intellect and interests were not, however, narrowly defined. He was intensely curious about a wide range of things, some of which did not appear in the curriculum, at least in ways that were accessible to Mark. There were aspects of his nature and intellectual life that were not being engaged by his work at school, and they should have been. By the time he learned about the IDP, Mark had decided to drop out of college, despite his own misgivings and the opposition of his parents. He simply did not feel whole or satisfied. He felt that he was fighting the system too much, and it was helping him too little.

Mark had come to his own critique of conventional education, focusing on the coercion of students and the prevalence of simulated rather than real learning. He also had begun to formulate an idea of what better education would be like, self-created education based on the autonomy of students. Mark had a big ego and an athlete's competitive temperament in responding to challenges. He saw the IDP as a challenge to live up to the educational ideals that he professed but against which he had never been able to test himself. He was also happy to find a way to remain in school and to end, at least for the moment, the conflict with his parents. And Mark was part of a lively artistic subculture on campus; it was an interesting group of people to live among and an additional incentive to remain in school.

The IDP attracted a number of students who, like Mark, were ideological proponents of open education. For them the IDP was not only a chance to do a variety of things that might be harder or impossible in conventional programs, but also an opportunity to live according to educational values in which they had invested thought and feeling. They had often joined or even helped to create one of the alternative programs that were popular in high schools in the early seventies.

The educational radicals in the IDP sometimes had more trouble adjusting to the program than the average student. They came to the program elated and overconfident. Their high school programs frequently rewarded them primarily for professing the correct values. Often the programs occurred during the senior year when all graduation requirements had been met and nothing was at stake that would affect future options. Although they believed otherwise, many of these students had never really confronted the problems of moving from a system that was basically coercive to one that was not. They lacked the skills required by the IDP, and they didn't have high levels of awareness of their shortcomings. The confusion that resulted was intense because they were deeply committed to the program's values. Some persevered and developed the skills they needed, and others did not.

Mark did not have these problems. Although his educational beliefs were important to him, there was something that was more important: to be left alone to work and develop as a craftsman and designer. The IDP's initial contribution to Mark's life was to give him back his time while allowing him to remain at the college and use its facilities. Although he already spent far more time at his work than other students in the field, Mark immediately doubled the number of hours he spent building and designing furniture in the wood shop and the design studio. Design was an established major at the college, and woodworking a recognized specialty within it. Mark's interests were not, therefore, excluded by the college's curriculum. But his passion for his work, the intensity and seriousness with which he approached it, did not fit into normal educational structures. Mark required days and weeks that were relatively uninterrupted by class meetings, exam schedules, and term papers.

His manual skills needed to be improved each day without gaps in his practice of them. He had to concentrate on and live with the design problems he posed for himself. He simply could not be attending five separate courses and taking weeks out at the middle and end of each semester to study for examinations. (Here, at last, was the "serious student" that faculty members are always yearning for, and the standard structures, ardently embraced by most professors, could not accommodate his seriousness.) As an IDP student Mark did other academic work which was to become important to him. But from the moment he entered the IDP, he was free to organize his time to reflect his real values. His education finally belonged to him.

Mark was also lucky. He had a superb teacher who would provide him with a model as a craftsman, designer, and thinker. Mark had taken woodworking courses from Wesley Brett, an older professor and craftsman. Mark continued to work in Mr. Brett's shop. Although humble and reserved, Mr. Brett is a thinker and a perfectionist. He is completely in control in his shop, where things are simply not done sloppily or thoughtlessly. He is also both kind and wise, and he genuinely enjoys talking with and learning from young people. He is, in short, irresistible, and for all practical purposes Mark apprenticed himself to Mr. Brett, assuming the dual role of student and assistant teacher for elementary woodworking students. Mark was one of three students, in thirty years of teaching, to whom Mr. Brett gave a key to the shop.

Although it developed slowly, his relationship with Mr. Brett was of great importance in Mark's life. Among other things it changed his orientation to formal education. Mr. Brett saw that Mark was serious about his craft. That was enough for him, and he was content to wait for Mark to move to define their relationship further. Mark did his work but steered a rather wide path around Mr. Brett. By his own report, Mark's previous experience with teachers had been dominated by dishonesty. The teacher's function was to judge, and Mark's response had always been to present the appearances of appropriate learning and docile behavior, at least until he did something disruptive. In such relationships one did not ask genuine questions, for they implied ignorance and made a person vulnerable. Slowly Mark tested Mr. Brett. He asked a few real questions, for there were many things with which Mr. Brett could help. Mark faced the dilemmas of his craft, and Mr. Brett's experience and skill were obviously too valuable to ignore. Mr. Brett gave direct and useful answers, and did not use the questions against Mark.

Now that Mark spent the whole day in the shop, he and Mr. Brett began eating lunch together. Every day at noon, Monday through Saturday and sometimes on Sunday, Mr. Brett invited Mark to join him in his small office adjoining the workshop. Mark usually had forgotten to bring lunch and would excuse himself to run over to the cafeteria to get a sandwich. Mr. Brett offered instead to share his lunch with Mark, and eventually Mrs. Brett began packing two lunches. They ate and talked and argued, for Mark was given to extreme and provocative statements of issues, and Mr. Brett was not. At lunch they talked about everything except design and wood: philosophy, art, science, religion, politics, human relationships, and even, in a polite but direct way, sex. In the midst of a large, crowded, bureaucratized campus of the State University of New York, an older man and a young man sat in a room each day and lived in a classic student-teacher relationship. Mark described the association with Mr. Brett as his first predominantly intellectual relationship with another person. The two men were right for each other, and they had the time to work together and talk.

Mark's work with Mr. Brett dominated his education, but it was never all of it. Mark was curious and had a lively mind, and the IDP gave him a chance to use it in new ways. It took him a while to trust the new system, to believe that he would really be allowed to follow his interests. But he was persuaded after some testing and probing. His work in poetry is the best example of Mark's use of the IDP to move into new areas.

Mark had always had a vague interest in poetry, but he never acted on it. Although he was intrigued by poetic uses of language, his English courses in high school had always made poetry seem boring. Mark saw himself as a craftsman, designer, and athlete, a physical and artistic person, not a scholar or academic. Each semester he considered but then rejected the idea of taking an advanced literature course, the only setting in the college in which poetry was taught. The turf was too far from his own. He did not think he was the sort of person who took poetry courses. Mark's intellectual life was active, but it was not easily expressed in the scholarly idioms and style that he would have encountered in English courses. He knew this from talking with other students and from his deep distrust of the academic world, and I think he was right.

Mark

Mark had read some of the Beat poets, and he loved them. They were iconoclastic, lusty, and rebellious. They wrote the way Mark would have liked to write. Mark talked about the Beat poets with Dick Tow, a young English professor who had joined the IDP core faculty. Dick didn't know much about the Beats, but he was curious and eager to please. Dick and Mark agreed to do a project on the Beat poets. The project was important to Mark. It was his first attempt to look at poems carefully and to understand how they grew out of experience. Mark became very involved, and his enthusiasm, according to Dick, was contagious. Dick was drawn into a deeper relationship with the poets too. Mark wrote a poem as part of the evaluation of the learning contract, and Dick wrote:

> Through his reading of and reflecting on the literature Mark achieved a good understanding of the "Beat" writers, probably a better understanding than mine. We met periodically to discuss the fiction and poetry. I tried to give Mark what help I could, but this was truly an independent study on his part. He did not "study" the literature in an academic way; he let it become part of his life.

By the time Mark completed his contract on the Beat writers, he had begun to write poetry with some regularity. Again he worked with Dick Tow. Mark was not as craftsmanlike and careful with his poems as he was with his furniture, but he was writing, something he had not done before. And he was learning a great deal. This time Dick wrote:

> Mark's poetry shows great promise. The poems he submitted for evaluation impress me mainly by their sounds. Mark plays with words to see and hear what happens when they are put together. Some of his experiments are incoherent in any "rational" sense. His better poems are unified through imagery and sound. The poems are all in free verse and seem to me to be influenced by Ginsberg, Ferlinghetti, Corso and other writers of the Beat Generation, whose works Mark was reading during the contract period. I think Mark should revise more extensively and experiment with the discipline of meter. But, in general, he has the love of words necessary for writing good poetry.

When Dick wrote, in the evaluation of the first contract, that Mark did not study the subject matter but rather let it enter his life, he was touching upon the central fact of Mark's education, the fact that accounted for everything from his rebellion to his discipline as a designer to his playfulness as a beginning poet. Mark did not do things unless they engaged him profoundly, and then he did them with passion.

Mark worked with George Hole, a philosophy professor who was also a poet, on the Don Juan books of Carlos Castenada. The books touched a spiritual and mystical side of Mark that was often hidden by his exuberance. Mark would return home late at night after working in the shop, and he would sit alone or take long walks, experiencing his isolation and thinking about religious and philosophical questions. Without drugs or an exotic cultural setting, Mark pursued a spiritual quest that had parallels with Castenada's. He was intrigued by the questions of the existence and the possibilities of entering realms of life not governed by the categories of ordinary experience. Mark's learning is best reflected by reproducing the statements about the project that he and George, very much under the influence of the Don Juan/Castenada world view, wrote at the end of their formal work together.

Mark:

> For the past four months I have tried to gain some understanding of Don Juan's ideas on life. At this point I feel that I will continue to keep on learning how to learn and perhaps someday I will become a man of knowledge. At this point all that I would like to discuss is some of the reasons for making this very strong statement.
>
> Many of Don Juan's rituals seem very silly, and perhaps they are. But then again the idea of drinking Christ's blood or observing the Sabbath can seem as silly as collecting power objects or storing energy from the wind, if these acts are viewed without their labels. . . .
>
> In all of my past religious experiences I never was helped in dealing with the here and now, but rather with the concept of gaining entrance into heaven. Don Juan has made me more aware of nature and I have found a great reverence for life in his philosophy. This is also something that I never experienced through any of my religious experiences.
>
> One of the most interesting ideas that Don Juan discussed was that of decision making. For myself I had always been a very poor decision maker. I hardly ever made a decision that was precisely the way I really felt or wanted to decide. All of my decisions were just part of my routine lifestyle. Now I am trying to make all of my decisions as though they were my last. Again even here I say I am trying, but the fact is that all I have to do is make my choice and then follow it up and that's where the difference is between being a hunter and just sliding by. Perhaps these few lines by Charles Olson can describe this situation as it is:

to dream takes no effort
to think is easy
to act is more difficult
but for a man to act after he has taken
   thought, this!
is the most difficult thing of all.

Realizing that I can gain control of my life was a very scary thing to discover.

George:

Mark discovered through reading, but more through a special kind of Don Juan experiencing, the problem of learning to learn where one is on his own. He worked though his initial fear and pride of this discovery towards a rare confidence and humility. I admire his courage and persistence in trying to discover the path, for himself, with heart.

Mark did a number of other projects. A few of them, like those in jewelry making, photomechanical design, and product design, were done to fulfill requirements of the Design Department. Others had the idiosyncratic quality of Mark's work in poetry and religion. One of these, done with Art Pitts, was on the art of biography. Mark read the biographies and autobiographies of artists, and he wrote a long autobiographical essay. The readings frequently illuminated for Mark his own inclinations toward a life as an artist. Occasionally he was stunned by another person's clear statement of something within himself that had hitherto remained vague and unformulated.

In another project Mark and I collected readings from a broad range of periodicals. We looked for themes in American culture, and Mark tried to relate them to the way design problems are solved in our society. It strengthened Mark's tendency to see design as determined by culture. He did not wish to approach it as an isolated artistic-technical discipline, which was the concept behind many of the design classes he had taken.

Mark's decision about his future came hard. He knew that he was becoming a skilled designer and craftsman, and he was faced with two possibilities for using those talents. He was strongly attracted to becoming a woodworker. As an IDP student in Mr. Brett's shop, he had begun to live according to the pattern implied by that choice: long, quiet, disciplined, painstaking hours in the shop, working out highly artistic solutions to design problems. Mark could, in that mode, look forward to a modest life designing and building a small number of superior and expensive pieces of furniture each year. They would have aesthetic impact on the lives of an elite group.

The alternative was to become a product or industrial designer. He would travel, make a lot of money, and be involved with large industrial or commercial organizations, of which he disapproved and was distrustful. He would be in a position to try to be a small force for sanity and good design in a world that was, in his view, crazy.

Mark decided to become a product designer. His decision was the result of several factors: his usual response to a challenge, a desire to be socially useful, an adventurous nature, an interest in money. Mark applied to an internationally prestigious graduate program in design that accepted five students each year. Without grades on his college transcript for his last two IDP years, Mark was accepted on the basis of his portfolio and letters of recommendation. Mark was the graduate program's only American student that year.

At first Mark had difficulty in readjusting to conventional academic structures and staying out of trouble. He was outspoken and provocative about design matters like built-in obsolescence, poor planning for repair problems, wasteful uses of materials, and inadequate considerations of the environmental consequences of design decisions. Although Mark's professors were by no means reactionary, Mark's way of raising these questions was not endearing. Had Mark been either less talented or less productive, his style might have gotten him kicked out of school. Yet he was clearly the program's best student.

The graduate program required students to complete large-scale projects. The students worked in a large shared studio. The projects demanded many weeks of concentrated and continuous work. It started with research on a problem, the various stages of the design process, model building, and finally ended with a presentation. Most of the students, as good as they were, could not sustain the effort. During the semester almost every one of them would disappear from the studio for a week or two, losing momentum and intensity, unable to mount the concentrated effort required to produce his or her best work. Mark, who was certainly among the most talented of the students to begin with, had no such work problems. He already had detailed knowledge of his strengths and weaknesses as a worker. He had learned in Mr. Brett's shop to discipline himself in the use of his time, and he had experienced the benefits derived from such discipline.

Mark

Mark received his master's degree, writing an innovative and excellent thesis on the subject of comfort and furniture. Mark was approached by Buffalo State College and offered the faculty position in woodworking located in the Design Department, soon to be vacated by Mr. Brett's retirement. Mark declined the position and took one as a designer for the American subsidiary of a major Italian furniture company. When I last spoke with him, he was still amazed to be receiving a salary for work that was so much fun.

23

The Rise and Fall of the IDP

A wise reformer ought to be more modest, claiming that only a particular reform will not harm adult society and that it will make life pleasanter for parents, teachers and students in the short run.

    This plea for modesty in school reform will, we fear, fall on deaf ears. Ivan Illich is right in seeing schools as secular churches, though we seek to improve not ourselves but our descendents. That this process should be disagreeable seems inevitable; one cannot abolish original sin through self-indulgence. That it should be immodest seems equally inevitable; a religion that promises anything less than salvation wins few converts.

    —Mary Jo Bane and Christopher Jencks

The IDP was a product of a typical mixture of accidents, significant forces, personalities, and ideas. Although there are idiosyncrasies in its history, such a program could have arisen on many campuses, especially during the sixties. The IDP was, if anything, a little late, somewhat out of phase with the latest educational fashions, for its first students entered college in 1973, after the most intense period of campus innovation had ended. Innovative programs were still, however, valued in the early seventies. They were seen as signs that an institution was healthy and that its administration was creative. That atmosphere was responsible for my presence at the college as the token innovating liberal administrator. I was usually, for example, introduced as having come from Antioch, which had a reputation for experimentation. Attitudes changed, of course, making it easier for the IDP and me to be swept from the scene.

THE RISE

The key figure in the early planning stages of the IDP was Bob Shoenberg. He did most of the work that made it possible for Buffalo State to wave back when the Carnegie Corporation unexpectedly waved some money at the State University of New York.

As associate vice president for academic affairs, Bob was my immediate supervisor. He was the person at the college who was primarily responsible for hiring me. His job was to see to it that the administrative apparatus of the academic program ran smoothly. New courses, requirements, and programs had to be properly introduced, approved, and implemented. Resources were allocated, programs were evaluated, the academic calendar was changed, regulations established, and exceptions made. Bob was a thoughtful person who did his job well. He found that these administrative responsibilities often brought him directly to the consideration of rather basic educational issues: How does a college choose among possible educational experiences that could be made available to its students? What rights and obligations should govern the relationship between professors and students? How should money be spent to best educational advantage? Et cetera.

Bob was serious in his search for answers to such questions. He sincerely wished to apply sound principles to the solution of the practical problems he faced daily. He was also ambitious. He strove for creative solutions, not only because he wanted to improve education at our college but because he was eager to compile a record that showed that he could handle greater respon- sibilities, either in Buffalo or elsewhere.

Bob brought together, for example, professors from various departments who taught courses dealing with the same historical periods but from different disciplinary perspectives. They scheduled and coordinated their courses so that students could have a new kind of coherence in their course schedules. They even tried some team teaching. As in many minor experiments, there was some enjoyment in this for faculty members, although they tended to be nervous about even the most friendly collegial invasions of their turf. These "course clusters" were usually not found to be exciting by students, but they were certainly positive developments, helping a few students and teachers and harming nobody.

Bob and I became friends, and our friendship was important to both of us. We discussed education several times each week over lunch. I argued the case for student freedom and nonauthoritarian structures, and Bob was in- trigued. He had taught English at Williams College and had been an excellent student before that. But he had been disappointed with his work as a profes- sor, and that was one of the reasons he'd become an administrator. Looking back at his teaching, it seemed plausible to him that some of the excitement and deeper involvement that had been missing might have been present if the educational structures had been more student centered.

Bob's administrative work continually raised other issues for him. A major consideration in many decisions was the FTE, the number of "full-time equivalent" students enrolled in a course or department or taught by a particular instructor. The FTE is a standard unit of academic accounting, and it is based upon the credit hour. The two related numerical units are often used to measure academic productivity and to allocate money among competing programs. Since FTEs are neat and quantitative, while other approaches to measuring productivity in instructional programs seem fraught with subjective judgments, the counting of FTEs is prominent in administrative decision-making.

Although there are few obvious alternatives, thoughtful administrators inevitably confront the disturbing distance between real learning and the credit hour (and thus the FTE). The credit hour is a measure of the time spent in an instructional activity. A moment of reflection and a bit of experience reveal that learning need not, and often does not, follow the pattern of time spent in a classroom or laboratory or in the presence of a teacher. Administrative reliance on the credit hour promotes the illusion that learning is uniform among a wide variety of teachers, students, subjects, methodologies, and settings. It encourages decisions that make the system less flexible and responsive to significant differences that exist among the people and factors that affect education. We offer instruction in units that are assigned three, four, or five credit hours, depending on how time-consuming they are. We know, however, that there is an enormous amount of variation among three-credit courses and in the amount of learning accomplished by students within a given course. Is there any reason other than administrative convenience and the myth of uniformity for offering all instruction in standard semester-length units? Some resources and intensive learning experiences are best available over shorter periods. Others lend themselves to longer periods. Why should students always be working on four or five different subjects? Some people probably learn best by focusing sharply and not spreading themselves too thin. Most basically, isn't it time to attempt to measure learning rather than time spent in an activity? Isn't our emphasis on time anti-intellectual at its core, especially when we are dealing with brighter students who may learn quickly?

These were the thoughts and questions Bob presented in a paper one night to a group of faculty and administrators that met occasionally for dinner and discussion. His critique of the credit hour as a basic academic measurement and his argument concerning its homogenizing effects were well reasoned. He developed some ideas for experiments with structures that were more open and responsive to differences among students. Bob's talk and proposals were well received, and a lively discussion followed.

Bob was pleased and encouraged, and he decided to do something concrete. He formed a committee to discuss the ideas further and to formulate a proposal for a new program that would be more flexible and attempt to incorporate more realistic assumptions about how learning actually takes place. The committee would consider alternatives to the credit hour for the measurement of learning and instruction. Bob's boss that year was an acting vice president who was concerned primarily with maintaining the peace. The committee presented no immediate threat to law and order, so the acting vice president didn't object.

I joined the committee at Bob's request, but I had little enthusiasm for it. The meetings were dull affairs at which the members in turn exhibited their pet liberal ideas for the admiration of the others. There seemed to be no real engagement of issues, no work being done, although Bob chaired the meetings and tried to put a good face on it all by discovering, or pretending to discover, agreement among us, common themes that we might use as a basis for an eventual program that we would propose. I was sure that nothing would come of so smug an operation. One day, however, some money appeared on the scene. There is nothing like it to give meaning to the work of a committee.

The president of the college got a memo from the State University of New York (SUNY) central office in Albany. The Carnegie Corporation was tentatively offering money to the university. The Carnegie Commission had recently published a report called *Less Time, More Options*. It urged new and more flexible academic programs to meet the needs of different types of students. One of its major themes was that increased flexibility would allow many students to finish college in less than four years, and this was seen as a partial solution to the problem of the rising costs of college.

Some discussion had already taken place between the top people of Carnegie and SUNY. Carnegie would welcome a grant proposal that involved several of SUNY's campuses in experiments with flexible and time-shortened programs. The idea was that SUNY was sufficiently large and diverse to provide a realistic test of the theses developed in *Less Time, More Options.* Each of the campuses involved would test a different model of an innovative and flexible program, the idea for which would have been developed indigenously, not imposed from above or outside. A thorough research component would provide information concerning the effectiveness of the new programs, especially in the financial realm. The ideas and experiences would be disseminated throughout the educational community, where they could stimulate further innovation. Executives of the corporation would consult with people from the university as the grant proposal was written, so that the interests of both groups would be served and the proposal would have an increased chance of being accepted.

The president of Buffalo State College passed the memo to the acting vice president, and it ended up on Bob Shoenberg's desk. This was a chance for everyone to look good, for we could truthfully say that for months we'd had a committee working on the development of a flexible and innovative program that was very much in the spirit of *Less Time, More Options.* The committee began to meet more regularly and seriously. Eventually Bob and I, in a few hours, wrote a proposal for a Degree by Contract Program, which was to become the IDP. The program was quite flexible, and although it was not necessarily time shortened, it was time variable. Some students might graduate early, while others might take the normal time or an extended time to earn their degrees. In any case, we would try to get away from the credit hour and allow students to earn a degree in a period of time, long or short, that was related to their actual learning. Many of the ideas for the program were derived from the experience I'd had in the First Year Program at Antioch.

Bob took the proposal to his boss, a new vice president named Don Schwartz. Don didn't like it. It was too liberal and fuzzy, hinting strongly at the pampering of students and deviation from disciplinary orthodoxy. Yet from his perspective the proposed program might conceivably have been a good one, given the "right" students and faculty. Don had in mind a group of elite students with conventional interests working in tutorial relationships with faculty. The projects would be similar to graduate work. It would also have been politically awkward for Don to reject the work of the committee. He agreed to support our proposal, but he insisted that it be submitted in tandem with another program of his own design, the Early Admissions Program. This program would allow high-achieving high school juniors to take a couple of courses in the college's summer session and, if they did well, stay on and matriculate at the college instead of returning to high school for their senior year. Don hoped that the program would provide an incentive for brighter students, who would otherwise go elsewhere, to enroll at Buffalo State. Don was firmly committed to a philosophy of institutional improvement that involved doing nothing different except "tightening up" regulations and getting better students.

The dual proposal, much of which would have been controversial under ordinary circumstances, was submitted to the faculty-dominated College Senate for approval. The administration backed the proposal, and the promise of Carnegie money and prestige settled the issue with little debate. The program was approved for submission as part of SUNY's proposal to Carnegie. We would implement the program if we got the grant. We were still in a period of abundant government and foundation grants to colleges for new programs. Both faculty and administrators had learned that grants could be used in many ways to provide extra money and prestige for people on campus and generally to make life easier and more interesting.

Our proposals went to Albany and came back in several draft versions of a larger document that contained descriptions of the programs that were being planned on other SUNY campuses. The comprehensive proposal was nicely written to show that SUNY was at once indebted to *Less Time, More Options* and had been thinking independently along similarly creative lines. The budget can only be called extravagant.

Within the year the grant had been made, and Buffalo State's portion had been allocated through channels. I became Director of Accelerated Programs with responsibility for the Early Admissions Program, which was to begin immediately, and the Degree by Contract Program, which I renamed the Individualized Degree Program. The IDP was to have an additional year of planning and development. The core faculty was selected, and we worked for a year on the details of the program, for the original proposal was sketchy. Students for the IDP were recruited from incoming freshmen during the spring and summer, and the program began the following fall. The results are described in the chapters on individual students and faculty.

THE FALL

The sixties were a decade of growth at Buffalo State College and in higher education generally. SUNY grew explosively. The national movement toward mass higher education, combined with the postwar baby boom, caused enrollments to climb and institutions to expand. Faculties grew, new campuses were built, institutions were transformed. Budgets increased substantially year after year. Innovative programs were seen to be necessary responses to new conditions, and they were financed out of increments of growth. Establishing new programs was virtually painless, for they competed for funds with expansion elsewhere in an institution, not with existing programs that would be forced to sacrifice to release funds for innovation.

The end of this era was widely predicted. Everyone in higher education, after a while, could rehearse the arguments of demography and economics. Yet at some level most people did not believe that this affluence would end. When budgets finally stopped growing significantly, a profound shock was felt on campuses. No longer would almost everyone get tenure. Raises would be smaller, and eventually we found that they would not keep up with inflation. Being highly educated suddenly stopped being sufficient grounds for being highly paid, and this gave one pause. Good program ideas would not get money. Employees, including professors, might have to work more for proportionately less pay. Whole institutions or parts of institutions might turn out to be unviable.

The IDP was not, in a strict sense, the victim of these developments. It ended because a coalition of administrators and faculty opposed the program, an opposition born of profound disapproval. We attempt to understand the depth of this sort of intramural conflict at several points later in this narrative. Here we simply describe it as a factor in our program's history. The coalition of opponents came to prevail in the politics of the college and simply controlled the decision-making apparatus that determined the IDP's future. The issue was often cast, however, as a question of whether the college could afford a costly innovative program. This was demonstrably not the question, for the actual cost of the IDP was small. The professors were already on the payroll, the rooms were built and in use, the buildings already heated and lighted. When spread across the college or, more realistically, across a group of the college's departments, the cost of the program consisted in negligible extra burdens to be assumed in the form of slightly larger classes. Similarly, although we spent thousands of dollars of Carnegie's money to start the program, an institution serious about such an innovation could have done so on a pittance. The rhetoric of a "budget crunch," however, presented us, the program's participants and supporters, with a difficult additional problem, since the faculty and administration were deeply shaken by the new realization that the long-predicted hard times were upon us. Faculty members were getting ready to defend themselves and their closest interests, and were not prepared for a careful analysis of the question of whether another group or program was really competing for funds. Concern for the general performance of the institution or for someone else's program was at its lowest ebb in well over a decade. People were running scared.

The history of the fall of the IDP was for some of us a complex and painful drama. There were developments almost every day for a year: meetings, hearings, conferences, negotiations, the rallying of forces, arguments made, data requested and interpreted and misinterpreted, etc. We were alternately hopeful and despairing. There was plenty of anger and a few tears. In retrospect, however, the whole matter seems quite simple; many of the intricacies and details that obsessed us were irrelevant. The simpler pattern was, in fact, visible during all the tumult, but I and others preferred to ignore it, for we wanted to believe we had a fighting chance. (Since the history of the IDP was determined largely by the orientation toward the program of a few top administrators, this historical sketch of the IDP's demise will be supplemented by a chapter on Buffalo State's top administrators of the era.)

At the end of the IDP's second year, the college president, anticipating budget problems, asked the College Senate to prepare a list of programs that might be eliminated. The senate was an elected body dominated by a couple of blocs representing the major factions of the faculty, the largest of which was the faculty union. Virtually all issues before the senate were defined in terms of the positions of these factions. Senate decisions had the status of recommendations to the administration. They provided a good map of the path of least faculty resistance associated with any particular issue. Although there was always an elaborate charade of consultation and democracy, in the absence of which there were agonized faculty protests, administrators regularly made decisions that were contrary to College Senate recommendations. When, however, they chose to follow a College Senate recommendation, they made a great show of acquiescence to the wishes of the faculty, democratically expressed.

With no evaluation of the program and with no attempt to contact the staff, the IDP was placed on the list of expendable programs by a committee and then by the whole College Senate. The list amounted to an inventory of programs with weak connections among the faculty who were members of the senate. Those of us in the program considered this a minor matter. The nature of the list was obvious; it was clearly not the product of a careful examination of programs and priorities. We had seen the president and the vice president repeatedly ignore such recommendations. We had hitherto been able to persuade the administration of the worth of the IDP, and we'd received the support and protection of a series of major administrators. We also had significant support among faculty, though not primarily in the dominant group in the College Senate. We expected to be able to continue to argue our case effectively, especially since it seemed to us that our case was getting stronger as we learned how to function better in our new program. We could not anticipate, however, the effect of a forthcoming change in the cast of characters.

Within the next month or so a new academic vice president took office. His name was Bill Sturner, and we were encouraged by his liberal educational views. He talked about affective education and the education of the whole person. He appeared to be more favorably inclined to the ideas behind the IDP than were previous vice presidents, and we were optimistic about gaining his support.

Sturner appointed a philosophy professor as his assistant. The professor had applied for the job of director of the IDP when I was hired. He had, however, opposed the program since the early stages of the development process that began when I took the position. As chairman of the philosophy department, he warned me at the very beginning that he thought it would be difficult for his department members to find the time to supervise contracts in the new program. He also gave every sign of finding me, my administrating, and my ideas repulsive, especially since I came from a background of academic philosophy and my transgressions could be considered a kind of sedition.

The IDP was scheduled for an evaluation by a College Senate committee during the program's third year. When we met with the committee, the chairwoman stated that its function was to formulate a plan to dismantle the IDP in an orderly fashion since it appeared on the College Senate's hit list. This was spectacularly inappropriate. The formal mandate of the committee had come from the College Senate, of course, and it specified that the committee would evaluate the program's quality. Decisions to continue or discontinue the program would be made by administrators who could base their decision on the committee's evaluation if they wished to do so. When challenged, the chairwoman said that her version of the charge of the committee had come directly from the new vice president.

The senate's list did not constitute a decision, and none would be made, formally at least, until after the committee's work was complete. After a few weeks the chairwoman learned to pay lip service to the nominal evaluative function of the committee. Under stress, however, she continued to refer to instructions from the vice president. A few months later, for example, when the committee's work was still unfinished, she came upon the IDP in the process of recruiting students for the next year. She told Wendel Wickland, who was the program's new director, that he had no right to recruit for the next year. She strode off to the vice president to complain. The vice president was embarrassed and tried to ignore the incident.

My best guess is that Sturner's philosophical assistant persuaded him, soon after he arrived on campus, that the IDP was a problem that had to be eliminated, and that the senate's list would be a convenient pretext to do the job. Sturner had little contact with the IDP's staff and students, and in fact he became increasingly isolated from campus activities as the year progressed. It is hard to imagine that his position on the IDP reflected much more than the opinions of one or two of the people on campus whom he trusted. Eventually, a good bit of material about the program was to reach his desk, but it all got there long after the chairwoman of the committee revealed his hand. A new administrator must, of course, rely to some extent on the judgments of others, and those others will necessarily have their own views. This seemed to us, however, like an extreme case, one in which the key people were unusually resistant to the consideration of new data.

The year was occupied with the process of seeming to evaluate the IDP. A member of the committee, friendly to us, confirmed our impression that it wasn't approaching its job objectively. After a short time neither the committee nor the IDP staff believed that the other was acting in good faith.

A contest developed in which each side's moves were designed to reveal the bias, the unfairness, and the intractability of the other. People in both camps were deeply committed to the battle. The details had great drama for the participants, but they are probably not worth recounting. Power had fallen into the hands of the opponents of the IDP or their allies. We had lost our administrative protection. The members of the senate committee were part of that body's dominant faction, so we could expect no help on the floor of the senate. We had many friends on the faculty, but they were no match for our opponents, and the mood of the campus encouraged people, as we have said, to protect their own interests rather than extend themselves to defend others. The committee wrote a report recommending strongly that the IDP be dismantled.

Bill Sturner used the report as the basis of a recommendation to the president that the IDP be ended. The memo lay on Sturner's desk. There was a delay in passing it on to the president. Many decisions were post-poned, and it seemed as if a decision was being made as to whether Sturner would continue as vice president. Eventually, he announced his resignation. The IDP might be reprieved if he left before the memo went to the presi-dent, or even if Sturner's replacement were to oppose his position.

Sturner was replaced by his senior assistant, Barbara Frey. She had been an ally of the IDP. As former (and first) chairwoman of the College Senate and as associate vice president, she had publicly insisted that the committee's real charge had been to evaluate, not terminate, the IDP. She had ample opportunity to observe the manner in which the committee functioned, and she had agreed on several occasions that the committee's evaluation had been less than fair. She had worked with at least one IDP student, Eve, and although that experience had some trying moments, she seemed to enjoy it and to feel that the IDP was a good program. In conversations with Wendel, she sympa-thized with us by recalling her experiences with innovative programs in the public schools.

Barbara passed Sturner's memo on to the president unchanged. The IDP was apparently too small an issue for her to provoke her first confrontation with the senate and its leading faction. Barbara wished to be vice president permanently, an ambition she was to achieve before long. She also wished to be president, and she almost made it a few years later when the position was vacant. She was not about to let the IDP be an obstacle. When Noel Simmons, a friend of mine and a conservative supporter of the IDP, asked her about the program's fate, she said simply that the IDP had not made its case to the senate. She was close enough to the process to know that that task was virtually impossible.

24

The Core Faculty: Art

Students are no longer numbers on a computer print-out, but individuals whom I know and care about. Once they understand that my function is not to sum up their work in a letter-grade, their behavior changes. They relax and talk more freely about what their real interests are, about their fears and hopes. It is a great pleasure to watch their development, especially when I know that I have been of some assistance. When there are problems or failures, we have time to examine them and look for remedies. When there are achievements, we can rejoice together. It was the hope for this kind of involvement with students that drew me to the teaching profession, and it has been refreshing and energizing to have those hopes realized and renewed.

—Art

I've already mentioned Art, the colleague with whom Donna and I spent so much enjoyable time. He was also mentioned as the professor who worked on writing with Debbie and on biographies of artists with Mark. The special quality of Art's work with IDP students is probably best described, however, in the story of his relationship with Adie, a frightened and unhappy young woman.

Adie joined the IDP after several years of being miserable in conventional college education. Her initial conversations about the program and possible learning contracts were with me. Our talks were painful.

Adie mumbled, whispered, giggled nervously, and looked away. I was often unsure that I'd heard her correctly. She gave short uninformative answers to questions. Sometimes she responded to a comment, joke, or inquiry, and sometimes she didn't, as if nothing had penetrated her consciousness or perhaps as if it would be too frightening to risk any response. Adie's alienation from formal education and from anyone remotely connected with it was virtually complete. She would permit only minimal communication in a setting that occurred within the educational system. Adie was simply scared to death. I wanted to assure her that I meant no harm and would try to respect her privacy, but such a statement seemed to imply a level of closeness that was not appropriate to our exchanges. It felt as if Adie would receive an attempt to reassure her, or any attempt to communicate personally, as an assault.

Adie would admit only to an interest in skiing. She was president of the college ski club. It was actually comforting to know that her conversational paralysis didn't extend to all parts of her life, to have grounds to imagine a social existence for Adie. When asked about goals, she talked about going west after college, and her wish seemed to be to disappear to some distant ski resort beyond the reach of professors and parents. She remained in school simply to comply with her parents' wishes. The courses, examinations, and papers had no meaning to Adie except as harassments. She was depressed and demoralized, and she had compiled a poor academic record which, despite her lack of interest in school, was humiliating to her. She joined the IDP in an attempt to escape from the pressures of normal academic life and to see if the program might offer a more bearable route to a college degree. She was not attracted to anything special about the IDP. She seemed to join it out of the conviction that nothing could be worse than what she was already experiencing.

In my first conversations with Adie I kept coming back to the idea that a learning contract might somehow be based on her activities in the ski club because, despite my better judgment, I was almost coming to believe that skiing was really her only interest. I asked if she might like to do some sort of formal study of group dynamics or of organizations, and she looked at me as if I was crazy. We fell silent again. Finally, during our third or fourth conversation, Adie somehow let out the information that she liked poetry and even wrote some. A learning contract in poetry, we agreed, would be a good place to begin her work in the IDP. Amazed and almost as relieved as Adie, I took her next door to meet Art. They began to talk and plan a project.

Focusing on my own discomfort, I didn't quite realize then that it took considerable courage for Adie, given her feelings about teachers and the academic world, even to mention her interest in poetry to me. Schoolwork and teachers were sources of suffering for her, and it must have been difficult to allow her involvement with poetry to cross the boundary from her private life over into her school life. And it must have taken even more courage for her to bring her poems to Art at their next meeting. Art, as a teacher and a person, was ideally equipped to vindicate Adie's gamble, to build upon it and to nurture her in future acts of bravery. He would also respect the fears and limitations that she would never overcome.

Art is gentle and rather quiet. Unlike most college professors, he almost always approaches a person or situation with his apparatus of appreciation, not of criticism. One knows immediately that he is intelligent, but one knows also that Art's intelligence is not a weapon. Art lets a person breathe and be herself while he looks for the common ground on which they can stand. Adie may well have sensed this at once, for her trust in Art increased quickly.

Art and Adie discussed her poems, and they read other poetry. Adie had little to say, but her silence was no longer complete. Art told Adie how her poems affected him, and he made small suggestions. Adie's conversations with Art would occasionally come alive. She explained the connection between her poems and the fears and problems that were dominating her life. The poetry improved, as Adie slowly worked with Art's comments. Adie remained ambivalent, and she sometimes disappeared and Art wouldn't see her for weeks. But she began to come back more regularly, and things got easier and more pleasant.

Adie was anxious to graduate, and she often asked Art about the progress she was making. Art tried to encourage her, and he was right to emphasize the positives. Adie had made enormous breakthroughs. There was now an important intersection between her schooling and the rest of her life, and she had established and begun to use a relationship with an able teacher. But the IDP was still governed by the college's degree requirements, even if there was significant new room for their reinterpretation. In those terms, Adie's progress toward a degree was still slow, and Art gently told her so. She was disappointed.

Art and Adie had to find other learning projects. Art asked Adie what she read, but again she was reluctant to say much. Slowly information leaked out, and Adie turned out to be both a science fiction fan and a devotee of several popular authors. Adie still seemed to feel that it was dangerous to reveal her interests, but a combination of trust in Art and the pressure to graduate pushed her to do so. Art and Adie worked out other contracts based on these interests. As was usual with Art, he found himself enjoying the books they read, most of which were new to him. Art loves literature of all kinds. Over and over again he found himself enjoying authors and genres introduced to him by IDP students. Occasionally he and Adie found themselves talking in the fashion of fellow enthusiasts. They became closer. It was easier for Adie to accept Art's suggestions for new directions. Their communication was clearer and more direct. A friendship arose between Adie and Art. Its style was not terribly demonstrative, and its base never expanded very far beyond their common interests in literature and Adie's graduation, but it was a friendship nonetheless, an intellectual relationship which would not previously have seemed available to Adie, especially with a faculty member.

As their discussions produced ideas for additional learning contracts, Art put Adie in touch with a couple of other professors, chosen primarily for their gentleness. Adie persevered with her schoolwork, helped enormously by the fact that it now grew out of her own life. In the end she graduated from college, an outcome that seemed quite unlikely when we first met her. I don't know if she went west.

Adie never stopped being frightened at college. Nor did she become a conversationalist, open about her thoughts or feelings, or an easy person to make contact with, particularly for a professor. One always felt that she might, at any moment, make a bolt for the door. But there were changes. The work that Art and Adie developed meant something to her. She was still often depressed, but a bit of joy and enthusiasm could nonetheless break through during their conversations.

From time to time I sat in my office and heard someone knock on Art's door. Knowing that he'd left, I'd step into the hall and find Adie and tell her when I thought Art would be back. When she was coming to see Art, Adie had an air of confidence and even enjoyment. She was more relaxed and less scared than at the other times I saw her. Art helped people feel that way. And although few people were as extreme in their discomfort as Adie, many others responded in the same way to Art as a teacher and a friend.

*

Art once described himself as a crow. Crows, he had heard, bring shiny things back to their nests. Art's shiny things were ideas, poems, books, and well-turned bits of language. Although Art is a quiet person, his enjoyment of glitter is visible and contagious. IDP students loved him for this and for his gentleness. They learned that there would probably be a bit of glitter for Art in anything that they shared with him, and that he would be grateful for it.

175

As a professor in the English Department, Art was highly respected for his intelligence, his scholarly turn of mind, and his humanity. His history as a Princeton football hero didn't hurt his reputation, either. But there is something about a crow that doesn't fit into an English Department. Art didn't pursue a single scholarly specialty, nor did he covet teaching assignments in advanced literature courses for the department's majors. Sometimes he preferred to teach a full schedule of English composition courses because he liked the energy of freshmen. Art's colleagues were pleased to have him carry more than his share of what is commonly considered a burden, but they were puzzled. They wished that he would be more serious and write scholarly articles for esoteric journals, and they wished he didn't take quite so much pride in his sabbatical piece on househusbanding in the *Ladies Home Journal.*

Although a few students in each of his classes came to appreciate him, Art was not an especially successful teacher in conventional classes. He did not give exciting lectures. The size of regular classes and the usual grading games played by students kept Art, who is basically a shy person, from making real contact with most students. When IDP students, however, were surveyed about their satisfaction with the work of core faculty members, every student who had worked with Art expressed the highest level of satisfaction permitted by the questionnaire. It was a remarkable display of unanimous praise by a group of students that was often critical.

When an IDP student walked into Art's office with an interest in literature, whether it was Barthelme or Chaucer, Twain or Sophocles, Art could almost always find something shiny in the project for himself. He and the student would learn together, enjoying the process and each other. Speaking from my own experience with Art, it is no small stimulus to work with someone when that person really loves what he's doing. Art's enjoyment of these projects was a wonderful mixture of appreciation of the subject matter and of his coworker.

Art also had the knack of getting to know students and helping them find interesting projects that might not come to mind immediately. All core faculty members suggested projects to students, but an especially large number of Art's ideas worked out. The suggestions of some of our core faculty colleagues had the automatic quality of one of my college professors who wrote on the term paper of every class member, "See the Cambridge Platonists." Art was likely to do more listening than the rest of us before he tried to help. He was sensitive and had good intuitions about people. His ideas for projects were responsive to the individual student involved. His suggestions were not the knee-jerk reactions of a faculty member who knows the right moves. Art is also blessed with a particularly good memory, so he could conjure up references to books and articles with which to help define the first step for pursuing an idea for a project.

I responded to Art the way the students did. His combination of appreciation and intelligence drew me to him. I found myself eager to talk with him about books and ideas that were new to me, for I knew that he would find a way to share my enthusiasm. I wanted to hear about the things he was reading and thinking, for he has a fertile mind and his enjoyment heightened my own. Our conversations often led me to new books and authors, and as I mentioned in my discussion of the work that he and I did with Donna, Art remains an important figure in my intellectual life. The IDP's structures, although they provided primarily for student-faculty pairs working together, allowed teachers to arrange collaborations easily. Art and I used those opportunities gladly. The excitement and vulnerability of working in an innovative program in which we both believed also drew us closer. We formed a collegial relationship that had strong personal and intellectual dimensions, the kind of relationship academic colleagues often seek but find only infrequently.

As friends who welcomed the opportunity to work together, and as the two IDP faculty most interested in writing, Art and I worked on a project that was to make a difference to both of us. Many IDP students, like college students generally, could not write well. The problem was especially acute and embarrassing in the IDP because a written document, the learning contract, was the program's central academic structure. Students in conventional programs often select courses and options within courses to minimize their need to write, but IDP students who were poor writers confronted their problem at the first stage of every project. It could, and sometimes did, block all future progress.

Art and I organized a workshop, described briefly in the chapter about Debbie, for IDP students who wanted to improve their writing. We were influenced by an article we had read about teaching writing. Most of the ideas in the article did not work well for us, but we and our students developed our own structure for the workshop. We had about ten students, and we met once a week for four hours. Everyone in the group, including Art and me, spent the first hour or hour and a half writing, although some of us also brought in work we had done at home. Sometimes Art would propose a writing exercise, but more often we each wrote about whatever seemed important or amusing at the moment. There was something psychologically right for our group to be sitting quietly, occupied in parallel by the solitary activity of writing. There was the intensity of people working in common, even though the task was, for the time being, private. There was also a sense of curiosity and expectation in the air, an eagerness to know what the others were writing.

We then read our work to the group and discussed it. Often a person's piece or portions of it were read several times at the request of others. The group was extremely diverse, ranging from Debbie, whose first piece was a breathless and juvenile fantasy, to Michael, who wrote rather sophisticated and complex long poems. The diversity didn't seem to matter, or perhaps it helped, for there was a sense among us of the variety of things that might be done with the written word. The group's members began to look forward to each other's writings. We had our own little jokes about our interests and idiosyncrasies as writers. Our expectations of each other were both serious and playful. It was possible, one week, for Cecelia to write a description of a terrifying conversation with a sexually threatening man in the park, and a week later for her to write a funny piece about a visit from a rebellious younger sister, which unexpectedly put her in an unlikely parental role. The group developed its own style of praise and criticism, which was clear and gentle.

Every person in the group improved as a writer. I am sure that one reason was our freedom to write about anything. Another reason was that the writing was not an abstract exercise; the cohesiveness of the group meant that there was a real audience involved. The writing functioned in our lives as attempts to communicate with known people. It was not an academic skill to be learned solely for its utility in the future. Art and I have both gone on to teach writing in other settings, and we have tried, each time, to reproduce this aspect of the IDP's writing workshop, although neither of us has quite managed to recapture the unique excitement of that group.

It was, I believe, important that Art and I wrote and then read our work. The students' central problem in the workshop at the outset was the vulnerability implied by exposing themselves through their writing. This is a major source of the well-known difficulty of teaching writing. Our willingness to take the same risks, along with our obvious imperfections as writers and people, made it easier for the students. Both Art and I entered periods of intense interest in writing as a result of our participation in the workshop, as did several of the students.

Much of the workshop's success was due to Art's qualities as a writer and human being. His tact and kindness were always part of his criticism. As a writer he was playful as well as meticulous, exhibiting an interest in style that showed that craftsmanship did not distract from content. There was no pedanticism in Art. He was also scrupulously honest in his writing. Above all, Art's appreciation of people, of the value of human experience, and of language set a tone for our workshop that made it possible for the rest of us to find joy in the attempt to write well.

Art was happy in the IDP. He knew his work with the program's students was outstanding, just as he knew his work in conventional classrooms had not been. The structures of the IDP matched Art's talents perfectly. The IDP also provided Art with a work environment that he liked. There was a small group of colleagues with whom he got along well, and a larger group of students whom one met in informal settings. Relationships were direct and honest.

Art was much less comfortable in his department, where his colleagues postured as scholars, condescended to students, and played politics incessantly. The sham and pomposity of standard academic settings and the distance from students were burdens from which Art was pleased, in the IDP, to be free.

Art had periodically been dissatisfied with his life as a college professor. He read the want ads and thought about other jobs. His most vivid recurring fantasy was that he and his wife, a brilliantly gifted teacher, would take teaching jobs at a prep school someplace in the country. He would teach English and also be the school's football coach. He would deal with small groups or individual students and thus use his talents to best advantage. He would be part of a small and compatible staff. Art also thought about other jobs, selling real estate, for example, that were more concrete and, in a way, seemed more intellectually honest than being a member of a college English Department. Art's large family, with a number of kids reaching college age at about the same time, restrained him from living out such fantasies.

As the IDP drew to a close, Art considered other jobs more seriously than he ever had. He was depressed during his first semester of teaching regular classes again. He missed the IDP, and he missed me, for I had left. Art took a part-time job as a janitor, partly because he needed some extra money and partly because it was an adventure in honest work. He wrote me letters full of elation, singing the praises of hard physical labor and the romance of cleaning offices at night. He urged me to try, but I've declined.

The janitorial experiment became less exciting, and more importantly Art found that he was teaching his regular classes with new confidence and skill. Drawing on his IDP experiences, he discovered ways to remove the barriers that had always kept him distant from students. In the IDP he had learned to apply his playfulness to his teaching, and he retained this when he moved back into regular classes. One day in his freshman composition class, for example, he gave each student a book from his own library, and initiated a round of literary gift giving that enlivened the class. Or when he thought that a course wasn't going well, he said so and started over, refusing to hide his feelings and thus allowing his students to express theirs. In other ways, too, he found that although it was harder in regular classes, it was not impossible to be himself.

It was, however, never the same for Art at Buffalo State after the IDP. One day, visiting his in-laws in a small Louisiana town, Art and his wife stopped in at the local Catholic school. On the spot they accepted jobs teaching classes at the elementary and junior high school level. Within weeks they had sold a house in Buffalo and bought another in Bunkie. Art resigned his tenured position at the college. He is now an English teacher, the coach of several of the school's teams, and a part-time writer for the local paper. As far as I can tell, he is very happy.

25

The Core Faculty: Peggy

Peggy's participation in the IDP was full of embarrassment for her and the students and colleagues who dealt with her. Her experience as a core faculty member was almost identical to that of the IDP students who had the most difficulty with the program's freedom.

In the course of trying to arrange for increased freedom for students, the new structures of the IDP conferred additional freedoms on the core faculty. There was a great deal of planning by the program's founders, a group that included Peggy, about how to respond properly to students who had trouble with the new freedoms. There was no discussion of the possibility that we faculty members would not be equal to the task we were setting ourselves, that we might, because of personal failings or problems, be unable to do what we were saying we would do. One reason was the assumption that professional people like college teachers are self-correcting and self-disciplining. Our failure to plan for faculty problems also expressed something about our hopes for relationships among IDP faculty. We wanted them to be collegial, nonauthoritarian, responsible, egalitarian. We didn't want to think that it might be necessary to confront each other with our failings and shortcomings. We were liberals. Peggy's work, or rather her lack of work, raised the problems of authority, power, and collegial responsibility that are usually avoided in academia until they are reached in personnel committees, where the remedy is dismissal. But whatever our difficulty in responding, it was not possible, in the end, to ignore the fact that Peggy wasn't doing her job.

I got to know Peggy as the work of the IDP planning committee progressed. She was bright, energetic, and enthusiastic. She held a full-time teaching job in the college's social work department, and she was a doctoral candidate in psychology at the University of Buffalo. She was liberal and oriented toward students, and she was, like me, influenced by the human potential movement with its emphases on personal freedom, affective education, and learning in groups. Peggy seemed to be a natural core faculty member. As soon as the money for the IDP was received and I'd been chosen director, I asked Peggy if she'd join the program, and she agreed. Long before the other core faculty had been selected and the core faculty's work in developing the IDP had begun, Peggy and I met for lunch each week and talked about the program. Along the way we became friends, a friendship catalyzed by jointly held hopes for the future.

We talked about education that would involve the heart as well as the head. The academic work of IDP students would be connected with their feelings because it would grow out of their interests and goals. We would not encourage students to deny these connections in order to achieve a cool academic detachment. We would value enthusiasm and feeling.

We hoped that IDP students would grow emotionally as well as intellectually, learning to be more aware of their own feelings and of their impact on others. We hoped that they would learn to be more expressive when they wanted to be, and that they would grow more skillful in their relationships with others. We intended to encourage these sorts of learning by being more open with students and each other, thus providing them with interesting and constructive models. We would not hide behind the artificial barriers of professional role that create such distances between faculty and students. (I simply could not believe the nameplate, complete with "Ph.D.," that appeared on Peggy's desk the week after she received her doctorate.)

Another part of our shared dream was that we would create an educational program that was not sexist. Women students would be encouraged to consider the full range of possibilities for careers and studies. In our roles as educators we would not add unnecessary barriers. Peggy, a young professional woman, would provide one important kind of role model, and it would be particularly important because it was an unfamiliar one for many of our students, who came from environments in which the traditional expectations of women were still largely intact. In all of this we believed that Peggy's training in counseling and therapy would be helpful as she fulfilled her core faculty responsibilities. The college had only a few women faculty who would have been suited to and interested in the IDP. I felt fortunate to be able to include Peggy in the program.

Remembering those conversations with Peggy, I am embarrassed, for our language and style were faddish and unsophisticated. Yet I would still profess those goals and those essential strategies for their achievement. I liked Peggy, and I liked our fantasies about the IDP. What astonishes me, however, is my inability to give credence to the clear signs of difficulty ahead.

In arranging for Peggy to join the core faculty, I talked with her department chairman. He was a friend of mine but also a person with whom I often disagreed. He complained to me and warned me. Peggy does not live up to her departmental obligations, he said. She misses committee meetings and doesn't follow through on tasks she accepts. She is hardly ever around the department, and so she has no significant relationships with colleagues. My friend said little about Peggy's classes or her work with students. I was pretty sure that Peggy was quite a good teacher. I also knew of dozens of cases in which good teachers, who were somewhat deviant in terms of professional values and relationships with colleagues, were penalized and criticized in just the terms being used by Peggy's department chairman. I believed that he was being a petty bureaucrat, worrying about the things that didn't count and responding from a preoccupation with his own authority and imaginary challenges to it. Peggy was probably, I thought, refusing to waste her time with foolishness.

My own experience with Peggy should have lent weight to my friend's warnings and given me other reasons to worry about her eventual work in the IDP. Although she always kept our lunch dates, Peggy had indeed missed many meetings of the original committee on which we both served. Once the full core faculty was recruited, a few months later, we began to meet frequently, and it became clear that Peggy would participate only irregularly. I did not discuss her absences with her. I was her friend, and the spirit of the group was collaborative and not authoritarian. I still hoped that her work with students would be excellent and that it would make Peggy's failings as a planner seem trivial. But I should have known better.

I tried to ignore the fact that Peggy talked about her personal life a great deal. It was in those conversations that she became most animated and energetic. She and I truly were friends, and much of the talk was appropriate to our relationship. It was an era of personal revelation, and much of Peggy's conversation was within familiar bounds. Yet it sometimes became excessive, and the content of her conversation was disturbing. Despite our shared feminist beliefs and her advanced education and professional training, she was totally absorbed in the details of her dealings with men. In the current jargon, she was strongly male identified.

Although one did not have to be a feminist to be a core faculty member, our hopes that Peggy would be a new type of role model for independent women were terribly unrealistic. Much more significantly, Peggy's conversations with me provided other clues, which I ignored, that she might not be equal even to the minimal requirements for core faculty members. Peggy's enormous investment of energy and thought in her relationships with men, along with the substantial academic pressures on her in connection with the completion of her doctorate, left her little in the way of resources for coping with the IDP. She had neither the ability to focus nor the energy to develop as a constructive worker in the IDP.

Peggy never came close to functioning adequately as a core faculty member. She missed office hours, appointments, and meetings with students. She made commitments that she did not fulfill: to read books, to respond to the written work of students, to write evaluations of completed contracts. For a year I had an office near Peggy's, and I watched dozens of students turn away from her door hundreds of times because she wasn't there when she was supposed to be. Their enthusiasm faded, replaced by anger or disappointment. Interesting ideas, which might have become productive projects with the help of a faculty member, were abandoned. Or I watched students leave Peggy's office without accomplishing what they had intended because Peggy had not done her part. The new program was difficult under the best of circumstances, but extra burdens were imposed on students by Peggy's failures. Working with Peggy was often worse than working alone. The demoralization was palpable.

When Peggy did appear, there were occasional bizarre episodes in which she talked about her personal life, her relationships with men, with students who were not really her friends. They were there to get on with the business of a learning contract, but they left frustrated in their goals and puzzled about what had happened.

An additional problem resulted from Peggy's being too full of herself in another way. She was working on a doctorate in psychology and apparently doing well. It was a source of joy and fulfillment for her to be emerging as a professional psychologist after the long labors of graduate education. Peggy was not, however, in our college's psychology department but was instead a member of an applied department that trained social workers and other people in human service areas. Responding to a casual remark by the chairman of the Psychology Department, who knew of her work and said that he might someday like to have her in his department, Peggy began to do learning contracts in psychology with students who intended to major in the field. Although she was clearly qualified, this work led to academic territorial disputes with the Psychology Department, which was particularly jealous of its domain. I don't believe that the students involved actually lost time in getting their degrees, for their work was counted as fulfilling other requirements. But a considerable amount of unnecessary anxiety and bad feeling was involved.

Peggy was not a fraud. It might have been easier if she had been. She was intelligent and knowledgeable. She had the instincts of a loving teacher, and she sometimes acted upon them, reaching out to students, offering them help, understanding, and even friendship. She followed some work with students through to completion, although even when the work was complete, it was rare for Peggy to do her part in the process of writing the contract evaluation. She also contributed to the IDP by providing support at critical times to students, especially short-term help during crises, and by organizing and conducting, along with a psychologist in the college's counseling center, a personal growth group for IDP students. The group was helpful to a number of students who were having trouble adjusting to the program or who needed to talk about problems. But along with these helpful relationships, friendships, and successful learning contracts, there were far too many unmet obligations and relationships ended without notice.

Adjusting to the IDP meant, for both students and core faculty, learning to manage one's time responsibly without the usual external coercion or guidelines. Peggy hardly ever, for example, missed meeting with her regular classes before she joined the IDP. She responded to the presence of clear expectations and probable sanctions imposed on any teacher who was neglectful of that obligation. Although the moral and educational responsibility to adhere to office hours in the IDP was identical to that of meeting with a class, its violation was much less visible and the punishment was much less certain. This is the most obvious example. There were many others.

It was necessary for IDP students and teachers to gain enough knowledge of themselves to make realistic commitments to people and projects. It was also necessary to respect the obligations imposed by the IDP's structures, obligations to appear, do certain types of work, etc., even though infractions would be relatively private and not subject to the threat of standard punishments for either students or faculty. There was an abundance of mistakes. People overestimated their interest in a field, their abilities to organize and use their time, the ease with which progress could be made. Making too many commitments of too great a magnitude was a common problem of IDP students and faculty. So too was an implicit assumption that with threats and sanctions absent or remote, one's responsibilities would somehow be met more easily and with less planning than were required by conventional authoritarian structures. In these respects, Peggy made every mistake in the book.

Learning about time and work and responsibility, and then making the required adjustments of one's goals and patterns of achieving them, are central elements of the task of taking effective control of one's life. These tasks themselves require a measure of discipline and considerable time and energy. There were students who never could learn to cope with the challenge of the IDP because their internal resources were occupied elsewhere: making money, dealing with parents, falling in love, seeking meaning, adventure, or status far from the academic world, and so on. Such students might have managed a conventional college program. They had already learned to cope with classes, grades, and deadlines, all of which would not have required the development of new levels of discipline that were necessary in the IDP. This was Peggy's situation. As a faculty member in the conventional program she fulfilled her minimal obligations. She met her classes, usually appeared for her office hours, submitted grades around the deadline. Her teaching was at least above average. Knowledgeable, humane, and energetic, she sometimes had group meetings at her apartment and would, occasionally, devote considerable extra time to her students. But Peggy had been working at her limit. The pressures of her graduate work and her personal life left no reserves to deal with the extra demands of the IDP. Her behavior at work deteriorated, becoming erratic, destructive, and irresponsible. It could not have made Peggy happy, and it did not help the IDP. In a vulnerable program with limited resources, Peggy's salary and office should have gone to someone else.

As her boss, starting out as her friend, I was confused by the conflict between the need to use my authority to see that the students got the help they deserved and my wish to avoid the inevitable hostility between me and Peggy. I also hoped that the problems could be solved without abandoning the egalitarian norm for relationships among core faculty. It took me some time to achieve any clarity about what was happening. Peggy and I shared myths and fantasies about our program and each other; they contained some truth, and they were also significant barriers to my understanding the situation. When I finally got around to talking with Peggy about the problems, she responded as many students did in similar circumstances. She had an elaborately constructed view of herself that admitted the existence of the problems, but only in the past. She said that she had new insights into her situation and had worked things out so that everything would be all right. Events proved her wrong. These were, of course, problems that had no easy or quick solutions. To break through Peggy's view of the situation required more strength or cruelty than I could muster, although I knew that it might be more cruel to refrain from confronting her with the truth about her work. It was not particularly compassionate to remain party to the fiction.

As bad as I feel for not trying harder, I doubt that I could have had a positive influence on Peggy's work. Wendel Wickland replaced me as the director of the IDP, and he was not as reluctant to talk with Peggy about her failure to do her job. He did not have the history with Peggy that I had, and his personal and administrative style was gentle but firm; it was, in fact, ideal for working with Peggy. Yet he got few results, and years after Peggy had left Buffalo, Wendel was still making long-distance calls to ask her for evaluations of learning contracts. The telephone calls finally ended when Peggy said that the last dozen evaluations, of which she had unfortunately made no copies, must have been lost in the mail.

The IDP was spared the ordeal of firing Peggy. Because she did not meet a specified deadline for completing her doctorate, a deadline that had been established before she joined the IDP, Peggy's contract was not renewed by her department. The matter was thus settled without the necessity of evaluating her work in the IDP. Peggy saved face, for she did earn her Ph.D. before she left for a new job, and she was indeed moving on to a good position. It was not, on the surface, an unhappy parting, and appearances were maintained without anybody having to deal openly with the consequences of Peggy's failures.

There was a final ironic and maddening episode toward the end of Peggy's participation in the IDP. After talking with a number of troubled students, Peggy called a general meeting of IDP students and faculty. The object was to discuss problems, but the spirit was one of insurgence. Peggy cast herself as the advocate of student interests. She and others made some points that were helpful. One that I remember vividly, a point that would probably not have been articulated without Peggy, was that some faculty were making many students feel terrible by emphasizing the achievements of the IDP's most productive students like Donna and Eve. The faculty was obviously trying to allay its own anxieties with this focus, but other students, many of whom were struggling, were sick of hearing about the program's superstars.

There were other complaints, many of them like those offered by Eve and *The Squeaky Wheel* people. A few could be acted upon, many could not; it helped to talk about the difficulties and frustrations of the program. The substance, however, is overshadowed in my mind by my exasperation at Peggy's assuming the role of the true advocate of student concerns. There was a clear implication in her conduct that day that the rest of us were not measuring up to her standards for working with students. Even then, when directly challenged, neither I nor the other core faculty could publicly or privately deal with Peggy's monumental failure to do what was expected of her.

When I started to write this chapter, I hadn't thought about Peggy for some time. I went to my files to see if I had correspondence from her. I found only one item, a studio card sent to me early in our friendship. On the front is a picture of a beautiful long-haired blond woman staring at a flower. The focus, of course, is soft. The message is "Thank you for being you." But I wasn't, in my relationship with Peggy, the person I wanted to be, nor was she. We never even came close. The obligatory good feeling and the cliché of the card seemed to sum it up quite well.

26

The Top Administrators

The work which produces progress in one's own profession is sufficient compensation for not being understood by imbeciles.

—Cézanne

Let us begin with a few simple reflections on the relationship between administration and innovation in higher education. They help to explain why innovation is at once attractive and fragile.

The top administrators of colleges and universities are perceived by members of their institutions as almost omnipotent in matters of organizational governance. College bureaucracies are not terribly large, and so these figures of presumed power are not remote. They are present and visible. Their proximity is emphasized from time to time by obligatory gestures of collegiality. When the administrators of a college rise from the ranks of its faculty, they are particularly well known. The politics and gossip of a campus, especially a smaller campus, are full of elaborate analyses of the personalities, morality, competence, ambitions, and policies of the institution's top administrators. These few men and women are also the victims and beneficiaries of people's needs to identify with or to rebel against authority. I have no way of knowing whether these impulses are stronger among college faculty than other groups, but they certainly seem to be. Perhaps they are nurtured by the leisure and lack of excitement of the professorial life.

The myths of administrative authority are supported by the formal distribution of power on college campuses. It is hierarchical in the extreme. The chief executive is empowered to grant tenure, leaves, promotions and raises, to hire and fire, to formulate budgets, to enter into contracts, and to seek and accept grants. The numerous representative bodies of students, faculty, and lesser administrators are almost always, at least in formal terms, advisory to the president or chancellor.

Although many organizational and psychological factors contribute to the impression that they are quite powerful, the top administrators themselves, when they are not posturing or trying to impress, typically protest their power-lessness. Their options, they point out, are limited from above and outside by governing boards, accrediting agencies, legislation and public policy, by the mandates of public relations and fund raising, and by the inexorables of economics and demography. From within the institutions they find themselves constrained by student and faculty demands for participatory governance, by tradition and reigning academic ideologies, and by the intractability of loosely organized and undisciplined institutions, whose many formal and informal groups can resist or sabotage the implementation of unpopular decisions. There is also typically a level of institutional inertia that can defeat the most competent and energetic of administrators. It might, for example, take the accumulation of a decade's worth of budget and personnel decisions to have more than a marginal effect on the real nature or performance of an institu-tion. Yet many of these decisions have symbolic meaning far beyond their practical importance to members of the faculty and student body. The poten-tial for conflict is significant and frequently realized. Presidents and chancel-lors, therefore, often describe themselves as nigh unto clerks, but clerks who are represented by no unions or professional organizations and who are not even permitted decent levels of obscurity and privacy. They do not add, as they might, that they are particularly well paid as clerks go.

The conflicting legends of administrative omnipotence and powerless-ness emerge from the fact that administrators win battles but lose wars. Chief executives can decide virtually any single issue, and from that perspective they are quite powerful. After the flush of their first few victories, however, all but the stupidest among them see that the overall impact of their decisions is small. They also pay high prices for prevailing on controversial matters, and anything can become controversial. Students and faculty, although not for-mally empowered to make decisions, are sufficiently powerful to make life miserable for administrators, and each new unpopular decision elicits a thirst for greater revenge. Administrators are more mobile than many faculty, who are, therefore, more committed to their institutions, less able to call it quits in an extended controversy with the administration. Tenured faculty have the protection to fight wars of attrition. Their powerful administrative opponents do not, and a board of trustees that eventually tires of intramural squabbling can dismiss a president but not a faction of combative professors.

In such settings, innovation is a temptation that is almost impossible for an administrator to resist. Top administrators *do* have sufficient power to establish new programs. The programs stand as visible, tangible results of administrative initiative. Innovative programs tend to be clear expressions of an administrator's values, and they can be presented as responses to problems, like racial discrimination, poverty, technological backwardness, and urban revival, that larger communities are concerned about. Innovations have great public relations value, and they gain attention in an administrator's group of professional peers. Although there will always be opposition to new programs, it can be discounted, sometimes truthfully, as the knee-jerk reaction of academic conservatives to anything fresh and imaginative. Indeed it takes only a little cleverness to turn this initial opposition into a political or public relations advantage. Also, at early stages, the actual or potential conflicts between innovations and established programs will be less obvious than they will be later. The decision to innovate can appear to be less sensitive politically than other typical administrative decisions that must choose among established interests that are in constant competition with each other. All of those advantages accrue to innovation but not to most other possibilities for administrative action

Many of the factors that make innovation attractive also function, in another time frame, to make it vulnerable and problematic. A new program that is established by the use of a considerable amount of administrative authority must be maintained in the same way for some time. (This is why the change of vice presidents was a fatal event for the IDP.) It will not have the traditional status that makes it seem indispensable to a college or university, the kind of status that protects, for example, most disciplinary departments. Its staff will usually have junior standing and may lack the credentials that provide some protection in personnel matters.

The content of innovation— new methodology or curriculum or population of students served —is likely to be liberal. With the exception of an occasional honors program or the revival of part of the classical curriculum, the area for conservative academic action is largely preempted by conventional programs. Innovative programs are thus ideologically vulnerable, irritants to conservative academics who are often active faculty politicians. Innovation, almost by definition, violates important norms of the academic world, norms that are not trivial or marginal, but that bear upon the way people, professors in particular, define themselves. We will deal with this aspect in more detail in the next chapter.

Administrators reap the advantages of innovation early in the history of a new program. From then on, the program is likely to become a liability. Its failures, even if modest, will be exaggerated both by the inevitable distance between rhetoric and reality and by the public relations spotlight in which the program was conceived. The routine failures of conventional programs, which are often substantial by many measures, are less visible; they are part of the perceptual background, and they simply don't count in many people's minds, especially when evaluating new programs.

Innovations, especially if they have been started with grant support, are eventually recognized as competitors for scarce resources. When they are known to have begun in a special relationship to an influential administrator who controls funds, it will be easy to overestimate the force of their competition and to see them as having an unfair advantage.

Innovations create a burden on administrators that was often not anticipated in the exciting days at the beginning. It is not rare for a top administrator to cool substantially or turn against a program that he or she helped bring into the world. Administrators may turn upon their fellow innovators, those who have become the staff of the new program. Often they echo the conservative faculty, saying that things would have been all right if only the program had been run by more solid conventional types, the very people who were hostile or indifferent at the beginning. Why couldn't these innovative colleagues of ours, they ask, have implemented our lovely vision without causing so much trouble?

There are, of course, forces that operate to sustain innovation. The successes of new programs can expand their constituencies, and natural opponents can be transformed into friends. The genuine commitment of administrators and participants to the core values of a new program can justify and energize continued struggles on its behalf. Some of the public relations benefits of innovation can be extended over considerable periods by shrewd presentation of the program. After time passes, a new program may become part of the establishment; former opponents may accept it, perhaps grudgingly, and it may even offer unexpected opportunities for new activities to people who were at first hostile.

There is no question, however, that it is easier to innovate than to sustain innovation, that a top administrator enjoys the benefits in early stages of the process and then, as time passes, may be required to pay higher prices for less. When administrations change, this pattern is more pronounced. An innovation established by one's predecessor is likely to be more of a burden than anything else. The previous administrator has gotten the glory. The new person has only the headaches of maintenance.

It is within this context that a group of top administrators were critical figures in the history of the IDP. Their behavior and personalities are as much a part of the story of the IDP as those of the students and faculty.

E. K. FRETWELL, PRESIDENT

I am taller than most people, and E.K. is much taller than I. In public he acts like the awkward overgrown boy he once was. He has a joke for every occasion, although the connection between joke and occasion is sometimes tenuous. He has a quick and handsome smile, youthful for his years. One sometimes feels embarrassed in his presence, for he tries too hard and misses the mark too often. Yet he has a certain boyish charm that is endearing.

It fits perfectly that E.K.'s hobby is reading and knowing about railroads. He appears to be encyclopedic on the subject, and although he is always lively, he seems most truly engaged when he's talking about the old express that used to run between someplace and someplace else. More than once I've seen Buffalo State faculty members, who obviously couldn't care less, involve the president in conversation about some obscure railroad fact that they stumbled over and stored away for the occasion.

Shortly before I left the college, I talked with the president about the IDP, and I tape-recorded the conversation with his consent. It was a year since he'd approved the decision to end the IDP. I began by reminding him of an incident he had participated in several years earlier.

Ida Baldwin was a middle-aged black woman who had just started college. She worked at night, cared for a grandchild for part of the day, and went to school; but this routine represented a relief from the life she had led until recently. Her children were now grown and on their own. For twenty years she had worked at two full-time jobs and raised three children alone. Her new life as a college student was almost leisurely for Ida in terms of time commitments,

193

but it was not easy. She was intelligent and hardworking, and she knew she was learning a lot. Yet she wasn't doing well. She had been out of school for years, and she couldn't take tests, didn't understand what was expected.

One day a teacher returned a test in one of her classes. Ida had failed. After class she tried to speak to her professor, a woman who was harsh and unsympathetic. Going to college had been Ida's dream for years, and it seemed to be slipping away from her. Weeping, she ran from the building and literally bumped into the president on the sidewalk. He asked her why she was crying; she explained, they talked, and he comforted her. He also sent her to talk with Wendel Wickland who was the director of the IDP. She joined the program.

Ida was a spectacularly successful student in the IDP. She studied both conventional and unusual subjects. She explored her strengths and weaknesses as a student without being tyrannized by unnecessarily imposed evaluational schemes. Aside from doing work to meet the requirements of her major, which was Vocational-Technical Education, she did contracts that involved extensive reading on the nature of racism and sexism, forces that had been determining the shape of her life for decades. Rarely have I seen a student gain social and personal insight as Ida did in those projects.

When the IDP ended, Ida returned to regular classes. With new skills and self-confidence, she was now able to pass exams and was, in fact, an honor student for several semesters. She graduated and got a good job that gave her the status, money, and work-related satisfaction that she'd never had before. It was clear to everyone who knew her that Ida would have dropped or flunked out of college without the IDP.

My first question to E.K. was a hostile one. I asked how he felt about having made a decision to end the IDP, thus making it unavailable to Ida and others who might need or prefer it. I reminded him that he had referred to Ida's story in public several times, extolling the virtues of pluralism in education. He clearly knew of the program's importance in her life. There were several obvious answers he could have given, all of them variations on the theme that it is unfortunate that larger factors force us to end desirable programs like the IDP. Instead he answered as if the IDP still existed, as if there had never been a problem. He spoke only of sending Ida to see Wendel, and he congratulated himself. "That was a good act," he said. When I repeated the question which he had not answered, the president changed the subject.

I worked with E.K. for about eight years. As far as I could see, E.K. simply refused to deal with negative facts in the presence of anyone but a few trusted assistants. He was accessible when people were happy. His subordinates were available to confront problems, pain, or anger. When he miscalculated, or when his presence was absolutely necessary in an infelicitous situation, he tried to invoke a kind of verbal magic, the power of positive talking, to dispel the negatives. Shortly after my talk with him, for example, E.K. was interviewed by a Buffalo newspaper. He was at the time making a concerted effort to find a new job, but he had recently refused or not been offered a particular job in New Jersey. That experience, he told the reporter, had made him and his family realize how well situated they were in Buffalo. They had decided to stay. He waxed eloquent about his attachment to the community and to his job, as if his words and the approbation they sought would somehow change the fact that he would almost certainly be leaving soon, was in fact in the process of trying to arrange to leave. Within two months the newspaper reported that he had, all along, been applying for another important job, this one in Albany.

When I came to Buffalo State, Fretwell was a new president who was enormously popular. Friendly, good-humored, smart, he seemed like a person who would represent the college well and encourage creativity within it. By the time I left, Fretwell was terribly unpopular, and his time at the college was clearly limited. He spent a good bit of time away from campus; on campus he seemed to be reclusive, and he tried hard to avoid people who might disagree with him. He was suffering from a natural cycle of decreasing popularity, for every decision creates enemies, and he had made many decisions. But it seemed to me that something else was happening too, for he had virtually no support left. He was widely perceived as superficial, indecisive, and scared, acting entirely on the basis of expedience. One hardly ever heard it said of him, "I disagree with his decisions on certain matters but I admire his honesty (or consistency or conviction)."

The IDP was important to E.K. for some time. He had a relationship with the Carnegie Corporation that was useful to him, and his ability to stay on good terms with the SUNY central office was central to his job. The IDP and Early Admissions Program were prominent in the president's public statements, and they were featured in the literature emanating from his office.

Buffalo State College was relatively small, and administrators who worked there for a while all knew each other. Both Wendel and I, therefore, had relationships with the president that would not allow him to ignore or avoid us completely. As we saw things going against the IDP, it was natural to bring the program's case to him. Fretwell tried but could not make himself inaccessible to us; we saw him during open office hours he had established. We told him that we thought the evaluation of the IDP had been unfair, and he said that his impression was consistent with ours. We said that we'd like to provide materials to him that would present another view of the program, and we did. Like all discussions with him, ours were pleasant and full of avoidance.

Our efforts were ritualistic, for there was little chance that this president would support us and reverse a vice president's recommendation. He had benefited from the program in various ways, but there was nothing left in it for him. Supporting the IDP would clearly entail more difficulty for him than it would avoid. I think that the president probably put more thought into finding ways of avoiding Wendel and me than into thinking about the program.

DON SCHWARTZ, ACADEMIC VICE PRESIDENT I

I'm glad I knew Don Schwartz, for otherwise I would have thought that people like him existed only on television. Whenever I see an athlete looking directly into the television camera, index finger raised, proclaiming that he or his team is Number One, I think of Don. Don unashamedly wanted to be Number One in everything—or anything. The nature of the venture—becoming acting president during the president's short sabbatical, acquiring money, coaching a Little League team, playing volleyball with colleagues on Saturday morning, administering academic programs—seemed to matter less to him than coming out on top in a competition. The enthusiasm, energy, and search for validation that Don brought to every remotely competitive activity seemed to obscure any awareness that becoming Number One might sometimes not be worth the effort, or that Number Onehood is a transitory state, or that it simply might not apply. I once persuaded Don to reverse a decision and grant tenure to an

IDP faculty member. I had many arguments, for the person did deserve tenure. The factor that got Don's attention, however, was the information that the professor in question was also a successful businessman who had no financial need to work at the college; indeed he may have lost money by doing so, because of the state's tax laws. In Don's world view, a person who was a winner in one realm, especially if it was financial, would be a winner in another, and it was just natural to confirm the fact with the positive tenure decision.

Don was succeeding in his own terms, rising as an administrator to more prestigious and remunerative positions. Between 1968 and 1978 Don held five jobs, each more powerful than the last. In the twenty-five years following his Ph.D., 1955–1979, Don held eleven positions. One can safely assume that Don sought at least a few jobs that he did not get, and it is a fact that one must often apply for a new job well in advance of moving into it. It is obvious that Don applied for some jobs relatively soon after moving to a new position.

Don's style was to burst upon the scene full of threats and promises. I have heard him describe his mode of administration to a group of department chairmen in such sophisticated terms as "using an iron fist." He would expend an enormous amount of energy and make changes in areas in which things could happen fast, like "tightening up" (a favorite phrase) academic regula-tions for dropping courses or changing grades. His immediate subordinates felt secure, but more remote administrators and faculty members were often frightened; Don would invade realms in which they had always been autono-mous, making them feel as if any judgment, no matter how trivial, might be challenged from above and thus precipitate a damaging crisis. To his few confidants he was devoted and completely loyal. Don would get out while the getting was good, full of stories about his accomplishments. When he left Buffalo State, I thought I could almost hear a collective sigh of relief arise from the institution.

Of the series of academic vice presidents involved in the IDP, Don was the one who supported it most and probably liked it least. He was the one with whom I worked most closely. He was also the one I liked least, a confession I make with little reluctance because Don gave me ample reason, harassing me, as was his way, until I wouldn't put up with it.

When Don arrived at Buffalo State College, his conversation was domi-nated by two ideas. The college would be Number One, which in this case meant the best of the SUNY system's liberal arts colleges. The second idea, really an assumption, was that most of what had happened before his arrival was of irredeemably low quality. For almost two years he spoke scornfully of "this institution," as if he had not yet joined it, as in, "You mean a professor in this institution can cancel a class meeting without the approval of a dean?" It was such matters that scandalized him. He may never have known that his stance toward the past was deeply insulting to most of his colleagues. When he confronted the results, usually in the form of sullen, frightened resistance, he thought he was dealing with the problems faced by all people of high quality when surrounded by mediocrity.

Shortly after he arrived on campus, Don let me know that it was likely that my job would shortly be eliminated. It was unlikely, he opined, that I would fit into his administration. He decided to move quickly, and he had a plan. There was a group of lower-level administrators, mostly associate deans, that met informally on a regular basis, calling themselves the Associates Board. They discussed their problems and coordinated their work. It was a remarkable group of young men who had the responsibility for implementing but not making policy. They wanted to do their jobs well, and they saw they could help each other. The group was a bit conservative, seeing themselves as "nuts and bolts" people, and they weren't particularly enamored of my interest in student power. But a high value among them was hard work and dedication; they saw these in me, and our relationships were good.

Don invited himself to a meeting of the Associates Board, and he asked them to do a comprehensive evaluation of the college's orientation programs, which were then my responsibility. His presentation made it clear that he expected them to find that the programs were a mess and that I was incompetent. The group simply refused. His suggestion violated their sense of fairness, and most of them probably felt that, with a few lapses, the orientation programs were pretty good.

I learned of Don's proposal, went to his office, told him that I thought he'd been sneaky and unfair, and defended my work. Don backs down when confronted, especially by a person who can give him a good argument and who is not clearly stupider than he. It helps to have a New York Jewish style that makes him feel at home. After a few minutes, grinning, Don told me that I'd misunderstood and that he didn't mean it anyway. From that day on I was at least a marginal member of Don's team. One way of joining it was to fight your way on. We continued to disagree and argue, for I perceived him to be rigid, opinionated, and not the most tolerant person of my acquaintance, and he saw me as mushy headed and probably worse. He would do nothing to help me personally, and we rarely enjoyed each other. But he was, when he made a commitment to someone, absolutely loyal and supportive, and these qualities henceforth dominated his behavior toward me in our work together. He helped to make the IDP possible, for which I will always be grateful. In the short time he was involved, he never attempted, even under pressure, to compromise his support of the program. Had he remained at the college, of which there was no chance, he would have defended the program and insisted that it get the reasonable hearing which was in fact denied to it.

I believe that if given his way, however, Don would have kept me out of any relationship with the new program, and he tried. He did some things that I thought were intended to accomplish that goal. When we got the news that the Carnegie grant had been approved, it was time to start thinking about selecting a director of the two new programs. Don told Bob Shoenberg that I would not be an acceptable candidate, and the message was intended for my ears. I don't remember having been particularly interested in the job. I was thinking more in terms of leaving Buffalo State and had begun submitting job applications elsewhere. I was not comfortable working under Don, even though the worst was over, and I had already gone to a couple of job interviews. I decided, however, to apply for the new job at Buffalo State. Don would have the authority to deny me the position, but my pride prevented me from collaborating with him by not applying. Also it might be an interesting job, in many ways just the sort of thing I was looking for.

The selection procedure favored me, for the committee was made up largely of members of the group that had planned the program, people with whom I'd worked on that task. Don saw the likely outcome, and he did two things that seemed to be designed to change it. He directed the committee to recommend three candidates to him without ranking the selections. And he decided that the academic deans would also be asked to screen the candidates and submit their recommendations. With three unranked recommendations, Don would be able to choose someone other than me without seeming to overrule the committee's desires. I had, moreover, a history of disagreement with several of the deans, and it seemed unlikely that they would prefer me for the new job. Don's freedom in the matter would be increased further if the two groups disagreed.

The selection committee sent my name and two others to Don, but an accompanying memo made it clear that I was their strongly preferred candidate. The deans interviewed the applicants, and they surprised both Don and me by choosing me. Judging by my interview with them, which was serious and businesslike, I believe that the deans thought that I was the best of the candidates. There may also have been a touch of defiance in their action, since they knew Don's preference, and they might have seen themselves closing ranks against him by supporting a staff member who, like them, had preceded Don at the institution. We had all been forced to suffer his certainty that nothing good could have happened so early in the college's history.

Although he could have decided not to follow the recommendations of the two groups, substantial resentment would have been caused in a matter that was not all that important. Don was stuck with me, and he tried to accept the situation with good grace. He called me in, grinned again, and offered me the job. I accepted, and we talked pleasantly for a while, each trying to be respectful and not provocative. Don had his limits, though, and as he walked me to the door, he put his arm around my shoulder and in a mock pleading tone said, "One thing, Dick. When you get those kids in the new program together for the first time, please don't show them a film about the starving people in Bangladesh." In other words, he hoped I'd limit the bleeding heart liberal bullshit that was so natural to me, and try to get some good solid academic work done, which of course has nothing to do with starving people. But Don was just making a gesture, and he knew I'd probably show such a film, or worse. He was resigning himself to having to take responsibility for a bleeding heart liberal bullshit program. One could almost see him realigning his priorities to trying to make it into the country's Number One program of its kind.

There were unstated agreements between Don and me in which we effected some compromises. A major price for my substantial freedom in creating the IDP was my commitment to doing the best job I could in administering Don's program, the Early Admissions Program, about which I was not particularly excited. Within the IDP, also, it was clear that I would do well to emphasize the program's more traditional achievements when they happened and to make the news of them available to Don for his own political and public relations purposes. The best example of this involved a proposal for a grant for an undergraduate research project that was developed by me and a group of IDP students. Don had worked at the National Science Foundation, and he believed that the ultimate certification of academic quality was the ability to win in the competition for grants from national agencies. I worked hard to get the grant, and the point was not only to help the students by getting money to support one of their projects, but also to emphasize an area of the IDP's operation with which Don could identify. We got the grant, the first of its kind at Buffalo State, and there were a few happy moments all around.

Although he was present only at the earliest stages, Don was loyal, decent, and generous in support of the IDP and me, even though he would have preferred another program and another person. His response was not pure altruism, for some benefit could be derived from the program's existence, though not perhaps as much as from a program in which he truly believed.

BILL STURNER, ACADEMIC VICE PRESIDENT II

I know less about Bill Sturner than about the other administrators who were important in the IDP's history. Bill was academic vice president for a short time, and for a portion of that he was particularly inaccessible. He was, however, the person who was most responsible for the formal decision to end the IDP.

My best guess is that, as I have said earlier, Sturner accepted an assistant's negative judgment about the IDP shortly after he arrived on campus. My evidence is that the chairwoman of the evaluating committee seemed to be set on her course by him early in the game. She said that her instructions from Sturner were to design a plan to phase out the IDP, not to evaluate it. As the year progressed, the IDP's director, core faculty, and students had a few opportunities to present their views of the program to the new vice president. He was cordial and encouraging, and we believed that he would give us a fair hearing. Viewing the matter retrospectively, however, no longer under the influence of my desperate hope that the program would survive, our meetings with Sturner felt empty and ritualistic. Perhaps I am wrong, and Sturner's early judgment and instructions to the committee were based on a fair and thoughtful personal evaluation of the program. My reluctance to accept this thesis is based on the fact that I don't know where or from whom he would have gotten his information about the IDP. His data gathering, early in the game, definitely did not involve those of us working or studying in the program. Fair or unfair, however, Sturner certainly did provide us with a few moments of entertainment, chiefly when he accepted an invitation to introduce himself in a meeting with the core faculty.

The meeting lasted for more than an hour. It was one of many sessions he scheduled with different groups shortly after he came to the college. Sturner took off his jacket, rolled up his sleeves, and spoke eloquently about himself. He is an intense man, but his demeanor changed, and he became even more intense when he discussed the drama of his own new position. "This institution chews up vice presidents and spits them out," he said, and one knew that Bill Sturner was determined to avoid being chewed up and spit out. To us it seemed more accurate to say that vice presidents chewed up the institution, for they were dominant in all matters because the president was passive. But I have already mentioned these differences in perspective on administrative power, and it was natural for Sturner to feel vulnerable.

The other theme of the new vice president's presentation of himself was that he would not be a rubber stamp, acting simply to ratify decisions that were sent up from the lower reaches of the bureaucracy. He used the word *conduit* a lot; it seemed somehow to epitomize to him a serious danger. He insisted that he would not be a conduit for other people's decisions. He expected his judgments and philosophy to be major determinants of decisions that would be made at the college. When he was finished, it was our turn to tell Sturner about the IDP and ourselves.

We described the IDP, and Sturner listened attentively. When he commented, it was to express a liberal philosophy emphasizing the education of "more than the head." It was the first time we had talked with a top administrator of the college who seemed to favor what we were doing and to share our ideals, at least in some basic intuitive way.

The talk turned to practical matters: the forthcoming evaluation of the IDP. Sturner suggested that we develop a statement of the program's strengths and accomplishments for him. He referred to the College Senate's list of dispensable programs as if it were a big problem for us. We were surprised, especially after all of his talk about not being a conduit. "But I cannot ignore the institution's history," he said—correctly, of course. We were a bit puzzled but also cheered by Sturner's educational thinking. If that was, in fact, his philosophy, we would be able to make our case to him. We would not encounter the conceptual obstacles that might have been presented if the new vice president had possessed, for example, Don Schwartz's view of education.

Bill Sturner's flair for dramatizing his burdens was visible again soon when the *Chronicle of Higher Education* published a short essay he had written. It emphasized the debilitating effects of the pressure of the dozens of trivial decisions that a top administrator is asked to make or review. The essay offers Bill's own detailed plan for structuring his work week to neutralize these pressures: begin each day with two hours of uninterrupted work; don't open the mail in the morning; play handball or at least take a walk every day; set aside one day each week for work on big projects; don't return telephone calls unless the caller leaves a message that contains a good reason; etc. High drama surrounds every phone call; there is a need to separate oneself from the ordinary people.

Our next contact with Sturner was entirely pleasant, though perhaps it was simply theater. We arranged a meeting of IDP students, to be attended by him and members of the senate committee. Sturner and even the chairwoman seemed impressed, perhaps moved, by the students' seriousness about their education and their wish to take responsibility for it. They encouraged the students to speak out, asked them real questions, and seemed to be listening. The students were beautiful. They had no strategies; they were not trying to manipulate the visitors. They just spoke about their attempts to learn.

After that meeting nobody in the IDP saw or talked with Sturner until we bumped into him on campus months later, after he had resigned and written the memorandum that recommended the termination of the IDP.

Wendel tried to communicate with Sturner through Barbara Frey, his associate vice president. How had Sturner reacted to the material we'd sent him? Could we provide more? Would it be possible to discuss the committee's bias with him? Barbara had no answers, and as time went on, she admitted that she also had trouble getting in to see him.

I assume that the faculty members and administrators opposed to the IDP and me saw the program as an unfairly favored creation of a particular vice president, Schwartz. (Wendel came to believe that the dismantling of the program was, for some opponents, primarily a device for ridding the college of me.) A new vice president and a new group of insiders simply reversed the process. Like us before them, one assumes that they sincerely believed in their educational philosophy and their judgments about particular people. Turn-about, fair play. Neither the IDP nor those of us in it, however, destroyed or were a threat to destroy anything that existed at the college. If we were threatening, it was in some symbolic realm. In fact we were relatively harmless. We created something to which we gave several years and our hearts. Some students got extraordinarily good educations that were not otherwise available to them. In the process of academic politics-as-usual, the opportunity for other students to get such education was destroyed and so were parts of us. Sturner, who seemed as though he should have been an ally, was the instrument, perhaps the *conduit,* of this decision to destroy.

BARBARA FREY, ACADEMIC VICE PRESIDENT III

Barbara Frey was a faculty stateswoman. Like many of the college's education professors, she was a former elementary schoolteacher. She had been a de-partment chairwoman for some time, and she carved out a unique position for herself in the politics of the college. Although there were a few angry murmurings about Barbara's political maneuvering in the education division, she was almost universally respected for her fairness and for a certain kind of clarity about issues. Barbara was not and did not pretend to be a deep thinker or intellectual, but she had a practical intelligence that is more unusual on college campuses. She could simplify a complex discussion and extract the issues that would have to be decided, and she could do so without producing a statement of the issues that was biased in favor of one of the competing parties. She was an old-timer on campus and widely known. She was pleasant and appreciative of people, and they liked her.

The College Senate was created in the early seventies to add some democratic forms to the governance of the college. It was a period of intense factionalism, and many people and groups had reasons to test the senate. This was partly a test of the administration's sincerity in opening itself to new influences. The first years were characterized by an aggressive use of the senate's advisory function. Barbara was a natural choice for president of the senate, a position in which she served for a couple of years. She handled impossible situations well. As she presided over a forum that elicited nasty competition among faculty and administrative groups, Barbara exhibited another personal characteristic: she would not be provoked or manipulated. People and groups tried to use her, by co-opting her or causing her, through emotion or miscalculation, to make an error. Had she allowed herself to make such mistakes, her credibility would have vanished rapidly. Barbara was shrewd and saw through the tactics of people who tried to use her. She was clear in defining her position, and she was tough in sticking to it. She gave no indication of crises of self-confidence.

One does not become a faculty politician like Barbara without having at least a passing interest in power. It was almost inevitable that Barbara would become a member of the college's administration. I have no way of knowing how deep or long-standing her ambitions were, but she must have had some. They would be fed and encouraged by senior administrators who would want to use Barbara's real skills for the institution's benefit and who would also wish to profit from their association with a faculty member of her status.

Whether by careful calculation or not, Barbara did indeed rise in the administration of the college and almost became president. She did not try to move too fast, the most common mistake, and she was almost flawless in building a record and positioning herself advantageously for the next higher position. Her failure to become president is probably due to the prejudice of strong factions of the college against people with education rather than disciplinary backgrounds. She is also handicapped by her inability to indulge in certain types of intellectual posturing, although she is more thoughtful than and at least as intelligent as other recent vice presidents.

When Don Schwartz left the college, he was temporarily replaced by the young associate vice president whom he had hired. The younger man asked Barbara to become his associate vice president, and she agreed. It was a significant political boost for him to have Barbara on his staff. (Did she see that he would be an easy act to follow? Perhaps.) Her presence gave his administration an added measure of credibility among faculty that it would not otherwise have had. I bumped into him shortly after she had accepted his offer. He was jubilant, and actually referred to Barbara as "queen of the campus."

Unexpectedly the young man was not chosen as permanent vice president. Barbara stayed on as associate vice president under Sturner, his successor, and eventually was given the post on a permanent basis. It was like

Barbara to continue as associate vice president, even though she had been passed over when Sturner was chosen. And it was like Barbara finally to be the obvious logical choice when Sturner resigned.

It seemed as though Barbara generally admired the IDP. She was encouraging and friendly. She worked with Eve and valued Eve's accomplishments while studiously ignoring her provocations. Barbara talked with Wendel and me about having worked in innovative programs as an elementary schoolteacher, and she recalled the controversies and difficulties as similar to the ones that the IDP was experiencing. Barbara was an ally during the College Senate committee's examination of the IDP, although the final effect of her contribution was to influence the group to pretend to be evaluating rather than simply following Sturner's mandate to design its demise. Perhaps we would have done better if the committee had continued in its early candor, for it might have discredited itself. Once the committee pretended to change its function, however, Barbara was satisfied, or at least her work on our behalf stopped. It would have been too radical and partisan an act for Barbara to have pursued the implications of the committee's early behavior. And for most of the year, she was a member of Sturner's staff and limited in what she could do.

When Barbara became vice president, she could have changed Sturner's recommendation about the IDP and advised the president to allow the program to continue. He would surely have followed her recommendation. If Barbara had done so, however, she would have provoked a major confrontation with a faction of the College Senate, and it was precisely that group, dominated by professors from the arts and sciences, that tended to be hostile to the education division and its faculty. It was this faction with whom Barbara would naturally be weakest. As an old-timer at the college and an education professor, she could count upon the support of the applied science and education divisions. But in order to be an effective vice president and make a bid for the presidency, which would clearly be vacated by Fretwell soon, Barbara needed to maintain her support in the arts and sciences. One important claim to such support was her identification with the College Senate and her record on behalf of faculty advisory structures. To come out for the IDP would appear to violate these commitments, even though the College Senate committee had done its work unfairly. Barbara would have implicitly been challenging the integrity of key faculty politicians. This she could not do.

I believe that Barbara's consistent words of encouragement and support for the IDP were authentic. In ordering her priorities as vice president, however, I think she simply drew a line beyond which she judged it imprudent to take risks for the program. Her hard-earned political assets would not be spent for the IDP.

27

The Core Faculty: Wendel and I

. . . and I thought how unpleasant it is to be locked out; and I thought how it is worse perhaps to be locked in. . . .

—Virginia Woolf

Wendel and I were unlikely partners. Our work together produced a friendship and a useful collaboration, yet when it began, those outcomes seemed improbable. When I was selecting core faculty members, the biggest problem was finding a person in one of the natural science departments. There was a geology professor who had a reputation as a good teacher with liberal educational values, but he rejected my offer. He thought that interesting things were about to happen in his department, and he was looking forward to a term as chairman. Many faculty members were understandably reluctant to join a program that would focus energies and perhaps loyalties away from their departments. Raises, promotions, and tenure would still be controlled by departments, and those units provided natural peer groups and academic homes for most professors, even if some of those homes were full of strife.

Few other science teachers were interested enough in the IDP's approach to consider a full-time commitment, and it seemed possible that I would not be able to find anyone in that area to join the program. There were one or two exceptions, people who were eager to join, but their liberal rhetoric was in sharp and obvious contrast to their practices with students. These people were highly authoritarian teachers, and their presence on the core faculty would have represented a serious compromise of the program's ideals from the start. I continued my search by asking students about the science courses and teachers they liked best. Wendel Wickland and his biology courses were mentioned several times. Students said that Wendel was permissive and understanding, and that his love of nature inspired them to learn. I made an appointment to talk with him.

The first thing I noticed in Wendel's office was the dog-eared Bible on his desk. It made me wonder how he taught evolution, but I didn't ask. I told him about the basic ideas behind the IDP and waited for him to respond. He said little other than that he agreed. I tried, with virtually no success, to get him to say more about his educational ideas. He smiled, seemed interested in hearing more about the program, and revealed nothing about himself. The conversation seemed destined to be a monologue, so I thought I might just as well use the time to tell Wendel as much as I could about my plans and hopes. I had no idea whether my statements were being received by him as good news or bad.

I told Wendel that I hoped the core faculty members would get to know each other well as we worked together, partly for the enjoyment of new relationships and partly because I believed that close collaboration was likely to lead to creativity in the development of the new program. I talked of the program as an unusual opportunity to express personal styles of teaching and to work closely with students. I said that we would share our power with students both in the development and implementation of the program, and I explained a little of the basis for my belief that students were likely to use their new power productively. I also said that since the program would let students follow their own interests, we would probably violate standard curricular assumptions, including the idea, almost sacred to many scientists, that it is necessary to study certain subjects in particular sequences. I also talked about closer relationships between students and teachers and the search for connections between academic studies and other parts of life.

Wendel nodded and smiled as I described a hypothetical program that would have angered many of his colleagues in the sciences and stimulated serious doubts in the rest. I assumed that Wendel was being polite, and speculated that he might be a little stupid. I was, however, desperate for a science teacher who wasn't obviously tyrannical, and I asked him whether he'd like to join the core faculty. Without hesitation he said that he would if the arrangements could be made with his department. After having spent less than an hour, I left Wendel's office with a new colleague. My best judgment was that the whole exchange had been strange and lacking in good communication. It did, however, occur to me, in what seemed like extravagant wishful thinking, that Wendel might genuinely have agreed with it all, that he might be a good core faculty member, and that he was simply not verbose with strangers. I would not have bet on any of those propositions except the last.

Wendel became an excellent member of the core faculty and a close and loyal friend. He is unusually intelligent, and I have often reflected on the assumptions that originally inclined me to equate reticence with stupidity. When I thought that it would be best for me and the IDP if I were to move out of the position of director, Wendel agreed to switch jobs with me. Our change of roles was smooth, enjoyable, and productive for both of us. We also experienced together the unhappy consequences of participating in the IDP, and together we lived through one of the most difficult periods of our lives. Because we both served as the program's director, we were the members of the IDP staff most visible to our colleagues in the rest of the college. Wendel and I were thus most vulnerable to the punishments visited upon violators of institutional norms. This was painful for both of us.

The easiest way for me to tell this part of the story is to begin with the period of transition in which Wendel took over as director of the IDP. I was director during the developmental year and the program's first year of operation. I thought I had done well in that period, but it was also clear that I would be happier and more productive as a core faculty member than as the administrator responsible for the maintenance and gradual evolution of the program. I also wanted to stop devoting time to the Early Admissions Program. Wendel then became the director, and I joined the core faculty. There was a strange interim period in the second summer when we worked together, sort of codirectors. The idea was that I would show him the ropes. Those were unproductive weeks in which we both moved through elaborate deferential dances designed to keep out of each other's way and to show that we weren't interested in violating new or old prerogatives. The ritual ended with my vacation. When I returned, Wendel had, as planned, really taken charge. His plants replaced my posters in the IDP office in the administration building. His behavior replaced mine, and it was from this change that I learned a great deal.

We sat and talked. Out of friendship, perhaps out of respect for my opinion and my previous work, Wendel filled me in on his work during my vacation. I listened and was stunned. Wendel's narrative gave me a clear view of what had happened to me over the years. What Wendel described was rather simple. He had begun to solve many of the IDP's problems, as I knew he would. He was bold and aggressive. Assuming the value of the IDP, he had begun to use the full array of campus resources to improve and strengthen the program. He felt no need to offer implicit or explicit apologies for what we were doing in the IDP. He requisitioned equipment and services, negotiated with departments and administrative offices, obtained new supplies, had changes made in our physical facilities. Wendel behaved, in short, as if the IDP deserved everything the institution and its people could provide, which it did, and as if it was his job to secure those things, which it was.

Wendel's behavior immediately showed me that over the years I had lost my nerve in acting in the public arena. Under the pressure of disapproval and hostility I had become defensive and scared about myself, my innovative ideas and programs, and now especially about the IDP. Although I felt competent, secure, and happy while working with students, functioning within my home IDP territory, in the larger environment outside our program I had learned to keep a low profile. I tried to get by without asking for help, even if it meant settling for marginal solutions to problems that could have been solved better. I had come to expect criticism and trouble outside my own turf. These things had happened subtly, unconsciously, and in strange ways, for I was still an outspoken advocate of freedom and educational change. I was still, in our institution, visible and sometimes provocative. Within our program I was always the person who tried to offer clarity, inspiration, and uncompromising statements of our ideals. But I had not done the simple things Wendel was doing. My rhetorical bravado existed along with functional fear. I had learned to internalize my enemy's view of myself in the way typical of minority group members. I had begun to feel ashamed of things that were not shameful. Worn down by fear and hostility, I accepted unnecessary limitations and thus did half of my opponents' work for them. Talking with Wendel, seeing that he did not have those problems, provided me with moments of powerful self-discovery.

I soon realized that I was getting insight into the effects of things that had been happening to me since the First Year Program at Antioch. I had learned early in that period that there would be conflict and politics connected with the sort of innovation I had become committed to. The unexpected anger, hostility, and ostracism had been painful. Yet I had not known, until I could compare myself with Wendel, how much these things had changed me and my behavior. I began looking for more information about what I had become and why.

I saw that I was being deeply affected by my colleagues' views of me, but I found that I actually knew little about those views. I knew that I had a wonderful group of friends and supporters, and that there was a larger group of colleagues that was more or less critical of me. I felt excluded from much of the faculty's social and intellectual life. I tended to avoid people who weren't close friends, thus acting myself to increase the isolation that I felt had been thrust upon me. I expected hostility, and without yielding completely to paranoid fantasies, I thought that I frequently saw negative preconceptions tainting initial contacts I had with colleagues. I suppressed many of my friendly instincts, returning suspicion for suspicion. Such behavior, obviously, did not give me a vast storehouse of information about my colleagues and their perceptions of me.

Wendel told me a story which tended to confirm this view of things. The incident occurred a year after he became director. The IDP was to be evaluated by a committee of the College Senate, a process that is described in a previous chapter. As the program's first director, I met with the committee early in its work to give my view of the program's goals and performance. The meeting was tense but civil. One of the committee's most energetic members was a biology professor who discussed the matter with Wendel, also a biologist, shortly after the session with me. The man told Wendel that he was confident of his ability to be fair and objective in evaluating the IDP in all respects except for my participation and testimony. He cited no reasons and gave no indication that I had said something in the meeting that made him believe me to be untrustworthy. (I may, of course, have done something during the meeting that offended him, but I don't think I did anything terrible. Nor had I ever had any other exchange with him that amounted to more than a few words.) The sense of his comment was that Wendel would understand that some general knowledge of me and my nature would justify this unwillingness to believe me or this inability to remain objective. It was said, according to Wendel, without explanation, as if none were needed, and it was said despite the clear friendship and partnership between Wendel and me. The assumptions were generalized and did not require articulation, as when a racist talks about "those" blacks on the other side of town. When Wendel thought about it, the only content he could give his colleague's statement was that I was obviously some sort of evil person, a fact that Wendel was expected to recognize.

I had a series of conversations with Evelyn, an IDP student, that told the same story in infinitely greater detail. Evelyn participated in the IDP and the Early Admissions Program, entering college while I was director of both. From the beginning she did excellent academic work, having no trouble using the structures of the IDP. Evelyn was, however, quite young, and she needed a good bit of general encouragement, support, and help in thinking and talking through the normal problems of families and personal relationships, problems that were somewhat intensified for her by going to college at an early age. I had many such conversations with her at the beginning of her college career. Evelyn soon outgrew the need for this kind of counseling. I became a core faculty member, and then Evelyn's teacher and friend. We enjoyed our time together and talked a lot.

Evelyn majored in psychology and graduated from college in three years after doing excellent work. The Psychology Department was, however, a center of bitter opposition to the IDP. Evelyn won the reluctant support and help of most of the Psychology Department by virtue of her intelligence, outstanding hard work, perseverance, good humor, and diplomacy. Since she worked well on research projects, some of the faculty support she received was the result of enlightened self-interest on the part of professors. She was, however, provoked and baited, even though the quality of her work prevailed in the end.

When Evelyn and I talked, she sometimes alluded to the opposition of her professors to the program and their hostility to me. For a couple of years I let her remarks pass, declining her implicit invitation to discuss the politics and personalities of the situation. I saw no way to make things easier for her, and on some level I really didn't want to know what Evelyn could tell me. The experience of watching Wendel perform my old job in a new spirit was disturbing, however. It increased my feeling of separation from colleagues and made me want to learn more about their images of me, images which I now knew I had been internalizing to my detriment. I decided to accept Evelyn's next invitation to gossip. It would, of course, be a limited and skewed sample, but hardly any information of this nature was available to me, and anything seemed better than nothing.

Evelyn did not lack for material. She was doing a major learning contract in the laboratory of a young psychology professor. It involved working on an animal research project. Especially toward the end of the day, as work drew to a close, Evelyn would have long conversations with her professor. Even though she was doing excellent work that was made possible, among other things, by the IDP's scheduling flexibility, the young instructor was outraged by the IDP, convinced despite Evelyn's statements to the contrary that it was an obstacle she had overcome rather than a help to her. He also turned out to have an extensive critical theory of my life and personality, although he and

I could not have accumulated as much as fifteen minutes of conversation in the course of chance meetings on campus and at faculty parties.

Evelyn spoke freely to me, almost with relief. Having felt only limited freedom to challenge the strong views of a professor on whom she depended, I think she had felt disloyal to me. She had carried around the contents of his attacks without answering him or telling me. I listened to Evelyn with astonishment, for she began to describe an elaborate view of my life, developed by a stranger, that was by no means confined to my campus or professional activities.

To begin with, according to my colleague, I was a lousy father. There was no way that my two young children could receive adequate care while both my wife and I were working at full-time jobs. My problem, he said, arose from a combination of adherence to trendy feminist values, greed for money, and a lack of concern for my kids.

Evelyn's professor was intensely interested in people's academic credentials. Since mine were respectable, indeed fancier than his, he believed that my choice of work was tragic. I could, presumably, be doing work in my academic discipline instead of trying to create strange new programs that were anti-intellectual. The causes of my tragedy were administrative ambition, fueled by the previously mentioned greed, and some kind of perverse desire to be liked. There was probably, he thought, an element of sexual manipulation in my work with students. (This hypothesis of his, as I shall mention shortly, seemed particularly significant as I thought about it further.)

Although I assume Evelyn's professor had to do a little research in order to gather the facts of my family life for his theory, at least have a few discussions with colleagues, some aspects of my political life were well known. I had filed a Freedom of Information Act lawsuit against the FBI, a suit that I finally won. Its details were described in the campus and city newspapers. I had also spoken at campus antiwar rallies. The psychology professor told Evelyn that he thought I was dangerous, just the sort of person who might be in touch with a foreign government. The FBI, he said, was right to keep an eye on me.

There was a variety of other less global things wrong with me. The professor said that I dressed improperly for my position, was wrong to encourage students to call me by my first name, and disturbed him and his sensitive psychology colleagues by laughing too loudly at parties. The idea of my writing a book on education was silly, he thought, because I didn't have formal training in English. Finally I was taken aback to learn that his theory of my personality ended with a note of anti-Semitism: I was said to have a typically Jewish knack for negotiating a high salary in my middle-level administrative job.

This psychology professor was, obviously, a bit of a nut. Nevertheless I felt I was hearing something significant. Especially since he was eager to share his views with Evelyn, I doubted that the young man had developed these ideas in total isolation. And Evelyn reported that other members of the department made similar comments about me, though none of them was quite so obsessed or rabid. Other students had similar but milder stories to tell, as did the few friendly colleagues who were not embarrassed to bring back tales from faculty lounge conversations and committee meetings. As I heard these anecdotes, I felt that I was becoming acquainted with forces that had been influencing my behavior. These stereotypic views of me, operative among some colleagues in my social and professional environment, had contributed to my tendency to stay out of sight, to run scared, and even to feel a little ashamed of myself. An evil persona had been supplied for me by a group of my colleagues, and they and others proceeded to relate to me, at least partially, on that basis. Without my quite knowing what was happening, they treated me as if I were dangerous and malicious and even powerful beyond my means. I responded with reactions appropriate to a person so regarded. It was a liberation and relief to begin to understand a significant portion of the experience that went back to the First Year Program at Antioch.

The saddest part of this story is that events contrived to offer me the chance to observe similar phenomena in Wendel's life, a confirmation that I wish we had both been spared. The similarities between Wendel and me are striking because we are so different in many respects. Whereas Wendel's style is moderate and conciliatory, I tend to be outspoken in matters of educational philosophy. I was bearded and wore jeans; Wendel was more conventionally groomed and even a bit dapper.

Most colleagues didn't know Wendel, but almost everyone who did know him liked and respected him. He was a very hard worker. He happily undertook tasks because they would contribute to the lives of students, and often they were tasks that other people avoided. He spoke ill of nobody. He steered clear of politics and never became involved in fights for money or power. He hardly ever got the yearly discretionary raises that were usually garnered by those willing to lobby for their own cause, so his salary was lower than average for his rank. Yet when he came up for tenure in a division of the college that was particularly concerned with credentials, Wendel's colleagues voted unanimously in his favor even though he'd never completed a doctorate. As a tenured faculty member, Wendel may have been unique on campus in lacking enemies (until the IDP). His bearing reflected that fact. He was confident and friendly. He knew that he'd be treated fairly, and he did his job accordingly. He was secure and as assertive as was necessary to satisfy his rather minimal demands on colleagues and the institution.

When Wendel met with the College Senate committee that was evaluating the IDP, he was eager to cooperate with it, confident that a good case for the IDP could be made and would be received. He returned from those first sessions optimistic about the committee's members and procedures and about our prospects.

I do not know precisely how things went bad between Wendel and the committee, for I saw only the goodwill with which he approached it. Before long, however, it became clear that an evil persona had been created for Wendel too, and that its effects, invisible for a while, were now becoming quite evident.

The committee and its allies among our colleagues received Wendel's statements as if they were designed to be deceptive. It was assumed that each document or statement was an evasion, as if he had something to hide. Wendel is an extraordinarily candid and fair person. The treatment he encountered, however, eventually turned his friendliness to hostility, his confidence to uncertainty, his normal contentment—in Wendel's case one might even say serenity—to unhappiness. Shaken, Wendel, along with the rest of us, fought back.

In the course of the controversy, as things got hot and heavy, bits of information about Wendel's evil persona leaked out, again through students and friendly colleagues. He was said to be an easily manipulated agent of mine. In fact, Wendel was fiercely independent. I would say that he may have occasionally emphasized his differences with me in the decisions he made, but he was generally too rational to give in to temptations to that sort of drama. And I have watched him teach botany to students as we walked through the woods, and I know him to be a highly intelligent and sophisticated teacher. I also knew him to be scrupulously honest and moral. Although my treatment of my own evil persona is self-serving, I know for certain that Wendel was simply perceived falsely.

The creation of evil personas is not, of course, a skill possessed only by the opponents of innovation. Our side returned the compliments, and I am not sure that my view of my conservative colleagues at Antioch or Buffalo was more realistic than their view of me. (Wendel, incidentally, because of his old-fashioned morality and stubborn commitment to fairness, is the person I know who is least susceptible to the temptation of stereotyping enemies and who is most generous toward them.)

*

Sexuality is often a prominent element in stereotypes of people we fear or dislike. This is true on college campuses as it is elsewhere. As we attempt to describe and understand conflict among educators, a short digression into the sexual dimension of campus experience is probably appropriate.

College campuses are highly charged sexual environments. Many students are young, attractive, and unattached. Dating and mating are in the air. Some students break away from parental strictures and home environments by exploring and experimenting with sexual behavior. Professors are powerful members of this community, and some of them, like powerful people in all environments, use their positions for their sexual advantage. Since most professors are men, familiar patterns of sexist exploitation appear on campuses, as one would expect, just as they appear in other workplaces. A recent study showed that a large percentage of female graduate students in psychology had experienced sexual contact with their male professors. Such a finding should surprise no observer of campus relationships. And one must add that all sex between faculty and students is not manipulative and exploitive. Fine relationships between men and women, even faculty and student men and women, can begin on campus.

My object is not to belabor the less than startling fact that students and professors are sexual. I do, however, wish to describe the manner in which liberal student-centered innovation and its attendant conflict may be affected by this fact. The stereotyping that occurs amidst educational conflict, the sort of thing I have described as it affected Wendel and me, is deeply influenced,

I believe, by the way professors handle the sexual aspects of life on campus. Great emotional power is added to academic conflict by these psychosexual dynamics, building on the already strong feelings aroused by educational issues themselves.

There are many reasons for formality, distance, and even pomposity in human relationships. I believe that one reason for the prominence of these qualities in relationships between professors and students bears on the sexuality of the participants. Formality, at least on superficial levels, denies sexual attraction. Needless to say there are ways in which all sorts of sexual messages may be purposely or inadvertently communicated within formal relationships. Yet a professor who lectures from a podium and addresses students formally is adopting practices, one of whose effects is to deny explicit recognition to sexual attractions that may exist.

Having acknowledged that the sexual use and abuse of professorial power are fairly common, it is necessary to state that the opposite is also common. For moral and other reasons, many college professors are uninterested or choose to refrain from sexual activities with students, finding ways, including formal professorial behaviors, to handle a sexually charged campus environment.

Educational innovations like the IDP and the First Year Program are inevitably perceived and judged partially in the perspective of campus sexual politics and dynamics. Such programs encourage, value, and depend upon unusual levels of informality and personal closeness in relations between students and teachers. If education is to be truly student-centered, the life and personality of the student must be drawn into the process of conversation between the student and the teacher, and it is more likely too that the teacher's life and personality will become involved in the same way.

The intimacy of the educational exchange is likely to be perceived, especially by critics, as potentially sexual, perhaps even intentionally sexual. Since formality is sometimes employed to deny sexuality, informality may be seen as a move toward sexual involvement. Stereotyping generally focuses upon areas of emotional life that are frightening and highly charged. The educational innovator, like the stereotyped black person, may well be supplied with imaginary sexual motives or active sexual lives by those who are fearful or in disagreement.

As I became aware of my evil persona and as I talked with Evelyn and watched Wendel, I came to believe that there was a sexual mythology surrounding the IDP and its participants. There was a moralistic quality to the fear and anger of our critics, and it began to make a little more sense when I associated them with sexual attractions and fears.

I have no way of knowing, but I suspect that there was less sex between IDP teachers and students than between teachers and students in conventional programs. I think that the closeness among us may ultimately have produced something like an incest taboo and that the program's egalitarianism partially nullified the attractions and potential exploitations of status and power. I feel sure, however, that the participants in the IDP were not unusually promiscuous or sexually active.

*

Occasionally a businessman who has become a professor writes an article about the comparative serenity and decency of the cutthroat world of commerce when measured against the standard of routine campus politics. Although opponents and competitors are certainly stereotyped and mythologized in all realms of human endeavor, there does seem to be a special quality to the character assassination involved and to the energy with which academic conflict is pursued. Observers have pointed to the scarcity of objective measures of success in the academic world. We evaluate our own students, and as teachers we often have widely divergent goals. There is, therefore, an enormous amount of room for disagreement about what we accomplish and how good we are at our work. It is possible to argue and disagree endlessly about the nature of the educational venture and our relative success as professional educators. There is no closure, no basic profit and loss balance sheet that is accepted by all participants. Disagreement need never end.

As I pondered my discovery that I had been deeply affected by my colleagues' views of me, and as I watched the same thing happen to Wendel, it occurred to me that there was another basic reason that our campus conflicts turn so ugly. A clue to it all is the way professors talk about themselves and their work, and it is perhaps most evident in the ways graduate students, as they are being trained to enter the system, talk about themselves. Academics are almost obsessed with what it means to "be" a sociologist, mathematician, psychologist, or practitioner of one of the other disciplinary specialties. Graduate students who are having their initial teaching experiences talk endlessly about "what I, as a psychologist, can offer the students," or about "showing the students how a sociologist approaches a problem." Perhaps more than most professionals, academics are supplied not only with a role and job but also with an identity. The widespread pedagogical rhetoric about teaching disciplinary methodologies to students comes close to expressing this fact, as does the perennial appeal of the apprenticeship as an educational model. Students are taught how to *be* a certain type of scholar or scientist in a particular discipline. The unstated corollary, the fact from which much of the passion is derived, is that students are to be taught to be such a person using their particular professor as a model.

Many teachers, including many college professors, are responding to a rather primal attraction to the process of socializing the young by offering themselves as models of what a human being should be. This connects easily, in higher education, with the emphasis on disciplinary identities and methodologies. Although the common ways of talking about college teaching are rather cool and detached, the reality of the educational process is quite passionate and involving. The mathematics professor may say that he or she is teaching ways of approaching certain types of problems with certain methodologies. The professor may add that other parts of the interaction, other characteristics of the people involved, are totally irrelevant to the exchange. The actual human fact of the matter, however, is that the professor is often offering himself or herself as a model of a kind of desirable person. Teaching in this mode is a daring and risky act. It's a bit like having a child, but in this case the "child" has the right to reject the person who wishes to be the parent. It accounts for the elation and sense of pride, sometimes almost inexpressible, when one succeeds or when one's students do well, and for the deep attachments that arise between students and teachers. It also explains the dismal and depressing feelings that accompany bad teaching experiences. Being a teacher is not, for large numbers of us, simply a job. It is putting a substantial portion of ourselves on the line in a basic way.

Educators like myself whose values and methods are a bit deviant are not simply doing things differently, nor even competing for a limited number of student disciples. We are offering alternate models for being human, models implicitly asserted to be superior, for students to adopt. We are an affront to our colleagues, as they are to us. Despite the rhetoric of tolerance and pluralism that abounds on campuses, the level of these challenges is too basic for us to coexist easily. We do not so much have disagreements with each other; we *are* disagreements.

I knew a mathematician who went to a meeting on logic that included both philosophers and mathematicians. He thought that the philosophers were full of hot air, and he came home enraged. His way of expressing his anger was to describe the philosophers as counterfeit mathematicians, not to explain the fallacies of their positions. "They dress and talk and smoke pipes and write on the blackboard just like mathematicians," he said, "but they're not."

Offering another sort of education, as we did in the IDP and the First Year Program, only superficially involves rejection of conventional boundaries, values, and methodologies. More basically it is experienced by colleagues as a rejection of their whole professional identities, which for many academics constitute a large portion of their total human identities, a larger portion than is the case for people in most other lines of work. It is the conflict at this level that leads to the bizarre stereotyping that we've described and to the bitter conflicts so common in the academic world.

28

Education and the
Myth of Mental Illness

Success as a teacher first came to me in circumstances in which I was able
to get to know students well. The relationship between preceptors and students in Antioch's First Year Program was designed to be, and actually was,
closer and more personal than standard faculty-student relationships. There
was, in that program, an unusually large array of educational options from
which students chose. Decisions were influenced by personal goals and preferences, and these became matters for discussion and exploration by the preceptor and student. At about the same time I began to teach conventional courses
without grading, and there too I learned more about my students, got to know
them better. When standard disciplinary subject matters were no longer obligatory, students often pursued studies that had stronger connections with other
parts of their lives. These interests entered the collective life of the class more
fully than before. Class work was quite concretely associated with the experiences, backgrounds, ambitions, and personal styles of the students. Our discussions in these classes were frequently intellectual and abstract, but their
grounding in nonacademic life was clear.

The Antioch campus was full of ritualized controversy about educational
philosophy. One part of the ritual was that critics of more personal education
issued strong warnings, especially to their younger and more susceptible
colleagues like me. Education is not, they would say in tones dripping with
ominous meaning, psychotherapy. In your enthusiasm for individualized education, they continued, it would be inappropriate, nay, immoral, to overstep
your bounds and meddle in matters that could be handled properly only by
a trained psychiatrist or psychologist. Beware of psychopathology. A bad
judgment in this area might even be dangerous. In these conversations there
was always a hint of potential or perhaps remembered disaster. I did not wish
to be the college professor with blood on his hands, the blood of a suicide
pushed over the brink by the inept interference of a well-meaning faculty

busybody who lacked the training to deal with serious mental illness. The assumption that there was a clear distinction between education and psychotherapy was accepted by educational radicals and conservatives alike. I remember that my first response to hearing Keith McGary's description of plans for the First Year Program was to say that there would be an additional need for psychologists to deal with the personal problems that would surface. I was, of course, voicing the party line. Why should I have thought that free people have more need of psychologists than others? Isn't lack of freedom a personal problem?

I tried to be clear and responsible. I was alert for signs that my conversations with students were passing into the clinical realm, the area which should be handled only by a psychotherapist. Conversation did indeed sometimes turn to intense personal matters, especially to sex and love, troubled relationships with parents, and confusion about the future. I often asked students whether they wanted to speak with a trained psychotherapist, and we would discuss that question. Some of them did, and I helped them arrange appointments. At other times I simply steered the conversation away from things I thought were inappropriate.

I was behaving properly according to the prevailing wisdom, but there were problems. Most notable among them was that the students who went off to see the clinicians often did not get help. At first I thought that this was simply rotten luck, that Antioch College in those years happened to have psychologists, counselors, and a consulting psychiatrist who could have been a lot more competent and sensitive to the problems of students. This was true enough, but only part of the story. As the years passed, I came to believe that I, as a friendly and concerned conversant, could have helped many of these students more than the clinicians did, despite my lack of training. Moving the discussion of a problem into the clinical arena often did not seem to help very much.

Besides the weaknesses of the clinical part of the system, there was the basic question, which I gradually allowed myself to ask because it was suggested by my daily life as a teacher, of the truth of the dogma that distinguishes education from psychotherapy. In practice I tried to remain scrupulous about respecting it, yet the dichotomy did not seem valid. Experience in classrooms and in discussions with individual students seemed to display a seamless continuity between learning and personal growth, between thinking and learning about the world and oneself. Indeed the very same questions were addressed in "both" realms: the existence of God, the meaning of life, paths to knowledge, the nature of love, the value of competing satisfactions, problems of good and evil. As I studied and taught the history of ideas, I found that it had often been so. The classics are full of instances in which personal problems (including the dreaded thought of suicide), feelings, and processes of growth were deeply implicated in the search for knowledge. My students and I were not great philosophers, but such intellectual gropings and journeys did occur among us. It was ridiculous to believe that one ought to enter the realm of speculation with a clinical scalpel: this fascination with suicide is morbid and pathological and must be excised, while this one is healthy philosophy; John's inquiry into the meaning of life is good clean academic fun, while Jane's is sick.

As my teaching improved and as, at the same time, I became more knowledgeable about the lives of my students, the distinction between education and therapy appeared more artificial. Intellectual learning was continuous with personal growth and problem solving. There seemed to be one type of learning experience with different emphases and tones. I could not help noticing, too, that people did not crumble when a serious personal problem or issue came up in conversation. Students talked about homosexuality, love and hatred of parents, troubled relationships, suicide, but they did not dash off and kill themselves. Every year or two there was, in fact, a real or attempted suicide, and the people involved usually seemed to have been isolated and lonely individuals who had not talked about difficult problems. Students might, in the midst of important conversations, weep or become angry or speak from deep feelings. From time to time the result of such talk was learning and insight. Perhaps, I came to believe, conversation between a college student and a teacher was not extraordinarily endowed with the power to harm psyches. Perhaps talk was only talk, and it had its normal potentials, quite impressive and also quite limited, to harm and to help.

I discovered the writings of Thomas Szasz, who articulated and argued a view of "mental health and illness" that helped explain my experiences. His position also seemed true when measured against larger standards. It is by now well known and ignored. There is no such thing, Szasz says, as mental illness and treatment, for the medical model does not apply to behavior. Behavior may be valued as good or bad, familiar or deviant, but it is not accurately described as healthy or sick. This neither ignores nor makes light of unhappiness and suffering. Nor does it deny the fact that special sorts of training can equip professionals to be useful to particularly troubled people. But it does deny the propriety of calling behavior an illness. According to Szasz, the practical and intellectual functions of psychiatric usage are, among other things, to give special pseudomedical status and respectability to some moral disapproval of deviant behavior and attempts to control it. Homosexuality, for example, can be a psychiatric illness in one decade but literally be removed from the list in the next. Pseudomedical institutions and professional roles are created to punish people, incarcerate them, persuade them that they are ill, coerce them into behaving differently, and most importantly to persuade them of the necessity of sharing control of their behavior with medical professionals. The truth of the thesis is especially vivid on a college campus, where psychologists often have special functions in controlling deviance on behalf of the administration. (This is not to deny that the control is often exercised with humane motives.) Thomas Szasz has spent nearly twenty-five years developing these theses. It is not my intention to reproduce his arguments even in abbreviated form. I do, however, wish to trace the major implications of Szasz's ideas for formal education. I can only note that I think his view of mental health and illness is literally correct, not simply stimulating and provocative, the patronizing terms with which the psychiatric establishment usually attempts to dismiss him.

Szasz's writings address educational issues explicitly, but formal schooling only rarely. Once clinical language, with its taboos and mystifications, is removed from the realm of behavior, however, clarity on certain questions of teaching and learning is easier to attain. Specifically, it is possible to approach perennial questions of values in education in a new way. And it is no longer necessary to deny experienced continuities among many types of learning and personal change.

Szasz's basic thesis is that clinical concepts obscure the fact that matters of mental health are really matters of human values. What behaviors are right and wrong? What sort of person is it desirable to be? Which is the best of the alternative definitions of the good life? In view of answers to these questions, how does an individual wish to change? These are the real questions of "mental health and illness," and they are also the real questions of education, for the two realms are identical.

The standard view of education holds that knowledge and intellectual skills are offered to students, and that this venture is essentially value free, aside from its commitment to certain core academic values such as honesty, truth, and scientific method. It is convenient that these are values with which hardly anyone would argue. Education is by definition removed from the controversial world of value conflicts. It differs radically from religion and politics, where guidance comes from a revealed or partisan system of values, and from psychiatry, which claims to be guided by a scientific theory of mental health. Education, when conceived of as a venture that is free of values, thus achieves a sort of immunity from criticism of its basic goals.

Aside from the fact that this view of education is rather hygienic and bloodless, it is universally violated by students and teachers. These violations are often benign in the sense that the values involved are not terribly controversial. Yet it is important to be realistic about how education is actually conducted. It is commonplace among educators, for example, to claim that we are not simply conveying knowledge of biology or philosophy, but rather using the knowledge as a means of teaching a certain style of thought, say empirical scientific method or a particular type of analysis of language. But we go further. We want our students to think in certain ways, react suitably to particular types of problems, be skeptical, appreciative, clear, or wise. We want them to be certain types of people: liberally educated people, critics, mathematicians, artists, scientists, aesthetes, intellectuals, etc. This is what makes education so exciting, involving, and important. It is also, as we noted in the last chapter, the source of the passion and venom that characterize arguments about education. Educational issues address the basic question of what sort of person is best.

Most professors describe their goals in disciplinary terms, thereby providing academic respectability and a thin disguise to their teaching of "whole people," a term they usually reject as too vague to describe proper education. Yet in unguarded conversations, their disciplinary definition of education is revealed to mean the training of mathematicians, psychologists, or philosophers, and these roles are not narrowly conceived. Not only does being a mathematician, for example, mean knowing certain things and solving problems in particular ways, but it means appreciating certain kinds of beauty, talking in certain ways, choosing among one of a few appropriate styles of seeing the world. Becoming a mathematician is becoming a type of person; teaching mathematics is teaching people to become that sort of person. It engages mathematics teachers fully because they are really presenting themselves, or themselves as they would like to be, as models. When the process reaches students, they too may become deeply involved because it touches the central question of growth, who *they* wish to be.

Formal college education frequently does not work, and one reason is the faculty's confusion about its function. Professors are deeply motivated to show their students a way of being human; they wish to help them become certain types of people. The prevailing educational dogma, however, characterizes teaching in a narrower way. It tells teachers to ignore whole people, themselves and the students, and to focus on the smaller domains of skills and knowledge. Trying to do the right thing, professors wrongly constrain themselves, muting their real message to students and rendering their profession much less joyful than it should be. Sometimes they do not accept the constraints, or their enthusiasm carries the day, yet they lack the concepts and language to talk about their work accurately. This is a serious handicap.

The putative distinction between education and therapy is a barrier to understanding the nature of education. Szasz's work helps. We see that education is inevitably value laden at its core. The proper response is not to overlay the activity with a philosophy of education that insists on a sterile disciplinary focus that seems to involve no significant value choices. Such pretending is no protection against the possible abuses of manipulation and propagandizing. As is the case in most matters of value, the real safeguards are disclosure and honesty. Instead of pretending to be free of all but the most generally accepted values, educators owe the student candor about the full range of values guiding their joint activity and the possibilities for other choices. Conceptually and empirically all education, not simply the liberal innovations that employ rhetoric about individualization and the whole person, is about what sort of people students are to become.

29

Falling Short of the Goal

*In sum, autonomous psychotherapy is an actual small-scale demonstration
of the nature and feasibility of the ethic of autonomy in human relationships.*
—Thomas Szasz

There is a harshness to Thomas Szasz's rhetoric that I don't like, and even less
do I like his political conservatism. It was with some surprise, therefore, that
I continued to find his writings illuminating as I worked on the possibilities and
problems of noncoercive relations between students and teachers. Lecturing
one night at Buffalo State College, Szasz was at his best: clear, brilliant,
forceful, nasty. He denounced the psychiatric establishment with great energy.
Skeptical questioners were quickly and skillfully confronted with the consequences of their assumptions about mental illness, which usually involved the
idea that people should be deprived of freedom or due process for their own
good. The audience went his way, and it was a fine Szasz show. After the
lecture I asked Szasz a question I'd been thinking about all evening. Did he
believe in any kind of psychotherapy? Was there a constructive side to his
negative thesis? Annoyed that I didn't know all about it, Szasz told me of his
book, *The Ethics of Psychoanalysis.* I read it and again found that his work
had strong relevance to educational philosophy and practice. It shed light on
some of the things we'd been doing well and badly in the IDP. Only after
reading Szasz, moreover, did I see that we would never be able to achieve the
ultimate nonauthoritarian goals to which we aspired. Szasz's view of psychotherapy, which is in fact a type of education, implied that the IDP would
necessarily fail, at least when measured against the ideal standard we had
implicitly set for ourselves.

Szasz proposes a version of psychoanalysis which he calls autonomous
psychotherapy. Its function is not to cure a mental disease but to increase a
client's personal freedom. This goal is moral in nature, knowingly chosen from
the realm of values by both therapist and patient; it has no medical source.
It is not the result of an obscure or mysterious psychiatric theory to which only

doctors and other specialists have access. The process itself is correspondingly easy to understand, although psychotherapy remains a force with considerable potential power in human affairs.

Szasz believes that a therapist should offer a particular service, a special kind of conversation in which a patient's behavior and discourse about behavior are interpreted according to certain principles. The core idea is Freudian. The interpretive information will allow clients better to understand their actions and choices; this understanding will put them in an improved position to control their lives, exercise freedom. Knowledge of self is liberating.

Szasz's "therapeutic" goal, an expression of personal and social values rather than the consequences of a theory of disease, is similar to the educational goal of the IDP. Our aim was to help students become autonomous learners, which is to say, really, to say, to encourage them, with education as the starting point, to become autonomous people. To accomplish this, of course, they would need to possess or develop insights into their ways of learning. But there would be more involved than technical training in learning skills. Freedom implied facing the basic value decisions at the core of education: What do I want to become? What do I want to learn? How shall I go about doing these things? Rhetoric about freedom and choosing goals is, however, cheap, among both educators and therapists. The value of Szasz's work lies in his discussion of strategies for implementing these ideas. How is autonomous psychotherapy or education to be conducted?

Szasz's cardinal rule is that the therapist must make no move in the relationship that is coercive, that abridges the client's autonomy. One does not learn autonomy without being autonomous. One does not prepare a person for freedom by enslaving him. It doesn't matter if the patient (or student) wants to be unfree or if the slavery is mild, humane, or even helpful in some ways. The therapist, guided by the central value, is prohibited from fulfilling a person's desire for dependence. The therapeutic relationship is therefore structured to maximize autonomy for the patient and to minimize the chances of the therapist's interference in the patient's life. The patient in autonomous therapy has the possibility, therefore, of learning from two aspects of the relationship: the content, which is the interpretive information contained in the therapist's conversation, and the structure, the experience of living in a noncoercive association with another person. Szasz writes:

> ... if the analytic situation is ... free of coercion, the patient will realize it. The analytic relationship will thus not only provide the conditions necessary for a certain kind of learning experience, but will also furnish a model of the autonomous noncoercive relationship.

Our intention in structuring the IDP was to set the stage for a teacher-student relationship essentially identical to the therapeutic relationship described by Szasz. The primary content was a subject matter, not the student's behavior. Once a joint decision on a course of study was made, based substantially on the student's interests, the faculty member was to offer information about a subject area and resources for studying it. Secondarily, however, the subject often became the student's behavior in trying to learn; this was an intentional shift of focus, one that we anticipated and hoped to build upon. "Did you abandon the approach you thought most promising because I mentioned another book?" "How do you wish to relate to the opinions of experts?" "Let us look at the way you have made judgments about how to pursue this study." The student's well-learned patterns of seeking instructions to obey are grist for the teacher's mill just as they are for the therapist's. But whatever the immediate topic of discussion, personal or academic, the relationship was to be noncoercive, because we believed that a person's best chance of learning autonomy is to experience it.

Szasz analyzes in detail the setting and dynamics of the relationship between a therapist and a client, giving special attention to the most common temptations for the parties, individually or in concert, to compromise the central value of autonomy. It is in this aspect of his treatment of autonomous psychotherapy that Szasz makes observations that are profoundly disturbing to programmatic educational efforts like the IDP, and it is these observations that also illuminate the day-to-day problems of such programs.

The client in autonomous psychotherapy, according to Szasz, has only one obligation: to pay the therapist. Patients need not come to appointments on time, talk about anything in particular, do anything special in their lives, or refrain from doing anything. The therapist may speak about any or all of these behaviors, interpreting them in the profession's special way, but the patient is free to ignore the interpretations or use them in ways that are contrary to the analyst's wishes or expectations. These, then, are the essential terms of the contract between two people: the therapist offers a service and is paid for it; the client has absolute freedom in deciding how to use or not use the service.

> These considerations converge on a simple proposition: to preserve the patient's autonomy in the therapeutic situation, the analyst must avoid all unnecessary coercion. Since the only thing the analyst really needs (or ought to need) is money, the only legitimate demand on the patient is money. Indeed, what other demands can the analyst, as an autonomous therapist, have? Surely he cannot require the patient to lie on the couch or free-associate, to refrain from sexual misbehavior or law-breaking, or any of the myriad things that therapists demand from their patients.

Although most psychotherapists do not act this way, it is possible for them to do so, and Szasz's version of psychoanalysis has a powerful moral clarity that might attract practitioners, if it did not contradict some of their favorite behaviors. A clinician in private practice can indeed make an explicit agreement with a patient following the outline formulated by Szasz, offering only a kind of conversation in exchange for a fee. Moreover, in order to be sure that they are agreeing to a realistic contract, the clinician and patient can experiment with the relationship during a trial period, and Szasz treats the dynamics of this critical phase in some detail. The trial period includes intricate implicit and explicit negotiations of the terms governing the therapeutic relationship.

Since an autonomous therapist contracts to provide only a conversational service, he or she must not provide anything else, including drugs, advice, interventions with school authorities, draft boards, or employers, and educational or psychiatric certification. Szasz believes that each of these things necessarily introduces substantial probabilities for coercion and manipulation, for acting on ulterior motives. They all involve potentials for the therapist to gain influence over the patient despite the goal of autonomy. Noncoercive purity is thus preserved at a high price, for many therapists, like teachers, love to help people, and they will not be pleased by a view that regards all sorts of help save one as invasions of a client's or student's autonomy. This brings us to the principal barrier to the formulation of the proper kind of contract, the institutional setting.

Szasz argues that the required contract cannot be negotiated between a therapist and client who meet in an institution like a mental hospital, counseling center, or clinic. The institution's purposes and interests are bound to interfere with the relationship, for the therapist's loyalty will be divided between the patient and the institution, and he or she will not be free to follow only the terms of a contract with the client. An institution has its own agenda which can subvert the analyst's contract. The fact that the therapist is paid by the organization actually rules out the possibility of a real contract, for the client has nothing to offer that can fulfill a need that is appropriate for a therapist to satisfy in the practice of autonomous therapy. An essential purpose of the contract and the monetary payment, according to Szasz, is to create approximate equality between two participants who come upon the scene with vastly different amounts of power. A contract must be reasonably fair and mutual, creating a large measure of parity between the two people.

> . . . the analyst can help or harm the patient more than the patient can the analyst. The client is in a weaker position than the therapist. The analytic contract serves in part to reduce this inequality and protect the patient from the analyst's power.

The autonomous analyst refrains from a variety of actions, most of which would come quite easily to many clinicians. The analyst simply analyzes. The client pays.

It is appropriate to argue with Szasz on the centrality of money. Is it the only available medium of exchange that will produce equality? Is a rich person disqualified from being an analyst because a client cannot contract to pay a sum that will be substantial to a millionaire? Is there absolutely no way to make analysis available to poor people? Cannot the inherent rewards of exercising professional competence be sufficient in some circumstances? Nevertheless, Szasz's position is insightful and useful. It provides the conceptual framework to evaluate and understand education that purports to be centrally governed by the value of autonomy. Turning to the IDP, it becomes obvious at once that no relationship between student and teacher in the program can meet the high Szaszian standards for preserving autonomy.

The most obvious difference between autonomous psychotherapy and education in the IDP was the existence of an academic subject matter in IDP activities. But this is not a critical difference. It is possible, though not common, for a teacher to hold noncoercion as a value that will not be compromised, even at the risk of decreased academic learning or of straying into unconventional studies. Academic subject matter in itself does not require the sacrifice of autonomy. (The prominence of subject matter as an ultimate value of faculty members does, of course, remind us that few teachers are likely to opt for autonomy.) Things are not so bright, however, when one looks beyond the question of the substantive content of the teacher-student relationship and considers the institutional setting.

American education requires the teacher's word for the certification of learning for progress toward a degree. We make only minimal use of alternatives like testing and outside referees that separate instruction from certification. The IDP was no exception. To have done otherwise, to have planned a program that severed the connection, would have assured the rejection of the proposal. But the teacher's evaluative function confers powers on him or her that are simply too great to be equalized by any contract that could be negotiated between teacher and student. There was nothing students could offer in exchange that would be comparable in significance in the teacher's life to the college degree in the student's. Money was not available to create parity, for the teacher was paid by the institution, and it mattered little that the money originated in tuition payments by students. In fact, the incentives of money, status, and career advancement, major factors that concern teachers, are used to encourage the coercion of students and loyalty to the institution. A "good" professor, in the eyes of those who routinely distribute monetary rewards, is tough and demanding, a fair but hard taskmaster. Exercising power is central to that concept. Even a teacher who wishes to abandon the power associated with certification is not permitted to or faces institutional sanctions. It is thus virtually impossible for a college professor, like an autonomous therapist, to offer an educational service, an intellectual exchange, without caring how the student uses it. Power will not be equalized between the participants, even approximately, and coercion and manipulation, subtle or not, are unavoidably built into the relationship. Only the student who cares nothing for the degree, who is either indifferent to the future or financially secure like the Vietnam veteran mentioned in an earlier chapter, might negotiate a contract for an autonomous relationship with a teacher. Only the teacher who is impervious to the values of the institution in which he or she lives could be the other party to such a contract.

The problem showed up clearly in the IDP's learning contracts. They were not contracts at all in Szasz's sense, because the two parties were not rendered even approximately equal in power. The typical IDP contract thus described a variety of obligations accepted by the student. Almost no obligations, either to perform certain acts or to refrain from others, were assumed by the professor. For neither party were penalties usually specified for failure to perform. But it was clear from the institutional context that students would be seriously penalized by weak evaluations of their progress toward a degree. Even in cases in which the contract, in the interest of liberal form or spirit, specified a professor's promised behavior, there were obviously no sanctions available to reinforce the moral commitment.

IDP students and faculty were often confused by this discrepancy between theory and practice. The program's rhethoric, especially my version of it, was not too different from Szasz's. The reality of the central relationship between student and teacher was necessarily quite different. The confusion resulted from our failure, from the outset, to understand fully the limitations on our ability to offer freedom to students. No matter how sincere our intentions to promote student autonomy, we could not formally sever the link between instruction and certification, nor could we exist unaffected by the standard institutional influences on faculty members.

Having made the theoretical point derived from Szasz's framework, it is nonetheless worth examining the different stances taken by IDP students and faculty on the matter of freedom. Teachers and students found a variety of ways to deal with the situation. We will also look at other characteristics of the interactions between students and faculty in our program, for they are often relevant to the questions of autonomy even when they do not address them explicitly. Despite serious flaws, the IDP did make progress in the pursuit of educational freedom.

Some teachers were truly committed to freedom for students, even in the radical Szaszian sense, or at least they were willing to experiment with it. They often succeeded in finding ways, both in words and action, to express to their students their wish for relationships of equality and noncoercion. They might choose to subvert the certification system by making the evaluation of a contract pro forma, or they might make it so mechanical and predictable that it was drained of much of its power to influence a relationship. Teachers pursuing such strategies faced a problem of credibility. Students had to believe them, develop confidence that the professors would not in the end revert to role and punish them for exercising independence. IDP relationships were often, at least early in their histories, dominated by exchanges in which the student tested and probed to determine the limits of a professor's belief in freedom. Yet some student-faculty pairs communicated well enough and were sufficiently inventive to achieve substantial autonomy in a system whose structural characteristics opposed it. The autonomy was not Szaszian, but it was not trivial.

Another group of professors believed in some form of the idea of freedom. They were also, however, committed to performing the certifying function with integrity. This commitment derived from loyalty to the institution, to their disciplines, or to an educational philosophy. They were often terribly disappointed and hurt, for their principled adherence to the process of certifying could block any meaningful expression of their interest in freedom. They assiduously built quality control safeguards into their programs of work with students. Students responded mainly as they had learned to respond, as adversaries who were almost inevitably tempted to follow nonlearning strategies to win the evaluational skirmish. Such professors genuinely wanted to achieve new levels of equality, closeness, and collaboration with students. Depending on the professor's personality, students were sometimes able to respond to both parts of the conflicting message. In such cases the relationship, though somewhat confused, could work. There could be an interpersonal closeness that encouraged learning, and an oscillation between freedom and friendly, well-meaning coercion. Sometimes the relationships were rendered almost useless by the conflict between evaluation and autonomy.

There was yet another group of professors that was attracted to the IDP by the prospect of working closely with individual students. These people were not, however, even mildly interested in autonomy as a governing principle of that relationship. Most often they had a highly authoritarian idea of the student as scholarly apprentice. The student would be totally subject to the control and rigorous judgment of the supervising scholar. In this model of the teaching relationship, the two people would be close and friendly because they would agree fully on the nature of the task and the need for paternalistic authoritarianism. Some students were repelled by this idea, for it represented a strengthening of the classroom tyranny that they were trying to escape. A fair number of students, however, fit into this paradigm and worked productively with these professors. Their relationships were intense. The authoritarian model of education was familiar and comfortable in many ways. In one way it felt right to be in such a relationship, for it was not violating basic norms of the educational world. It might also be a relief to be temporarily rid of the tensions and ambiguities associated with the attempt to work autonomously. And real learning took place, although some of it was quite different from what had been intended in the creation of the IDP. A few students joined the IDP and proceeded systematically to establish such relationships with professors. They used the structures of the IDP to abandon autonomy rather than to learn it. Yet this, as Szasz pointed out, is one of the uses to which freedom can be put if one finds an authority figure who is willing to collaborate.

Pure autonomy never existed in the IDP, for even the most egalitarian and noncoercive relationships were subtly haunted by the absence, to use Szasz's term, of a reliable equalizing contract whose basic terms could be negotiated by two individuals without outside interference. Yet considerable degrees of autonomy could and did exist, and these depended on the complex interactions of the values, skills, and personalities of the two participants. For a complete picture of the IDP's ability to encourage autonomy, however, we must leave Szasz behind and look beyond the most obvious facts of the participants' inability to form a contract. That issue is central, but it doesn't exhaust the subject. The question is how fully could students influence, if not control, their educations. There are contextual factors besides certification and institutional power that determine the answer.

On the most obvious level, IDP students met with professors individually, usually in faculty offices rather than lecture halls or seminar rooms. Those offices, of course, are not without the trappings of status and authority; and some professors play them to the hilt. Yet coming to a professor's office to initiate a conversation is active and personal, much more so than appearing among a group of students in a class, the result of a bureaucratic act of registration, often in fulfillment of a requirement. Students presented themselves to make a request and possibly to begin a process of negotiation. The negotiation, to be sure, was not to be between equals, yet the request was grounded in a personal interest or goal. Even the most formal and authoritarian professor could hardly avoid responding to the student's unique personality and proposal. This is in stark contrast with the classroom setting, in which even the most informal teachers have difficulty in treating students like individuals. The IDP's change in the arena of academic action, emphasizing the individual student, was not a small accomplishment in a world in which many students routinely add their social security number to their signature on any document given to a teacher or other institutional representative. It is best, of course, to enter a relationship having equal power with a professor, but it also is better to enter a relationship with the dignity of some individuality rather than simply as a member of a group defined by bureaucratic contingencies.

The elimination of the letter system of grading was in itself liberating and elating for many students. There is something particularly offensive and humiliating about having a portion of one's life summed up and categorized by a single B+ or C−, especially when these may affect one's future. There is barely a pretence made, in that system, of attempting real communication with the student. The grade's apparent precision is in stark contrast with the complexity of the real learning experience, and it demeans that experience. The IDP's written evaluations were supposed to be jointly formulated. This provision was often respected in significant ways, and it represented another substantial gain in autonomy for students. To some extent, evaluation became something in which they participated, not something that was done to them. Not only did they have a measure of control over it, but the format was not an insult to their complex experience. The evaluation was discursive. It could be lengthy. The student who cared to do so, and there were some who did, could almost always help develop an evaluation that tried to capture the subtlety of the experience.

There were other important gains that bear on the question of autonomy. Subject matters and methodologies for studying them were worked out between teacher and student. The results were sometimes quite imaginative, though often they stuck fairly close to the standard curriculum. Even in the latter cases, the slight deviations from familiar syllabi had considerable meaning for students because they were *their* deviations. Students did influence, more profoundly than in conventional programs, the subjects and methodologies of their studies.

The determination of a daily schedule was a problem and an opportunity of enormous magnitude in the lives of IDP students, and it represented a major increase in autonomy. Students in conventional programs go to classes according to an imposed schedule; they are given assignments with deadlines; they live according to the standard academic calendar. Their use of their own time is largely determined by these externals. From moment to moment during most of their academic lives, IDP students had the freedom to use their time as they saw fit. It is hard to overstate the importance of this concrete condition of life. The substance of freedom exists within a person's minute-by-minute decisions concerning the use of time.

It is commonplace to observe that people can feel liberated when they stop exercising power over others. Professors found opportunities in the IDP that were related to some of the freedoms experienced by students. Many college teachers are constrained by conventional academic structures. Standing in front of a class, they may feel love for their students or their subjects which they can't express in that setting. Discussing term papers, they may wish to offer help or support but can find no outlet for these because the focus on the grade is too intense. Unable to know about or take into account the special circumstances of students' lives, professors may have tried to increase flexibility in their courses by experimenting with curricular options and various other gimmicks, when they really wished to participate in a deeper process of collaboration and individualization. Conventional structures may have made this impossible for many teachers, but the IDP provided the opportunity. Just as IDP students often found that they could become engaged in their studies more fully, professors found that they could teach with more of themselves. This was no small reward for the teachers who experienced it, and it redounded to the benefit of the students. It was not a payment negotiated with the student, like the autonomous therapist's hourly remuneration. Yet it was something important that many teachers received from the experience of working in the IDP with particular students. When it happened, it also contributed to the feeling and reality of the student's autonomy, for it was clear in these cases that he or she counted for something, had affected a professor's life for the better. Occasionally this developed into a deeper sense of adventure and collaboration, a sense that student and teacher in some ways were exploring new ground together. A type of equality between student and professor could emerge that essentially obliterated the formal inequality of power that was a necessary institutional fact. Freedom and autonomy can characterize relationships between people engaged in a meaningful joint venture. The negotiation of the terms of a contract may be implicit, emerging from the relationship. And questions of power may simply drift into the background and disappear, and when this happened, it was one of the more wonderful consequences of struggling toward freedom. It happened often enough in the

IDP for us to know that it was at least a possibility for any student-faculty pair that entered upon a project that had real meaning for both partners.

We started the IDP with stars in our eyes, promising too much to ourselves and our students. Quickly and painfully we became aware of the constraints that we could not remove, and our rhetoric moderated. Students could not have total freedom to learn and to live autonomously. Such freedom may be unavailable except under the conditions of a more limited construct like a psychotherapeutic relationship, and it is probably rare there. It cannot exist in a college or university. Yet students did have much more freedom than was available in most educational programs. It was incomplete and confusing, but it was substantial.

To return to an argument we mentioned earlier, conventional education is supported as realistic by proponents who claim that oppression is everywhere, and students must learn to cope with it. IDP-style education is vividly supported by the same argument stood on its head. Limited freedom, flawed and complex freedom, is available in many places in the world. One may, as an educator or student, choose the task of learning how to use it as fully as possible. One may choose to create a program like the IDP that addresses this educational goal directly. Freedom in these programs, in all schools, will be imperfect, as it is everyplace else. But such education can provide valuable practice. Students can develop the skills necessary to deal with the freedom they find. They can develop the moral and empirical acuity needed to make the delicate factual and value judgments necessary in a life with this emphasis. This is what we were doing in the IDP, and there was a period in which we didn't know it. The task was more subtle than the one which we had consciously undertaken.

30

Learning from Margaret Mead

A prefigurative society is by definition a society with an unknown future, and an unknown future is inevitably frightening. The sense that the children are a little better prepared to face these unknowns because they are at least birthright members of the newer order can be either comforting and give hope or be twisted into a philosophy of despair. But there is a constant danger, more constant than I realized ten years ago, that the struggle will prove too difficult, and the by-products too destructive.

—Margaret Mead

I returned to Antioch College as a teacher at the age of twenty-three in 1963. It was the era of the generation gap, an image and figure of speech that was prominent in our media and our thoughts. The phrase was used to describe and to attempt to explain the fact that all hell was breaking loose and that young people seemed, in one way or another, to be responsible.

Only a few years older than my students, I was a marginal participant in the new youth culture. Like all teachers, I faced the new culture and politics of young people as part of an educational problem. My response was, for reasons I have described, progressively to abandon my professorial power, to allow and encourage students to make the central decisions in their educations, at least in those parts of their educations in which I was involved. Students reacted by using their freedom to bring new subjects into the curriculum: rock music and its poetry; media; curiosity about Eastern cultures; antiwar, civil rights, and ecological politics. I felt, as I have said, that my classes were enlivened by the new materials, although many of my own interests, formed by my training as an academic philosopher in graduate school, remained conventional and changed much more slowly. A respectful tolerance and curiosity existed between me and those of my students whose interests were quite different from mine. In another part of my life, one marked by fewer reservations, I was drawn into the civil rights and antiwar movements.

240

Learning from Margaret Mead

As a teacher I felt that I was improving and that this encounter with the special features of the 1960s was productive. Yet despite pragmatic progress, there were both enormous gaps in my understanding of these things and other painful practical problems that left me baffled. The most serious development in the latter category was the hostility of most of my colleagues. They had recently been my teachers, and they had welcomed me to their profession enthusiastically. I saw my new practices as consistent with the traditions of Antioch, and I was stunned when my colleagues turned against me. They, of course, undoubtedly thought that I had turned against them. I was unprepared for the depth and finality of their rejection of me, and labored for years to explain myself and to build bridges to them, unwilling to accept the obvious fact that the problem was not that they misunderstood me.

I did not understand the source of my colleagues' anger. The best I could do was to say that they were "threatened" and to divide the faculty into two groups, the small band of good guys (my friends and me) on one side and everyone else on the other. Nor did I know what to make of the competing claims that were being staked out on all sides of the generation gap. Were we really at the dawn of a new and better era of world history, as some young people and their older supporters claimed? Were we witnessing the rise of a new barbarism that threatened all culture, as my more hysterical colleagues asserted? If neither extreme position was true, what in fact was really happening? My daily reaction was to experiment with more radically open educational structures and to become more deeply involved in the civil rights movement. On one level these were productive responses; on another I knew that there was a lot I didn't comprehend. Almost everyone felt that something large and unified was taking place, but none of the available ideas seemed to capture it adequately. And in my heart I believed that my own direction as a teacher involved something more interesting than the next step in a liberal tradition or an adjustment to new subject matters. There was a rightness and timeliness to it that felt as if it arose from something deep and new that I was at a loss to articulate or explain.

I don't remember exactly how I came to read Margaret Mead's *Culture and Commitment,* but I have vivid memories of seeing Mead at a scientific meeting during the sixties. She was a major speaker, and the ballroom was inadequate to handle the crowd. The overflow was created by hundreds of students who came to the session because Mead was known as an establishment figure of the highest status who was nonetheless interested in and sympathetic to radical young people. I was in the crowd milling around outside the room, disappointed and hoping somehow to get in. Before long Mead and the person in charge of the session made their way through to the door with difficulty, and she was saying, "Try to get this lecture piped into other rooms; if you can't, I'll give it two or three times."

Later that evening, my wife and I attended a meeting of a caucus of radical scientists, mostly graduate students. I was participating in their program, which began with a review of the schedule of the next day's meetings. Sessions were identified whose subjects had political implications, especially those that might have connections with the way science and technology were being used in the war in Vietnam. Members of the group would go to the sessions and raise questions and make statements. In the midst of this evening meeting I turned in my seat and saw Margaret Mead with a friend in the back row, sitting and listening. She stayed the whole evening and said hardly a word. She certainly seemed to respect young people and to feel that she could learn from them. I loved her for her presence and her silence.

When *Culture and Commitment* was published in 1970, I read it with feelings of elation and clarity. More than anything I'd read, the book helped to make sense out of experiences I had been having. It also suggested a deeper conceptual basis for the educational strategy that I had been adopting. My approach had developed out of a variety of practical and ethical considerations. I had been searching for a rationale that was less personal and more in touch with social realities. I had an intuitive sense that such a rationale existed and that perhaps I would eventually be able to formulate it myself. Mead's analysis was a virtually complete statement of a position toward which I had felt myself groping. It had a global perspective and a measure of wisdom that was beyond me and my experience. But I believed I could use her insights once I learned of them.

The central thesis of *Culture and Commitment* is that a group of unique and significant changes occurred in the world in the 1940s and 1950s. They were mainly technological developments that had profound cultural ramifications. First and foremost was the atom bomb and the unprecedented prospect that war might destroy virtually all of the human race. There were also worldwide electronic communications and jet transportation which greatly increased information flow and physical access to all parts of the world from all others. Space exploration dramatized the ecological view of the world as a small and delicately balanced unit in a large universe, and it seemed to place human life and values in a new and more realistic perspective. Computer technology began to remove long-standing limitations on a variety of human endeavors, limitations that arose from the amounts of data that needed to be processed and the time that the processing took. The range of human culture had been explored by anthropologists, and there was little expectation that many hitherto unknown forms of human life would be uncovered; the cultural census of the human family was nearing completion. Geographically, the world was almost fully explored.

Mead's thesis was that children born after 1940 were born into a new world, one that was qualitatively different from the world of their parents. This radical discontinuity in experience was being strongly expressed as the first generation born after 1940 reached college age. This was not the familiar perennial conflict between generations, but a unique gap in experience between two generations, a gap produced by a particular group of events that would occur only once in the history of the world.

> . . . Adults, over thirty or so, had to realize that there would never be people like ourselves again, people reared in a partly explored world, a world in which there was no atomic bomb and so no danger of total destruction, no TV and man-made satellites to send messages around the world in seconds, no possibility of going to the moon, no computers to condense a lifetime of calculations into a few minutes. We, on our side of the gap, had been born and bred in an age before the second Fall, incapable of destroying the whole human race, and innocent of the terrible responsibility now upon us all. The ancient lure of parenthood, which had kept men and women of the past reproducing and laboring for hundreds of generations, so that others like themselves could live as they had lived, is gone. Our generation, in a curiously final way, will have no successors. . . .
>
> Today, suddenly, because all of the peoples of the world are part of one electronically based, intercommunicating network, young people everywhere share a kind of experience that none of the elders ever have had or will have. . . .
>
> Today, nowhere in the world are there elders who know what the children know, no matter how remote and simple the societies are in which the children live. In the past there were always some elders who knew more than any children in terms of their experience of having grown up within a cultural system. Today there are none. It is not only that parents are no

longer guides, but that there are no guides, whether one seeks them in one's own country or abroad. There are no elders who know what those who have been reared within the last twenty years know about the world into which they were born.

Mead, undeniably an elder, stated a simple, clear, and powerful thesis. The world had changed radically and quickly, and the younger generation, born into the new world, knew or at least intuited critical things that were not normally accessible to older people. It is not surprising that the book was carefully ignored, especially by educators, the group for which it had the clearest practical consequences. Not only did Mead's position imply radical changes in the conduct of education, but her book had an intellectual range and a disrespect for boundaries that would make many academics uncomfortable. More disturbing still, Mead was consciously addressing global problems. One could almost feel, especially in the revised edition published a decade later, shortly before her death, her straining to summon the wisdom she possessed to trace the outlines of solutions. Such a book and author were not likely to be embraced by an educational world that was turning back to the "basics," poring over enrollment projections, and becoming infatuated with the potential of behavior modification.

Building on what she had learned as an anthropologist studying socialization, Mead distinguished three modes of the transmission of culture. There are "postfigurative" patterns or cultures, the most familiar and seemingly natural ways of socializing the young. The culture is shared, with no question and little change, by three or more generations living together. In such settings older generations are clearly best situated to teach the young what they will need to know. Elders prepare new members of the society for a way of life that they have lived. There is no reason or inclination to doubt their authority or qualifications in the matter.

"Cofiguration" is a pattern that obtains when socialization occurs as peers learn from each other what they could not learn from their elders. Perhaps the clearest case is among immigrant groups; when young people went to school and learned how to be Americans from others their age, they quickly surpassed their parents in their assimilation and had nothing to learn from them in that realm of life. Whereas in postfigurative patterns "the future repeats the past," in cofigurative patterns "the present is the guide to future expectations."

Mead's thesis becomes most provocative and useful when she discusses "prefiguration," a situation "in which the elders have to learn from the children about experiences they have never had."

> Even very recently, the elders could say: "You know, I have been young and *you* have never been old." But today's young people can reply: "You never have been young in the world I am young in, and you never can be." This is the common experience of pioneers and their children. In this sense, all of us who were born and reared before the 1940s are immigrants in today's culture. Like first-generation pioneers, we were reared to have skills and values that are only partly appropriate in this new time, but we are the elders who still command the techniques of government and power.

Mead wrote about developments on campuses that seemed close to my own experience:

> And so all over the world there were strange and sudden capitulations by the perceptive, responsible, and concerned elders, as well as angry, often vicious reactions from those who felt that the very essence of all they held dear was being completely destroyed.

I was not much of an elder, and I acted more out of instinct than perception or responsibility, but Mead did help me to understand what I had been going through. Throughout her book there were short passages like this one that explained the unexpected role of outcast that I had been forced to assume.

Some writers moralistically condemned young people, treating them as cynical and evil agents bent on destroying sacred values. For almost ten years I was the teacher of hundreds of those students at a particularly radical college, and I knew most of them to be gentle and well meaning. Other writers took worshipful stances toward each new youthful enthusiasm; one wanted to believe them, but it was hard. The enthusiasts tempted one to dishonesty. Mead, sympathetic to young people and respectful of them, presented a version of developments that was global and descriptive. She was specific and clear about the crucial changes, their effects, and their significance. Not only did she seem to get to the core of things, but she did so from an engaged position, struggling to glimpse ways in which the future could be influenced and molded for the better.

Prefigurative though the new situation might be, Mead did not suggest that the older generations discreetly remove themselves from the scene. She did, however, propose a shift in power and a process of experimentation with new forms of collaboration. (Many people of course, like my professorial colleagues, would experience the loss of even a small amount of power as equivalent to removal from the scene.)

> So the freeing of the human imagination from the past depends, I believe, on the development of a new kind of communication with those who are most deeply involved with the future—the young who were born in the new world. That is, it depends on the direct participation of those who, up to now, have not had access to power and whose nature those in power cannot fully imagine. . . .
> . . . the development of prefigurational cultures will depend on the existence of a continuing dialogue in which the young, free to act on their own initiative, can lead their elders in the direction of the unknown. . . .
> The children, the young, must ask the questions that we would never think to ask, but enough trust must be reestablished so that the elders will be permitted to work with the young on the answers. As in a new country with makeshift shelters adapted hastily from out-of-date models, the children must be able to proclaim that they are cold and where the drafts are coming from; but father is still the man who has the skill and the strength to cut down the tree to build a different kind of house.

By the time my colleagues and I began to plan for the IDP in the early seventies, the theses of *Culture and Commitment* were important parts of my thinking about education. Mead's ideas provided a social and conceptual basis for an educational strategy based on increased student power, and it was derived from a view of the world that seemed true and insightful.

The relationship between student and teacher in the IDP was to be based on a student-initiated and student-centered learning contract. There was considerable curricular freedom for students to determine the content of their projects. I saw the student-faculty relationship in the IDP as one model for the new kind of collaboration that would formalize prefigurative learning, capture its vitality while still operating within the context of an existing institution. Within the IDP generally we attempted, given the constraints of our larger academic system and its ethos, to shift both control of the learning venture and responsibility for judgments of relevance toward students. These changes were made in the belief, encouraged by Mead, that the students were culturally well situated to find productive ways to use this power, and that they could be helped to acquire, in such a setting, the requisite skills and knowledge they lacked.

The IDP existed for only a few years and had a couple of hundred students. Such a body of experience is minute compared with the scope of the ideas we've been discussing. Moreover only a fraction of the IDP experience got far enough to be relevant to even the most preliminary test of these ideas against concrete facts. There were, as we have seen, organizational and emotional barriers to the implementation of the new kind of collaboration we sought, and there were also simple human failures to do what was needed. Yet despite the incongruity of burdening the experience of a few students at an ordinary state college with the weight of global theses, it would be worse still to discuss grand ideas without ever looking at one's available experience, no matter how small. Certain students come to mind at once. Most of them have already been described. Let us recapitulate briefly, bearing Mead's ideas in mind.

Eve carefully selected portions of the current professional teacher training curriculum and rejected others. She created an education for herself that constantly engaged her in practice as well as theory. Eve's education was always motivated by ethical commitment and later by political values; she executed a consciously planned process of abstract political self-education and a parallel process of gathering practical skills. Eve's politics and a sense of adventure brought her to a Turkish migrant-worker neighborhood in Berlin. By then she had developed skills as a teacher and child-care worker, and she brought them to a setting in which action in pursuit of her political goals was possible.

Mark became Mr. Brett's apprentice as a craftsman, but he also studied ecological politics and advanced design, not to mention poetry and other matters of the spirit. He is aggressively eclectic and disrespectful of intellectual boundaries. He refuses to accept separations of technical issues from questions of values. He has become an industrial designer, and one feels that he brings a new twist or two to that profession.

Donna was scholarly, artistic, brilliant, and energetic, and to these qualities, like Eve, she added political commitment during the course of her education. She went to graduate school in England, but found that the university setting seemed to subvert her attempt to synthesize her interests in literary scholarship, art, and politics. Donna returned home and got a job in the publishing industry in New York. She is studying languages and filmmaking. She writes, takes photographs, draws, and reads voraciously. One gets from Donna the sense of a person reaching, extending herself toward an idiosyncratic amalgam of involvements. Her interests are diverse, but it is like Donna to create or discover a unity in them.

Evelyn was one of the best students of psychology Buffalo State College ever had, and she may be the person of my acquaintance who is least afraid of hard work. As an undergraduate she was, with her professors, coauthor of several research studies. She also did a number of IDP projects on children's television. Evelyn went to graduate school in psychology but stopped short of a Ph.D. despite the urging of enthusiastic professors, for she had continued to be a productive student. Her success as a student and her genuine interest in psychology were overshadowed by the repulsion she felt at the careerism, politics, and elitism of academic life. She simply couldn't stand the pretenses in which her professors invited her to share. She returned to work in educational television. In addition, she and her husband live in the country and are striving for a high level of self-sufficiency in living on their land.

Kathy, whom we haven't mentioned before, was also interested in television. She spent all of her time in the IDP working on a couple of major video projects. Her work attracted the attention of a local station, and she left school after less than two years to accept the kind of job she had been aspiring to.

Glen was a film freak who arranged his entire academic life to touch, in one way or another, on the subject of movies. Not only was his knowledge of the medium encyclopedic, but he sincerely and energetically expanded his education into larger fields, literature and art history, for example, so that he could understand film in broader perspectives. Glen continued his education in a graduate program in American Studies with an emphasis on film. He has become a part of the artistic life of his community, pursuing many of the activities that began as part of the IDP learning contracts. He acts, directs plays, makes films, runs film programs, and shoots documentary footage for the local historical society.

Neia became a teacher of handicapped children. She was always ambivalent about the standard professional training required in the field, and she remains ambivalent about the assumptions of her profession. Yet she finds utility in some of the skills she was taught, and she loves her work. Neia is organizing young teachers like herself into support and discussion groups to deal with the problems in their work. She has a gift for picking and choosing, for working within the system and finding the soft spots where change may be possible.

Debbie too became a teacher. Married, a feminist, a gardener, she works with her husband toward an independent rural life and their dream of establishing a school. Her life has the same special self-created feeling that came to characterize her education in the IDP. She has continued to grow in self-confidence, and in this respect the frightened, timid teenager who entered the IDP is hardly visible any more.

I am not inclined to claim, and it isn't necessary to, that these students are terribly different from others of their generation, nor to argue that anything that may be distinctive about them can be attributed to the IDP. Although some of them and their teachers believe in such cause and effect, there are many contributing factors to a life, and formal education's efficacy must always be held suspect, despite the obsessions of educators. There are, however, observations to be made about the way these students used educational freedom and the kinds of lives they have created for themselves.

The ambitions and temperaments of these people are quite different. Mark and Eve, for example, are by nature critical and antiestablishment, whereas Evelyn and Donna's styles are to study thoroughly before venturing a careful criticism. Mark and Donna probably dream of achievements that will be recognized in national or international arenas, whereas Glen and Debbie are likely to see the neighborhood or the small local community as their realms of action. Eve and Debbie and Neia are inclined toward action, whereas Donna is intellectual by nature, although she is likely to push herself in the direction of action. There are, in other words, great variations in character and life orientation among this small group of students.

These students used the increased freedom of the IDP to synthesize an education to suit them. Each one, with the exception of Donna, chose options with strong elements of practice or fieldwork. All of them were touched by feminism and environmentalism in ways that affected their education and the lives they chose to live after graduation. Most of them displayed, in the course of their educations, an interest in and respect for communications media. Technology in general was not frightening to them, and it was often seen to offer opportunities.

Social values, sometimes explicitly political values, were particularly prominent among them. A stance of strong commitment in some arena of endeavor, not primarily private, was the motivating force in their education. It was in allowing increased room for the expression of such commitment that IDP education differed most markedly from conventional college education.

There was also, among these students, a sense that they were somehow trying to do something new. They were not assuming roles that had already been defined by people whom they accepted as models. Mark loved Mr. Brett, but he wanted to be quite different from him. Mark was not particularly tempted by the flattering offer to take the faculty position when Mr. Brett retired. Neia admired and learned from Win, but neither Neia nor Debbie had known teachers of handicapped children upon whom they would model themselves. Donna had nobody to follow in the creation of the special combination of artist, intellectual, and activist she wished to become, and I doubt that Eve had such a model for her life. These people may or may not succeed in the lives that they have chosen, yet their aspiration to new syntheses are significant.

My biases are clear, and we are on vague and intuitive grounds here. Yet it is my sense that these people are reaching toward public and private lives that are informed by the kind of feeling for the future that Mead ascribes to their generation. And if there is anything to all of this, there is reason to be cheered. For although these students went their own ways in significant fashion, those ways were not *that* foreign or disturbing to their professors or the institution. Each drew very significantly upon teachers and established knowledge, and usually it was done with a sense of gratitude and respect. Each had at least two or three especially good relationships with professors, relationships that were significant to both people. Yet not one of them put together an education that routinely comes packaged as a major subject in our standard curriculum. And questions of gratitude and respect aside, each was practical. Not only did they fail to slip into educational chaos, but none of these students is a helpless idealist, dangling without ways or means at the fringes of society. Both the IDP and this group of students had their problems, but they were not these horrors that the educational conservatives constantly promised us.

Mead's revised version of *Culture and Commitment,* published at the end of the seventies, was not sanguine. As she indicated in the passage quoted at the beginning of this chapter, she was taken aback by the strength of the anger of older people toward members of the younger generation and their new beliefs. She had underestimated the difficulties of reconciliation and of the creation of new forms of partnership, prefigurative partnership. In the newer portions of her text, one feels Mead straining to find the grounds for continued optimism. Even Mead, certainly one of the more tough-minded of the intellectuals who were sympathetic to the young people, was at first seduced into unwarranted optimism about the ease with which prefigurative forms might be invented and sustained. She was talking about questions of power, and power does not shift easily.

In the attempt to draw conclusions I find myself facing stark contrasts. Students and teachers confronted formidable barriers in trying to use freedom, to live within educational forms that sought to institutionalize prefiguration. Although large numbers of professors—between 150 and 200, constituting about 25 percent of the faculty—worked satisfactorily, often happily, with IDP students, our problems were exacerbated and our program finally terminated when a dozen or so faculty became enraged and destructive. Somehow they cared more or spoke more directly to the values, beliefs, and biases of the institution than did the more positive experiences of others. Yet some students and teachers did exceedingly well, flourishing and finding joy in new ways of collaborating. Looking at the lives of these students and teachers, widespread radical freedom in education is not hard to imagine, nor does it seem particularly frightening. Those people followed their lights to results that were useful, interesting, and seem to present somewhat novel ways to move into the future. There is a certain feeling of rightness to it all, the kind of feeling one would expect if Mead's position were valid.

As I write these words, I hear the protests of professors of education and of social scientists, objections to my attempt to use these anecdotes, feelings, and intuitions. Can't we get better data? Must we be content with such fuzzy thinking? Ought we not conduct extensive longitudinal studies, examining the success in later life of students who have participated in different types of educational program?

We know, of course, that the empirical search for any effects of formal education, separated from the effects of family, class, race, personality, etc., has not been particularly productive, at least when the methods of contemporary social science are used. We also know that the tides of innovative education (and the accepted styles of conventional education) ebb and flow rapidly, hardly standing still long enough for program-specific empirical research. But these matters, essentially issues of methodology, are not to the point, and it is really not by reference to these criteria that the case must be considered.

A concept like prefigurative learning brings us into a realm that is too abstract to be handled by the kind of inquiry that would be used to measure the consequences of dropping a language requirement. Mead is providing a philosophical framework, a set of ideas through which to view the social world. No single empirical test will confirm or deny her thesis or any meaningful application of it. If her ideas are attractive and seem plausible, one must try to live with them, within them, as one would adopt and experiment with a political philosophy or an aesthetic. The value of the ideas will show itself, or fail to do so, in the illumination and connection of disparate events, in the creation of new ways of seeing developments in society and culture, in the process of stimulating insights, in providing guidance for action that turns out to have been wise. The ideas will either gain in their cumulative power to explain and unify, or they will fade away, clever thoughts that produced little. In education we base our actions on such frameworks all the time; almost any meaningful educational strategy derives rather directly from core ideas about human nature and culture. We are here on the kind of intellectual ground from which we have no choice but to exercise our best intelligence and humanity, and then risk a commitment to a position. One simply cannot, by the nature of the case, wait until all the data are in. It's not that kind of issue. This is even more decidedly the case since Mead's thesis is historical. It characterizes the nature of the moment in which we live. There are existential choices to be made, and there is no avoiding them.

My intuition, obviously, is that Mead is right and that we live in an era in which prefiguration is the timely mode of learning. I feel that I have glimpsed it in the informed and intelligent gropings of my students and colleagues. I believe also that power will shift because events are requiring it to shift. Whether we create IDPs or oppose them, young people, both in and out of school, will respond to the imperatives of their environment. The outcomes, of course, are uncertain, and catastrophe, especially of the nuclear or ecological variety, is a prominent possibility, as Mead well knew. Perhaps the odds against disaster will be minutely increased if teachers and institutions of formal education join the young people, befriend them, and offer to collaborate. If Mead is right, such would be the only alternative that has any utility, honor, or grace.

31

Freedom in Conventional Classrooms

The class was walking to the park, and we had to go past some men who were putting in a new sidewalk. Anders was at the end of the line and he wasn't looking, so he accidentally stepped in the wet cement. One of the workmen took him by the shoulders and shook him and scared the hell out of him. He started to cry. When Mrs. Bradley saw what was happening she came back to the end of the line and told the class to keep walking. She stayed behind and started to bawl that guy out. He was big and she stuck her face right up into his and really gave it to him. We kept looking back, and even after we'd gone two blocks she was still going at it. I think that big guy was more scared than Anders.

—Josh

I began writing this book in earnest after leaving Buffalo. I was full of the anger and sense of defeat that came with the demise of the IDP. I thought I had learned significant things about freedom in education, and I'd wanted to write about them for some time. I settled down to the task sadly, for it seemed that my book would inevitably strike a negative, even a bitter note. I wished that it might have been otherwise, but my experience did not seem to argue for an optimistic view of the place of freedom in education. I saw freedom working in the lives of many students and teachers, and I was enthusiastic about what I saw, but I also watched its destruction when it was structured into the programs of institutions.

Like others who had become deeply involved as IDP core faculty members, I did not feel much like teaching in regular classrooms. Having experienced the intimacy, the sense of opportunity, and the challenge of the educational exchange in the IDP, the potential of normal course and classroom structures seemed pale. At the risk of being misunderstood, I sometimes explained my loss of enthusiasm for classroom teaching by using a sexual image. It was as if a relationship between two people had reached the stage where they had just begun to make love, and then they were constrained forever only to shake hands. They would, to be sure, learn a good bit about the potential of the handshake, but that seemed like small comfort. I had also painted myself into something of a rhetorical and ideological corner, if only in my own eyes. My work for at least ten years had been based on an emphasis upon the limitations of conventional structures. It would be hard to give up, simply to say, "Never mind," and go back to the old forms. It was an unhappy situation to have taken major practical and psychological steps toward removing myself from doing one of the things I felt I could do best—teach. Yet that is how I felt: uninterested in conventional classroom teaching and apparently destined, as a writer, to project pessimistic views about my most valued educational ideas.

Our family moved to Ann Arbor where my wife took a new academic position. One result of the move was that the formal education of our children was no longer entrusted to Win Evers and Cause School, and I immediately found good reasons to worry about finding suitable schools for them. Also, overnight I became a househusband and a fledgling writer, a development that provided other things to worry about. Although I had pondered the move and tried to prepare myself for it, the loneliness of my new life was a problem. For the first time in fifteen years I was not working with students and colleagues. I had few social interactions. Although I did not pine for some aspects of life in the institutions in which I'd felt oppressed, I did miss others. I also felt a sense of being unused, almost a sense of waste at not employing skills and knowledge that had come to me during the long, complex, and sometimes painful struggle to be a teacher, a process that had occupied most of my adult life.

I suspect that I would have avoided a return to teaching if it had not been for the economic shock we felt when our family tried to switch, in an inflationary time, from two salaries to one. After a year, then, I began asking around about part-time teaching jobs, and I found some. I indulged myself in a secret sense of martyrdom, convinced that my return to the conventional classroom would be depressing and boring, dominated by the constraints associated with traditional structures. Since it wouldn't be the IDP, it wouldn't be good.

My negative expectations about these jobs were to some extent accurate. I didn't, for example, enjoy the experience of entering, in middle age, an academic system in which I was subject to the indignities of being at the very bottom of the professorial totem pole. In all my previous jobs I had been a high-status person in whatever local system I had worked within. The new indignities were even greater than those one suffers as a teaching graduate student, for the advanced student, unlike the middle-aged househusband working part time, is assumed to possess the possibility of a bright future. I also had to deal with some of the problems I'd anticipated about conventional course and classroom structures. Yet to my surprise and delight, the main impact on me of these part time teaching jobs was positive. I became involved again in an exploration of the possibilities of freedom in conventional structures, and found that they were more ample than I had allowed myself to believe. I found that much that I had learned during the IDP years was adaptable to the courses I was now teaching. I had expected a dreary chore, and I found myself truly engaged in work that I liked very much. Conventional structures were not the simple dead ends they had appeared to me to be while I was deeply involved in exploring alternate forms. These teaching experiences were therapeutic as well as instructive. Bitterness about the IDP left my heart more quickly.

The search for a decent education for my children was a bit harder, but we made progress there too. As I tried, therefore, to order and write about my ideas on educational freedom in innovative settings, events in my work and family were providing me with a new personal inquiry into the question of freedom in conventional structures. As the end of the work on my book drew closer, I felt more optimistic and less doctrinaire. In a period in which accepted educational rhetoric was becoming more conservative—"back to the basics" —I found myself gathering evidence, almost in opposition to an intellectual program that I'd followed for years, that things could be pretty good if one pursued educational freedom in regular classrooms. Some positive innovations did not require radical structural changes. I had earlier resigned myself to writing a book whose emotional weight would come down on the side of the problems of freedom. Instead I found myself with new reasons to talk about the promises.

It is probably best to begin with the search for educational freedom for my children in a new community. Unlike the parts of the story that deal with my life as a part-time teacher, these episodes are relatively untouched by my professional vanities, my reactions to institutional politics, and my responses to reentry into the system after a brief absence.

*

Our school system has a policy of allowing open classrooms, which it calls "informal" classrooms, in some circumstances. Our first experience with such a class was instructive, for it illustrated a point made earlier in the cases of several college professors, namely that valuing freedom doesn't create freedom. Certain knowledge and skills are required to make it all work.

The story concerns Josh, who was eight years old when we moved to Michigan. Josh's first teacher, whom we located after a careful search, extensive scheming, and the purchase of a house in the right neighborhood, was a young man, suitably long-haired and bearded, blue-jeaned and smiling. He sincerely believed in freedom for students. The atmosphere of his class was decent and open. The classroom was free of the most common oppressions and petty rules, the things that are often most annoying to children. One did not have to ask permission to do normal human things like go to the bathroom or get a drink of water. There was free movement around and between the two rooms occupied by the class. Things were quite comfortable and relaxed. The teacher worked hard to involve the kids in a variety of projects and activities. He liked his students, and he was good with them although, like most human beings, he seemed sometimes to feel like screaming in response to life among a few dozen children. (As a househusband, even though I had only two children, I knew how he felt and could not begrudge him a normal nervous system.)

This young teacher tried hard, but at some basic level his classroom didn't work. His projects were the sorts of thing that sounded good but that didn't truly engage the students. There were patterns to such projects and to the interpersonal dynamics that surrounded them, and they were familiar, for I'd seen them at many levels of education among teachers trying to be more responsive to students. The teacher would propose a project that sounded good, a groovy idea: let's write a play or make a movie or have a theme for everything we do next week. There was usually, however, a hidden agenda behind the project, and it arose from anxieties about freedom. These anxieties produced, in turn, various types of subtle coercion. Teacher, students, and parents were worried that "nothing" would happen in the class if there was too much freedom. There was concern floating around about whether the class was really "doing" something. (Peg Bracken's "Don't just do something, sit there!" is always good for a laugh, but people aren't easily persuaded of its wisdom.) The principal item on the hidden agenda was to look good.

The kids also liked the teacher, and there was a genuine inclination among them to give him the benefit of the doubt. Usually a group of students, or perhaps the whole class, would commit itself to the idea out of a mixture of interest, affection, and concern. The project, however, would rarely get off the ground. There is an enormous difference between assenting to a teacher's idea and finding that the idea is good enough to elicit time and energy willingly for its implementation. The teacher would be hurt and indignant, and there would be a fair amount of moralizing about living up to commitments and responsibilities. There was, of course, little analysis or understanding of the context in which commitments were made and how that context affected the ultimate behavior of the students. Projects would sometimes be carried to completion by a small group of kids, the ones who happened to be interested or, as was more often the case, were particularly responsive to pressure from the teacher. A major problem was that the teacher chose projects that were not terribly interesting to him. They were the sorts of thing that would look good to an observer. Although I'm not sure he knew it, he was driven to produce visible products testifying to the viability of this open classroom. But there was little depth or excitement in his engagement in the projects and therefore no possibility that he would communicate these to his students.

Freedom for students does not mean only acting on student interests. It may mean creating activities growing out of a teacher's interests and giving students the opportunity to join in. Students of all ages seem willing and often eager to become interested in a teacher's interests, but they are also particularly sensitive to fraud in this matter. If you, as a teacher, would like students to share your enthusiasm about something, it had better be a genuine enthusiasm. The sad fact about this young man was that he exhibited a genuine interest in open education, but if he was concerned with other things, he didn't let the world know about it. There was no intellectual contagion in this classroom because there was little in the air, or in the young man, to catch.

The teacher also lacked the ability to respond to the enthusiasms of his students. He didn't have the knack of picking up on their interests, extending them, and building upon them. Although the structure of the class, when the teacher was in one of his more permissive periods, formally valued the interests of students, there was little effective encouragement, guidance, or help. A commitment to freedom does not entail a belief that students of any age are completely equipped to produce their own educations. Teachers are needed, although not coercive ones. A teacher in an open classroom who has a total policy of passivity simply doesn't understand the complexity of the educational problem.

The situation is the same, though more complex and subtle, when one enters areas of life that are more value laden. There was meanness among the kids in this informal classroom, and Josh, as a newcomer, and also because of his temperament, was particularly vulnerable to it. He was often frightened and hurt, and he stayed home as often as I would let him. Interpersonal relationships in the classroom were obvious reflections of those in our neighborhood and families. There was only a small amount of intervention by a teacher that would have been appropriate or effective. Yet the young teacher seemed to me to be completely passive in this ethical sphere, as he was essentially in the intellectual sphere. It would have been wrong and unrealistic of me to expect the teacher to change the kids' behavior, to force values upon them, to solve Josh's problem. But I did want him to be a moral actor in the play, representing, as each child who was a member of the class did, some values other than a passive acceptance of the behavior of others.

The teacher himself, of course, was under a great deal of pressure. Parents, principal, and therefore students worried about academic achievement, although our neighborhood is upper middle class and dominated by university families, so most of the kids had no problems in that area. There was also pressure from other teachers, who found this class disruptive or simply offensive. I have no doubt that this young teacher was treated badly by his colleagues, in ways similar to those I had known. And being young and normal, I'm also sure that he had self-doubts and internal conflicts which added to the external pressures on him.

One way the teacher reacted to these pressures was to vacillate, and the most obvious realm in which he did so was that of scheduling activities and insisting upon commitments. When he felt strong and confident, he ran a rather relaxed class, assuming that there was value in the spontaneous activities that students defined for themselves during large blocks of free time. When he didn't feel quite so strong, he required students to plan their time in detail in relation to stated goals, whether or not these were felt as genuine goals. For some time the kids had to fill out a form each morning describing their goals and their schedules for achieving them. During these periods this open classroom, therefore, was more oppressive than a normal classroom in which the teacher provides the time structure for the day. In the conventional classroom there are dozens of little ways to subvert the structure and gain some psycho-logical, if not physical, space. One doesn't, in regular classrooms, have to pretend to have goals that one doesn't have. One simply follows instructions. Nor is one encouraged in feelings of guilt by a teacher who is generally sympathetic but who insists that one must live with false goals and schedules to achieve them. This teacher, like the college professors who try freedom but don't have the requisite skills and understanding and are unwilling to take the time to develop them, had a tendency to blame the students for his failures. Unlike many of the professors, however, this young man persists. He does a better job each year, and he may eventually create the kind of education he values.

Most poignant to me about this teacher's dilemma was his isolation, which I, of course, had also experienced. His ability to ask for or receive help and support was very limited, however, because he found it necessary to keep up appearances. Things were always great; if there were problems, he had just figured out the solutions. Never mind that the kids sometimes noticed him out in the hall with tears of sadness or frustration in his eyes. He had the painful and destructive arrogance of a very young man: willing to offer advice, unwill-ing to seek it, for that would amount to owning up to his partial failures.

Josh was in this man's class for two years. They weren't terrible years, since a modicum of freedom counts for a lot. Josh was, like most of the kids in the class, mildly bored. The teacher established some of the necessary conditions for real educational freedom. He removed many of the barriers. There were things he could not manage, however, things that need to be done once barriers are gone. Most of them depend on having a teacher who is intellectually alive and stimulating.

I walked Josh to school almost every day. Josh and the other kids moving through the street were generally high-spirited and energetic. They laughed, chattered, shouted, ran. There was a sense among them of being engaged in life. Sometimes I'd walk Josh to his classroom. In the school building I looked through the doors of classrooms. Kids took their seats, in most cases in rows facing the teacher. To my eyes it seemed as if the children had learned to turn off large parts of themselves, to hold themselves in abeyance, suspended animation, until recess. To me it felt heavy, dull, full of coercion, and extremely familiar from all the hours I'd spent in college classroom buildings. Josh's class was more relaxed, much better. The kids moved around, had some freedom to choose among activities and places. Yet although I have said that those years were not terrible for Josh, I always left that building feeling depressed and guilty. It *is* terrible to take a young human being who grows and learns naturally as he goes through the day—and I am not rhapsodizing, I am describing what I and other parents see if we bother to look—and unnecessarily limit for most of the day, in the name of education, his range of play and inquiry. Josh's response was to feel bad and read books. Since he was reading, nobody bothered him much. To read, and not to act out one's bad feelings disruptively, is a fine adaptation to school. At least it avoids big trouble. He was basically bored and living in a constraining and impoverished environment during school hours.

*

Toward the end of our second year in Ann Arbor, my wife began asking everyone she met about informal classrooms in the public school system. We heard about a few, collected gossip and rumor, and visited some classes. We found a teacher we thought would be good.

The story of freedom in Lovie Bradley's classroom has special significance because Lovie is a survivor. She intends to be around as a public school teacher for a long time. She will probably not burn out, for year in and year out she seems to have an inexhaustible supply of energy and good humor. She will definitely not be removed against her will.

Lovie is a middle-aged black woman, and it is fitting to mention her race at the outset because it was a major factor in her particular route to a commitment to freedom for students. Lovie's family moved to Detroit from Georgia when she was an adolescent. She attended segregated schools in both places, but found herself at an academic disadvantage when she entered the Detroit schools. She quickly rectified her deficiencies, but for a short while some of her teachers may have thought she was slow. Lovie also had an independent and defiant streak in her character. These factors combined to accentuate the routine stereotyping visited upon black children by teachers and counselors. Wherever she turned in the schools, Lovie met people in authority who discouraged her and suggested that she limit her ambitions and lower her sights. She vividly remembers seeing the words "not college material" inscribed on her records, and she remembers those words taking effect in the behavior of the teachers and advisers with whom she dealt.

Bright, energetic, determined, with deficiencies in her educational background, Lovie set out to overcome the disadvantages she faced. It is not necessary to recount the succession of schools and jobs that brought Lovie to her present work, although it is appropriate to mention that she worked in a prison where she had ample opportunity to observe the fate of people who fail, as she did not, to get out of their traps. Details aside, Lovie emerged with a deep belief, based on firsthand evidence, in the idea that an injustice is done to students when they are expected to learn according to someone else's schedule. She knew that she was capable of doing what was necessary if allowed to do it when she was ready. She also knew that her ambitions and sense of self had been placed in grave danger by the imposition of other people's ideas about when things had to be done. This is one source of Lovie's belief in educational freedom, and it is also the source in her of what may be a teacher's single most important personal quality in the implementation of educational freedom: patience. Observing Lovie and talking with her, one sees that she loves her students. One also gets the sense that she loves them not only for what they are, but for their secret hidden potentials, those people that they might become if they are given the freedom, stimulation, and time they need.

Lovie believes in freedom, and she has the skills, insights, and personal gifts to make it live and breathe in her classroom. She has a genuine, deep-seated respect for the interests of her students. It is not pro forma, not simulated or ideological in its origins. It is not manipulative or designed to extract from students a project that will look good to the outside world. She listens, watches, questions, learns. When Josh was in her class, the game Dungeons and Dragons was popular among the kids. She talked with them about the game and watched them play it. She came to understand the challenge and appeal of the game. She valued her students' involvement in it, and her understanding was put to good use in the classroom.

Lovie has interests of her own. Often they involve social problems and current events. She brings them into her classroom. Students aren't required to share Lovie's interests, but sometimes they do. It helps that Lovie is passionate and articulate about them. The intellectual environment in her classroom is lively and genuine. People do projects because the projects elicit enthusiasm and contain meaning. They aren't just nice ideas that may produce something that looks good to the outside world. The projects aren't the occasions for moralizing about living up to commitments; they are occasions for feeling and acting upon commitments.

Lovie and her students do not live in a world of their own. There is a school board, some of whose prominent members are university professors, whose ultimate goal is to install reading and math "systems" so that there will be a computer printout on someone's desk describing the exact progress of each of the city's students in each subject. Henry Ford is still the dominant intellectual force in our part of the world. There are also nervous parents and outraged colleagues. Lovie is honest and realistic about the constraints on her. She tells the students exactly what the externally imposed tasks are, and she finds ways that they can be done with the smallest hassle. But although Lovie is constrained in her ability to create a free learning environment, she does not vacillate. Her students do not get mixed signals from her, as they were constantly getting from Josh's previous teacher.

Lovie is quite sensitive to the quality of human relations in her classroom. She knows that educational freedom among children in a classroom is fragile, easily eroded by negativism and interpersonal coercion. She is skillful in intervening among the kids to clarify their interactions and discuss the consequences of their behavior. She knows the power and limitations of discussions among people who are in conflict. In all but the most extreme cases—physical violence or serious dishonesty—she will not try to coerce the kids into certain patterns of relationship. But Lovie *is* a force for fairness and psychological freedom in her classroom. Her groups avoid the tyranny of the aggressive and energetic that is so prevalent in badly realized open classrooms, a tyranny that is enhanced by a passive teacher.

Although things are generally harmonious in Lovie's classroom, she does have problems with colleagues from time to time. She violates the unspoken rule of teacher solidarity, and she is fearless and outspoken in defense of students against teachers who are unfair or mean of spirit. Although she is an active member, Lovie will publicly criticize the teachers' union when she thinks it is wrong.

Lovie also makes alliances that serve her well. She has a knack for creating a group of supporting adults, mainly parents. This goes a long way toward combating the loneliness and isolation that wear away at most innovative teachers. Lovie has guts; she'll take risks, and she'll go it alone when necessary. But she also knows that it's better to be fighting in the company of friends and supporters.

Lovie's gifts as a teacher are partly gifts of God or nature, partly things that can be learned. Wholly located in the former category, however, are two final qualities, among Lovie's most obvious: an enormous amount of energy and a capacity to enjoy life and find fun in it. It is hard to maintain a depression or a fit of boredom in Lovie's presence. To her classroom structures of freedom, Lovie brings intelligence, curiosity, high spirits, a capacity for fun, and a deep love of her students. These fill the open gaps, and Lovie emerges as a spectacularly successful practitioner of free education.

For the first time since Win Evers was his teacher at Cause School in Buffalo, Josh enjoyed school. He saw that problems, when they arose, would be solved. He found that his interests and, more basically, his unique personality, would be respected. At bottom, I think, he came to know that there was someone in school at his side who would push to the limits on his behalf.

When the behavior of more restrictive teachers or the racist positions of the school board get her down, Lovie sometimes talks of forming a small school of her own with a few sympathetic families. It seems to me, however, that she is not really serious. The strange challenge of creating freedom within existing institutions seems right for Lovie. It engages her fully, and she is brilliantly suited to it. She hardly ever makes a wrong move.

I wrote this chapter in the weeks immediately following the school year that Josh spent in Lovie's class. The Little League baseball season had begun, and Josh was on a team with some of his classmates. A story, possibly apocryphal but with the ring of truth, circulated among the parents of these kids as they sat on the sidelines watching the baseball game. Its substance was that, after a long and exhausting school year, Lovie was seen leaving the school on the final day of the year with tears in her eyes.

32

An Introduction to This Course: A Talk to Students on the First Day of Classes

> *We had learned from Canopus that argument does not teach children, or the immature. Only time and experience does that.*
>
> *—Doris Lessing*

When a class meets for the first time, you expect a professor to introduce the course to you. He or she will present a general definition of the subject matter and then talk about books, articles, schedules, and requirements. Finally the instructor will tell you about grading in the course. That is when full attention is given. It is also when probing occurs and the strategic questions are asked: "How many pages do the papers have to be?" "Do the exams cover only the material assigned since the previous exam, or do they cover all the materials from the beginning of the semester?" "Does class attendance count?" Etc. In general it is a time when students try to take the true measure of a teacher. Are the professor and the grading system fair? Is the teacher organized, honest, and clear, or is the system likely to be changed halfway through the course, leaving students off balance and awash in wasted effort? Can this instructor be trusted? How devious do I have to be in this course? Educators who write articles or give seminars about teaching always recognize these crucial dynamics between teacher and student. They repeat over and over to each other, "Be clear about your expectations," as if clear expectations, especially an explicit grading system, will somehow solve all educational problems, as if expecting is teaching.

When a teacher talks about grades in a class, there is electricity in the air. The students strain to understand each nuance; the teacher strains for maximum clarity. This common experience stands for me as a concrete symbol for much of what happens between students and teachers and of much that is wrong in education. Students undertake a complex set of maneuvers, first of all to establish the real nature of the grading system in a course and then to get the best deal out of the system that is possible. Getting the best deal means getting the highest grade for the smallest amount of work. The teacher devotes a great deal of energy to being fair and to resisting the manipulations of students. An economic analogy is, I think, fairly accurate: The teacher is the boss; the student is the worker; learning, appearing to learn, or performing a set of specified tasks alleged to be related to learning, is the work; grades are the money. The teacher's main function is to be sure that the money is paid out only when the work is done.

I reject this system because, although it effectively encourages obedience and the appearance of learning, I don't think it is a good way to encourage real learning. And even if this system produces some learning, it also involves the kind of relationships among people that I don't wish to have with you. Over the years I have found that I teach best and that my students learn most when we are not adversaries in a game of manipulation, deception, and eternal vigilance. I want to be on your side. I don't want you to be tempted to try to fool me in order to gain an advantage and get a higher grade. I don't want always to be on the alert to catch you. I don't want you to be scared of me. I don't think I will be the best teacher or you the best student if a gulf of grade-related power exists between us. I therefore abandon that power. I will not grade you. At the end of the semester I will ask you to write your grade on a piece of paper, and I will copy it on the form that I submit to the registrar.

If my past experience is a guide, you will have many questions about this way of doing things. There are also some predictable problems and dangers in structuring a course in this fashion. I'd like to try now to anticipate some of your questions, talk with you about some of the problems that are likely to arise, and share some initial ideas on how we might try to solve them.

First of all some of you probably don't believe me. Not only does this way of grading seem peculiar, but you may well have had other instructors who said that they would back away from conventional ways of grading. Such teachers often have little tricks or loopholes in their arrangements that serve to maintain the power over you that they say they are giving up. Some liberal changes actually turn out to be more stringent than the ordinary grading system, for they often depend upon making you feel guilty, and then in the end the teacher exercises the power that has not been abandoned but has only been disguised behind a smile. During the next few weeks some of you will ask me many questions and pose hypothetical cases to me to see if I'm serious. You'll find that I am serious about not grading even in the face of preposterous possibilities. Some of you may not believe me to the end, and you will follow a conservative course, essentially pursuing requirements you think I would have imposed had I done things in a more conventional way. But you will probably realize, after a while, that such contortions and attempts at mind reading are not necessary.

Besides setting the stage for a less troubled relationship between us, my act of giving up power over you has another important consequence. I will not, indeed under these circumstances I could not, force a syllabus or course of study upon you. In this course, therefore, there are no requirements, tests, assigned papers, materials to be covered. There will be activities in class, but you are not forced to come to class. Required activities are absent not because I think books and articles and term papers are unproductive, but because I believe you'll learn more if you come to such activities for your own reasons. I am not, you may be sure, opposed to reading and writing. I spend large portions of my time engaged in both those activities. I believe it is important to know about the world and about the things people have thought and learned. These are contained in books, and you must read them in order to become better educated. I don't assign books to you because I think such explorations are most productively pursued when they arise freely from your interests or ambitions, or simply from plain old spontaneous curiosity. I also spend a lot of time writing, and I find it an invaluable activity for communicating to other people and clarifying my own thought. I would probably not be as enthusiastic about writing, however, if someone forced me to do it.

The question that almost all of you will ask, directly or indirectly, will be "What am I supposed to do for this class?" You may ask it out of suspicion, wondering whether I, like some other liberal teachers, have really reserved some element of my power in order to clobber you if you don't do what I want you to do. More often, however, you will ask it sincerely, because you will want to do the right thing, and the absence of requirements seems bewildering. What are you supposed to do for this class? It seems like a proper and simple question to ask, and it seems to deserve a clear and simple answer. But I have trouble answering it. On one level it has no answer. There is nothing, no one particular concrete thing, that you're supposed to do. There is no reading list to follow or term paper to write or exam to prepare for. On another level what you are "supposed to do" is answer that question for yourself. This suggests the larger task I hope each of you will begin to work on immediately. Examine your life. Locate an area in which important learning might take place for you. Then, with my help and perhaps with the help of other members of the class, or simply on your own, begin to work on it.

By not assigning tasks to you and by not enforcing the performance of assignments by means of a grading system, I intend to create in this class a certain sort of educational freedom. Since it is real freedom, you may use it in any way that is appropriate for you, and you also may choose not to use it at all, although I must admit that it will sadden me if you make that choice, and some of you will.

The challenge, then, is to learn something, work on something that is important. What is important? I don't know for you. You may or may not know for you. If you don't know, then you should try to find out, and this class is an opportunity to work on that task. I have taught classes like this before, and these prior experiences may allow me to provide you with some help.

I have a suggestion. It's only a suggestion, not a requirement. (Someone once said that if God had been a liberal educator, the Ten Commandments would have been the Ten Suggestions.) Take some time at the beginning of this course to look carefully at your life, to reflect upon your past, present, and future. Do you want, in some way or other, to be a different type of person? Are there areas in which you want to be more knowledgeable, skillful, competent? Are there ambitions you would like to achieve? Perhaps this course is a time and place to work on those areas. There are other questions: What are you interested in or curious about? Are there topics or skills that you've always wanted to pursue more aggressively but have lacked the time or resources or courage? Are there things that have touched or intrigued you that you did not or could not probe further? Answers to these questions may be the beginnings of an answer to the question of what you're supposed to do in this class. We'll come back to this subject in a few minutes. Let's talk for a while about another obvious question.

What are we going to do together in class? That's another good simple question, and it's easier for me to answer. In the process I may shed a little light on the matter of your personal work in the course. Basically we'll do two things in class. I will share with you, and you will share with the rest of us. I will come to class prepared to talk to you about things that interest me and are important to me. I will try to engage you in discussions of these matters, and I may also initiate activities connected with them, sometimes even games that involve their players in certain subject matters. In doing these things I will be sharing with you the results of my own participation in the process that I have just recommended to you. I will begin, have already begun, by examining my life and world just as I hope you will. Then I will select ideas, books, films, news, information, questions, and activities that I want to share with you. Some of these things will inevitably reflect my past experience as an academic person, as a professor and graduate student. Some of them will not be particularly related to my discipline. They may arise from other parts of my life.

When I come to class with things from my world, it will be with the hope that they will become interesting, even exciting to you. That is what sharing is all about, and it is one of the great rewards of being a teacher. But I know that this will happen only part of the time. My interests will not always become yours, sometimes because I have not presented my material well, sometimes simply because we are different people, come from different worlds, lead different lives, have different tastes.

There may be times when you respond to my presentations in class in ways that I think are inappropriate. I will talk about a book or idea or problem, and you will think to yourself, "Oh, *this* is what we're supposed to do in this class." You'll decide to read the book I discussed or do research in the library on the topic I explored. My reaction to such a decision may be confused and confusing. If I have really stimulated you or gotten you interested in something new, I will be delighted. If it seems to me that you're pursuing my interests as a way of avoiding a search for your own, I will be disappointed. I will ask you questions, probe, and prod you to examine your motives and reactions. You are, of course, free to follow my interests automatically, just as if I had assigned them to you. There is no way that you can be punished for doing so, and such behavior will only rarely lead you to more harm than some wasted time. It would seem to me, however, that to follow such a course of action would be to squander an opportunity to do something more central to your own life.

Students or colleagues sometimes tell me, when I organize a class in this way, that I am being lazy and irresponsible. I am laying extra burdens upon you, the burdens of grading and of deciding what to do in the course. I also seem to be abandoning a teacher's critical function. I seem to be saying that anything goes, whereas a teacher's basic job is to say that anything does not go.

Here are my responses: I am indeed laying extra burdens on you, but I feel that I have good reasons to do so. You will grade yourself, because I've found that grading in the conventional way will hopelessly contaminate the relationship between us, a relationship that is more important to me than anything else. Some of you will agonize over the grade, and some of you won't. All I can do is apologize if it is a big problem for you and explain that my reasons involve what I believe to be central educational principles. I think that we will collectively profit from the arrangement in the end. I have weighed advantages against disadvantages and made my decision.

Giving you the burden of deciding upon your own studies is also the result of another important principle. And here, from my perspective, we're getting down to significant questions. I am most interested in autonomous, self-directed learning as opposed to learning that arises from following another person's instructions. If you make only small progress toward being an independent learner, I believe you will have accomplished something more important than you would have if you absorbed a great bulk of information by following a teacher's orders, even if I happened to have been that teacher. I want to be involved in a process in which people develop their abilities to function freely, not a process in which they exercise their capacities to be obedient. This is a question of basic educational philosophy. My actions spring, I believe, from a kind of responsibility to principle, not from irresponsibility. Nor do I think, or should you, that it is easy or politically advantageous to teach a course in this fashion. If you doubt this, consider what you know of the faculty and administration of this institution. Imagine how they will respond to a class like this. Imagine what they will think of me. I am not taking the easy road to success and advancement. I may be gone from here before too long. I'm not asking for your sympathy or support. I'm simply explaining and trying to be clear about what I'm doing, my motives and what the consequences might be.

On the question of laziness, I simply invite you to examine my work in this course. I will be well prepared to do my part in each class. I will work hard in class. When there is a chance to be of assistance to you, either in the search for a definition of your work or in its actual implementation, I will spare no time or effort to help. You may be surprised at the strength of this commitment. You, however, must be the one to initiate our interactions. You must invite me to help. I will not pursue you or force my assistance upon you. You are free not to relate to me, not to be bothered by my help. Only if you have that freedom, I believe, will our encounters be genuine. I will not, therefore, set up a schedule of required conferences or anything of the sort, but I will be available to you and very happy to see you.

When I say these things, people sometimes respond that I am trying to do something impossible. They say, "You are trying to create a relationship of equality between us, but we can never be equal. You are the professor. You are better educated than we are. You will inevitably be judging us, no matter how hard you try not to."

I do not, however, claim that we are all the same. All I claim is that, by eliminating a particularly important difference in power between us, I can improve our relationship. I do have more of certain types of knowledge and experience than you, and these are often especially important to the kinds of things that happen in a classroom. You may have superior knowledge and skill in other areas. I do not say we are the same. Thank God we are not the same.

I will definitely criticize and judge you, if I am moved to do so and if these behaviors seem useful and appropriate to me. I assume you will return the compliment. Since I will not grade you, I feel a paradoxical increase in my freedom to be critical and evaluative. I can speak my mind without fear that you will feel that I may punish you unfairly with a low grade. Since you are free to reject my criticisms without immediate practical damage being done to you, I feel free to be completely honest and candid, without worrying that I might misuse my power. I will judge, criticize, and evaluate to my heart's content, and like free adults, you will be able to decide whether my comments are useful to you.

This question of misuse of power is related to another issue that is probably bothering many of you, even if you can accept most of what I've said so far. It is the issue of fairness. Is it fair that one of you might give yourself an A while another of you gives yourself a B for the same amount of work? Or is it fair that students in this class might get unearned high grades while students in another class must struggle and sweat for their grades? No, it's not fair, and I'm sincerely sorry that this sort of fairness gets sacrificed in my system. Fairness and learning do not, however, have a great deal to do with one another. Sometimes they are antithetical. It is my experience that students and teachers in ordinary classes get obsessed with fairness and grades, and that learning, good education, is sacrificed. I feel that I am forced to choose between fairness and learning, and so I choose learning.

I have, by way of introduction, things to say about two more subjects: sharing in class and defining your work. I believe I've had enough experience to predict some developments in both these areas, and I'd like to tell you about them before you ask questions and we move on to an open discussion.

First the question of sharing in class. When you are to be graded, it is almost inevitable that the class focuses on the instructor. This gives him or her a lot of influence over the minute-by-minute development of the discussion. Even, for example, when a student is assigned to run the class, a great deal of attention will be given to the teacher's response. Is the student doing well, doing what the teacher wants, earning a nice fat juicy grade? The teacher's judgment, in the end, will either harm or help you, so it is only smart to be as attentive and careful as possible, to follow the teacher's lead in class, for there is the danger that you will be punished if you don't. Now I believe that I have things to teach you, and I hope you will be simply fascinated when I speak. I also believe that the class collectively has more to teach one another than I have to teach all of you. This may seem to you an unrealistic and romantic statement. I think it is hardheaded and accurate, derived from a considerable amount of experience in education. When I enter a new group like this one, I have learned to have a sense of anticipation and wonder, feelings that I did not have, by the way, when I started out as a young teacher. Although I don't know the details yet, I know that there is great diversity and depth to the skills, knowledge, and life experience you possess. Those things will emerge and become public among us as we go along. I am almost certain that there will be wonderful surprises. I hope that my decision not to give grades, along with the various gimmicks I will use in our class sessions, will help us to focus on the entire group as a learning resource. There will be many times that I encourage you to share your work and your reactions to other people's work. You are free, of course, to pursue your work in private without arranging to share it with the class. Such might be your simple personal preference, or that decision might arise from other considerations. Yet if you do take the opportunity to share, your work will almost inevitably be more productive and other people will learn from you. If you are undecided as to whether to go public with your thoughts and work, I will push you to do so.

This talk about sharing reminds me of previous classes that have been organized like this, and it suggests an important warning. The dynamics of a class change when the normal rules are altered. There are new problems and new opportunities. The new rules are obvious. There is no need for you to worry about being harmed by anything you say in class, at least in terms of a grade. Also, my own program for the contents of the class is only partial. I plan to do various things in class, but I don't have a complete schedule or syllabus for the way we should use our time. I expect the definition of the class to be completed by your interests and personalities. This part of the definition will take some time to emerge. But more is involved than time. An unfamiliar process will occur among us, and it may at times be a bit wild and chaotic. It will undoubtedly be particularly frustrating to some of you.

Early in the semester especially, there will be many times when our directions in class are unclear. One person will speak, and the conversation will go one way. Another person will speak, and the drift of the discussion will be in another direction. There will be dead ends and exchanges that seem pointless. There will be times when you get angry at me for not avoiding these problems and steering the class in more productive directions. You may well be tempted to say, "I'm not spending all this valuable time and money to listen to bullshit coming from all these people, who know no more than I do." Or, "You are, as an instructor, acting irresponsibly when you fail to control the class." Or "Aren't you supposed to set some clear-cut goals for the class and then show us how to achieve them?" Or simply "You're the teacher, why don't you teach?" The frustrations reflected in these questions will arise from the undisciplined character of our discussions.

The challenge of our classes will be to create discipline of our own. At first there will be a vacuum created by my decision not to provide a complete agenda and make sure that we stick to it. The usual teacher-supplied discipline will be absent. The discipline that will arise to fill the vacuum will be an assertion of this group's character. It will take time to develop. If there is widespread participation among us, an implicit compromise combining our various interests and styles will be worked out. No individual or small group need necessarily dominate the class, and nobody need be bored, although these things may happen. A collective definition of our goals may emerge and also a respectful process by which we exploit the experience, knowledge, and even the wisdom that you bring to the class. All of this may or may not happen.

It is more likely to happen if we have widespread participation and if, occasionally, we stop to talk about how things are going. When you feel that things are going badly in our class, I plead with you not to withdraw in anger or frustration. If you respond in that way, you allow things to continue in directions that are dissatisfying to you. If you intervene, express your opinion or your feelings, things will usually not change immediately. But there will be a cumulative effect. I believe that in the end you will be able to see the benefits of your participation. If you give this process a chance, I think you will come to feel that you've made an important contribution to the class.

To repeat, it *is* possible for a group to develop its own forms of discipline and self-control. I've seen it happen, and it will happen, in some form or other, in this room. The new discipline will be better and more productive to the extent that it derives from wide participation. I ask you to give the process the benefit of the doubt. Participate in it. My last comment on this matter will be in the form of a promise, a promise I think I can keep with your help. Look around the room now and see how it feels to be here. We are a group of strangers. We don't feel particularly knowledgeable about or connected to each other. We don't really know whether there is much we have to offer to each other. I promise that, at the end of this course, it will feel quite different and a lot better to look around this room. You will see people with whom you have laughed, argued, shared, become angry. We will have come to appreciate each other, and we will have learned from each other. It will feel wonderful. I am not certain about this, but I know that it can happen. It is mainly for the sake of this possibility that I am structuring the class as I do.

And now I'll conclude by making a series of comments, not about our work together in class meetings but about your work alone.

I have not provided you with the curricular guides you have come to expect. In similar circumstances in the past I have found that students have tried focusing on the title of the course to see if it could provide answers to the question "What am I supposed to do?" I don't think this is particularly productive, and I urge you to avoid the temptation. If I could, I would give this as a course with no name. Each of you might supply your own course title. The fact that there is a phrase of a few words associated with the course should not be allowed to short-circuit a process of self-examination and self-education.

A more serious potential difficulty is the tendency of students to settle upon a premature solution to a tough and unusual problem. When given freedom in the definition of an educational task, it is tempting to grasp at the first or second idea that comes along. The idea is often plausible. It may even be a little out of the ordinary, which gives one the feeling of being involved in a significant use of educational freedom, but it may be close enough to the regular curriculum to feel reasonably safe. By prematurely committing yourself to a concept of your work in this course, you may avoid the bothersome initial process of self-examination and reflection. You will enjoy the envy and admiration of other people in the class who are having trouble deciding on their own work. But if the commitment is really premature, you will pay in the end. The end is the process of implementation. Working as a student who is not told what to do will, for many of you, be quite difficult. In order to have your best chances of success in the face of predictable difficulties, you must be working on something that is inherently important to you. Don't settle for less. It may take a little time to decide on a course of action. The time will be well spent.

Even if you work in an area that is terribly important to you, there will be problems. You will have unforeseen obstacles to overcome. These may be poor work habits, lack of discipline, unavailability of resources, lack of confidence in yourself, inadequate academic skills, insufficient background in a subject, etc. Each of these things is an opportunity as well as an obstacle. Confronting each of them can produce learning. Whenever you deal successfully with one of these problems, you have increased your ability to learn on your own. There are dozens of such problems, and I have found that there is one factor that is critically important in determining whether you will deal with them well. If you are able to ask for help, you are decreasing the odds against completing a task that is, to begin with, difficult enough. If you can't ask for help, you're probably in trouble.

Many people do not find it easy to ask for help. We feel that we are supposed to be rugged individualists, completely self-sufficient. It sometimes appears to us that we admit a shameful inadequacy when we ask for help. The simple act of seeking assistance, however, sometimes itself helps solve a problem, for it causes one to organize and clarify the situation, and it summons up some new emotional energy. Even if this doesn't happen, people come at problems from different starting points of knowledge, style, and experience. A formidable problem for me may be a trivial one for you, and so when we ask for help, we put ourselves in a position to profit from these differences among us. Ask for help. There are always a million reasons not to do so, and they are usually terrible traps.

I am quite sure that the reasons for all of this have become evident to you. People often have hidden agendas. Mine is this: I want you, as students and as people, to make progress toward greater independence and autonomy. I want you to learn how to learn. I want you to identify things that are important for you to know, and then I want you to figure out how to learn them. These skills—they are emotional skills as well as academic ones—are more important than any particular subject matter I or anybody else could teach you. I see only one way to accomplish the task. That is simply to get on with it. I get on with it by granting you freedom within this small domain, showing you how I do it, trying to demonstrate that I care about you and am willing to work alongside you. When I first started to talk, you might have thought that this was all going to be an easy exercise. By now it may seem to you, as it does to me, quite difficult. I think that it is worth the effort.

33

Fourteen Men

The class met one morning each week during the summer quarter. There were fourteen men and no women. They were attending Wayne State University's Weekend College, an adult degree program. Most of the students were Vietnam veterans using their government benefits to go to college. A few were sponsored by their unions or the companies that employed them. The Weekend College possessed an elaborate educational rhetoric about the special qualities of older students and the innovative programs to be provided for them. The rhetoric was belied by spectacularly conventional programs and faculty. In essence the Weekend College was a fiendishly clever educational innovation designed to transfer funds from the Veteran's Administration to the coffers of Wayne State University with the least possible trouble to the parties involved. The ease of the transfer was the occasion of more than one lawsuit against the university challenging its interpretation of VA regulations. The students collaborated because they had traditional hopes that a college degree might do them some good and also because they, like the university, received a monthly stipend that involved little exertion.

The class met in a large seminar room on an upper floor of an office building that had been taken over by the university. The weather was hot, and the men wore sports clothes. They worked afternoon or night shifts. Some of them left class to go directly to work. Others came to class after working all night, having had a chance to catch an hour or two of sleep at most.

At our initial class meeting, I gave the current version of my first-day talk about educational freedom and grades. It was received with the usual mixture of enthusiasm and skepticism. Since we had three-hour class meetings, there was plenty of time left after we had completed a thorough discussion of the way the class was to be structured. I had decided to use a gimmick I had learned in sensitivity training. I gave each person a large piece of paper and asked him to draw a picture of himself in his world. Deflecting further questions, I deliberately left the task vague and open to a variety of interpretations.

After about fifteen minutes I asked for a volunteer to show and explain his picture, and one person hesitatingly agreed. Once we got started, there was no further reluctance. Although this does not always happen, in this class there were many people who wished to talk about themselves and show their pictures. It became quite an interesting session.

Most of the pictures were dominated by a workplace, usually portrayed as oppressive. Dollar signs appeared in a few. Forced to work at jobs that were difficult and unpleasant, the men filled the rest of their pictures with their children, wives, houses, sports and other recreations, automobiles, and sometimes hedonistically appointed vans. Some of the men, married, or unmarried, had pictures of several women on their papers. A few depicted their unions as important factors in their lives.

As a man described his picture he might well be interrupted by questions. This was a talkative group. One man, for example, was a deer hunter. "Do you eat the animal, or do you kill only for the sport?" another man asked, and there was clearly an emotional debate placed on the agenda. They asked each other about their jobs, their positions in their unions, their places of employment. They discussed neighborhoods, home improvements, cars, vans, bars, nightclubs, and experiences in the military.

About half the class was black. Some of the whites were "ethnics," men of Polish or Italian ancestry, conservative in their social and political views. There was a radical union activist in the class, an insurgent engaged in starting a plant newspaper opposed to the current union leadership. Before the first class was over, also, cynics and idealists, hustlers and solid citizens, had shown themselves.

There was a moment in that first class that was particularly important to me. I had talked about the picture I drew to reflect my own life. It involved not having a full-time job, trying to be a writer, caring for my children, and my wife's employment as a scientist at the university. My place in our culture was fairly well defined and quite different from that of most of the other people in the room. I had an exchange with one of the men; it was probably about feminism and women's liberation, although I don't remember that clearly. Certainly it was prompted by the fact that my wife was then the family's main wage earner. He was one of the more conservative men in the class, a skilled tradesman, a person who presented himself, probably accurately, as a hard worker who had pulled himself up by his bootstraps. He spoke well, but I felt that he was holding back a fair amount and was hostile toward me. I looked at him and tried to figure out what was going on between us. I played a hunch and said, "You think that I've never put in an honest day's work in my life. If I had to put my muscle and sweat into earning my living, you think, I might not be so liberal and idealistic. Is that what you left unstated in the exchange we just had?" The young man laughed and allowed that my mind reading was essentially correct. I said that I may never have worked as hard in a single day as he did each day and that he would come to see that I respected his skills and experiences, which were so different from mine. I said I intended to conduct the class so that I and others might learn from such a body of experience. I added that it would strike me as intellectually dishonest for him to dismiss my views because I didn't have his type of job, just as it would be wrong for me to discount his statements because he had not attended graduate school. I felt that we had had an important dialogue, that it was useful to recognize in an explicit fashion the cultural, educational, and class differences between the students and me. My hope was that these differences would be the source of richness and complexity rather than barriers.

As I drove home from the first class meeting, I felt that I was in luck. The interpersonal chemistry of that class seemed special. An unusual number of people had spoken freely and intelligently. There did not seem to be anyone who would cause problems by dominating discussions or acting out personal problems in class. There was an interesting diversity of people who professed a wide range of values. And although there had been a bit of arguing in the first class, and it was sometimes strongly felt, there had been little irrationality and anger. The exchanges had seemed honest, with antagonists listening to and answering each other with some clarity and sense of dialogue.

My plan for the three-hour class meetings was to break the ice and get some external stimulation into the system by playing a social science simulation game for the first hour of each session at the beginning of the term. The simulated society involved jobs, money, communication, minority groups, unions, and political parties, and I thought it would be amusing and involving. The rest of the time would be spent in discussions of the game, of topics I introduced, and of subjects that arose in the contributions of students.

As it turned out, I liked this class better than any I'd ever had. It was a group of people that happened to work well together. The class was lively and serious. We often had fun, but we also had heavy moments in which we touched difficult thoughts and feelings. In the following pages I offer some anecdotes from this class as examples of things that can happen in a rather open classroom. I do not argue for them as proof positive of my abilities as a teacher or of the total correctness of a philosophy of freedom, for in other classes I have done the same sorts of things in pursuit of the same ideals with results that were much less satisfactory to me. Yet as long as one does not ignore failures, it is useful, it seems to me, to examine one's successes carefully, for they demonstrate the potential inherent in methods and structures. Potential is that to which we must cling. Every structure can fail, every game can be lost. It is interesting to know, however, what the prize will be if one happens to be successful.

DAVID

David approached his participation in the class with a strange mixture of openness and caution. He was the only person who had played the simulation game previously, so he understood some of its characteristics long before the rest of us. This was something he didn't reveal until close to the end of the term when the game was over. However he made only marginal use of his knowledge of the game. In talking about his war experiences, David told of being wounded in Vietnam, shot in the arm. He was shot because he'd been high on drugs and did some careless and reckless shooting of his own (at animals) and unnecessarily drew enemy fire. David told other tales of a rather wild youth. He seemed like a person who could be dangerous. I was, because of his own stories, suspicious of him, wondering whether he could be trusted. But the evidence provided by his own statements in class, and even more so by his general manner, indicated that he was being absolutely open and truthful with me and the others. Although his actions may sometimes have been flamboyant, his way of speaking had a calm eloquence. He spoke softly and directly, and he appeared to be able to say precisely what he meant. It was beautiful to listen to him.

Toward the end of our second or third class, we were going through a period in which the discussion languished. No particular topic caught on. I asked whether there was anyone in the class who had something on his mind that he'd like to talk about.

David began to speak. He was black, and he worked in the security department of a utility company in Detroit. He was hired with five other black people as part of an affirmative action program to integrate the security force. David had a wife and two young children. He owned a house. He was concerned to provide well for his family, and he wanted to accumulate enough money to be able to return to Alabama where part of his family still lived. He had come up North for a better job, but he now felt that he'd be happier in the South. David had good reason, therefore, to be ambitious for job advancement and a higher salary. Even without the stimulus of concrete goals that required money for their achievement, he was probably ambitious by nature. David routinely applied for promotions and for better paying assignments; for example, he wished to transfer to a new nuclear facility where security guards were paid more. He complained that he was constantly facing racial discrimination in his attempts to get better jobs.

Some of the white men in the class began to question David. Although their questions were respectful, they clearly doubted that David was facing discrimination. Their questions were designed to determine whether David was using his race as an alibi to explain his failures to get promotions or transfers that simply weren't deserved. One man, Terry, was particularly skeptical. Working in the automobile industry in a skilled trade, he believed himself to be surrounded by blacks and women who were being favored for positions they did not earn and were not qualified for. Terry doubted the existence of any racial discrimination in the workplace, except for discrimination against white men like himself.

I began to get nervous about where this discussion might lead. Instead of growing angry, however, the exchange actually became gentle without losing its directness. I think David was relieved to hear Terry say what he actually thought. David smiled and began to tell more of his story. Terry, although convinced of the position to which his experience had led him, was willing to listen and reconsider.

The five other blacks hired with David no longer worked for the company. David told the story of each one, and he made a plausible case for the idea that the bosses in the security department had manipulated the situation to make them vulnerable to dismissal. David told of occasions in which he thought he had been set up but which he had survived by good luck and cleverness.

David said that he had become acquainted with a black woman in the company's personnel office and that she gave him important information. The most dramatic example was an incident in which a guard from a private security agency had been hired and put under David's supervision, ostensibly to perform a particular patrol function. In fact the man had been hired to spy on David, and David had obtained copies of the reports submitted by the man. On another occasion the results of a psychological test, not routinely administered to other applicants, were used to deny a promotion to David. The company backed down when David asked to have the test results interpreted by an independent psychologist. David had many other such stories.

Almost everyone in the class came to believe David's version of events, but he was asked some hard questions by Terry and others. The possibility that David was paranoid and obsessed by race was rather rigorously tested by those questions. I feel certain that Terry, like many members of the class, modified his views on race somewhat, although he was not a person who readily admitted to changing his mind.

At each class David talked for at least a few minutes about what was happening at work or in court, for he had filed a lawsuit against the company. If he didn't volunteer, I would usually turn to him and ask him if he wanted to talk about his situation, and he always did. Sometimes his stories were the occasion for an extensive discussion, and sometimes they weren't.

During the last class meeting of the course I asked David whether there was anything he wanted to say. Tears came to his eyes. After class I wrote down what he said as best I could remember it. This is fairly close to his exact words:

> It's hard for me to keep fighting. It was pretty bad this summer. Some days I couldn't face it. I'd take a vacation day and just stay home. All I felt like doing was crying. Every Wednesday morning I would come here and talk about what was happening. I knew that you guys were interested and that you cared about what happened to me. I don't know whether I would have been able to make it through these weeks without you. Thank you.

ROBERT

Robert was usually disruptive. He could not or did not care to follow arguments closely. He felt strongly about many things and would often express his feelings when something in the discussion, germane or not, brought them to mind. His comments were usually irrelevant to the thrust of the discussion.

Other members of the class would let him finish and get back to the topic as if he hadn't spoken.

Robert felt beleaguered in this world. He said that he worked hard at his job but was never promoted because he didn't have the right connections. He was the poor working stiff who never got a break. He described himself as having been wild when he was younger: often drunk, a brawler, a troublemaker. He had been in jail, and he told of some of his prison experiences during a class discussion. On another occasion he made passing reference to having a brain-damaged child in his family. During a break in class I asked Robert about his son. He talked willingly about him, and I asked him whether he'd say some of the same things to the class.

When the class reconvened, I said that I'd asked Robert to talk about his son. Robert began by saying that a few years earlier he would have been unable to do so in public. He'd been ashamed of having a brain-damaged and retarded child. He'd cut off his relationship with many friends, and he and his wife had associated almost exclusively with other parents of handicapped children, people they met through various programs and social agencies. But mainly they were isolated. This had recently changed for him. He and his wife had begun making friends again. In a way he was eager to extend this development in his life by speaking to the class. It was practice in not being ashamed.

Robert said that the doctor who delivered his son suggested withholding treatment and letting the baby die. Robert said he never considered that option and did not regret his instinct: "This was my flesh and blood. I could not let him die." Robert had grown up in a religious environment, and for years he believed that his child's handicap was God's punishment for an immoral life. This was only one source of his shame and guilt. He described these emotions, along with a sense of persecution and self-pity, in detail. Although Robert did not have a gift for argument or logic, he did have a talent for the powerful and clear description of his inner life. Shortly after he began to speak, the class fell into one of those total and electric silences, and it lasted for as long as he continued. After a while, other members of the class began to ask questions. They were good questions, the sorts of things one wonders about but has always been afraid to ask. They were asked with respect, for it had become immediately clear that Robert, who until now had been mainly a source of annoyance, was someone from whom a person could learn.

Robert described the evolution of his own feelings toward his son. He talked about the experience of watching the child's limited development. He talked about his love for his son, his heartbreak at the boy's limitations, the joy of watching small increments of growth, his feelings of valuing his son despite the boy's handicaps, the problems that arose in this relationship with his wife. He spoke also of his anger at the boy and his resentment of the burdens that had been added to his life. He was most eloquent, and most angry, as he described the way outsiders, people who were not members of the family, behaved toward the boy. Their actions, Robert said, denied the child's humanity, and he hated people for it. Robert probably always had a chip on his shoulder, but since this boy's birth, he had good reasons for his anger. And the chip was now gigantic.

Robert's descriptions of the reactions of ordinary people to a retarded child—mainly fear and repulsion—had enormous power for members of the class. In spite of Robert's vehemence and anger, people in the class began owning up to such feelings about retarded and handicapped people. They tried to understand and explain why they had reacted so negatively to such people, and they said that they were beginning to see the cruelty and wrongness of their responses. Robert came down on them hard. He wasn't interested in understanding their feelings, for he was too immersed in the pain on the other side. Nobody really minded his attacks. The nature of his ordeal was too clear to the rest of us, and there was too much to be learned to allow oneself to be drawn into a fight with Robert. Members of the class conjured up memories of their experiences and feelings involving retarded people. Robert told dozens of stories about his son.

Robert's current stance in relation to the world, which was consistent with the pugnacious streak in his personality, was to be maximally aggressive in his advocacy of his son's right to access to normal experiences: Boy Scouts, Sunday school, movie theaters, skating rinks, supermarkets, etc. His son was sometimes disruptive, but Robert believed that special considerations were appropriate. He confronted people with their lack of thoughtfulness or understanding. He was a terror. At some point he had decided that he would not collaborate in the denial of advantages and experiences to his son.

Robert had traveled a painful and difficult road, and there was a long way to go. Most of us in the classroom would probably not have adopted his strategy for dealing with the outside world, yet its integrity, a kind of purity, was visible to us all, and we admired Robert for his strength, clarity, energy, and commitment.

The discussion continued for almost two hours, never losing its intensity. It was an event that would stand out in our minds, not only as the high point of the course, but as a special human experience. It was an exchange that had the power to cause people to examine their own attitudes, behavior, visceral reactions, and assumptions about human nature. Robert's comments demanded that we consider new standards by which to evaluate these things within ourselves. Robert had been something like the class clown. He never ceased to be somewhat odd and amusing, almost always slightly unaware of what was going on among the rest of us. But he also came to be seen as a person of some wisdom, a person tested and hardened by experience, and someone to learn from.

ED

Everybody in the class remembers the time Ed got arrested. He wasn't really arrested, of course; it was part of the social science simulation game we were playing. Ed was furious. He freaked out and stormed from the room. I followed him, and it took considerable effort for me to persuade him to come back to class. Everyone else laughed, and I had a hard time keeping a straight face and not making things worse by laughing. But it was not unusual for people to laugh at Ed, and it sometimes seemed as if he was encouraging them to do so.

A seriously unequal distribution of wealth and an overall scarcity of food were structured into the simulated society. By the luck of the draw, Ed was one of the food brokers in the game. He periodically received food coupons and could distribute them as he saw fit. He made a variety of different kinds of deals for food. Ed's behavior brought him into conflict with the dominant group of players, a group that was affluent and powerful and had decided to try to create a new, seemingly more rational social order in the simulated society. They saw Ed as a threat, for he was unpredictable, he controlled important resources, and he seemed determined to enrich himself and increase his power. He was indeed accumulating wealth. Using a provision in the game that allows players to buy simulated force with their money, the group arrested Ed and took over his assets just before he became, from their point of view, too powerful. That was when Ed became outraged with the injustice of it all.

Weeks later when we discussed the game in detail, Ed was still indignant, and everybody else was still amused. The people who arrested him insisted that he'd been dangerous and immoral in his "pimping" of food. Ed was self-righteous in the extreme, truthfully pointing out that he had sometimes given food certificates to needy players who could not pay. I was never sure exactly what to believe about Ed's motivation during the game, but I tended to agree with those who arrested him, that he was a threat to their project. He was clearly in business for himself, although there was some dispute as to his goals. Perhaps his goals changed as the game progressed.

When Ed got angry but then was persuaded not to leave the class that day, he became a rather visible member of the group. He was teased, albeit gently, about his anger and his alleged machinations. He and the others laughed, and bringing up Ed's arrest was a surefire way to start a good conversation about the game, which had turned out to be very absorbing to this particular class. Ed also volunteered for a number of activities. One day in class, for example, I talked about a few of Goffman's papers in microsociology because I was intrigued by the enormous body of meaning to be found in observations of minute daily behaviors, observations that could be made by anyone. Ed decided to take a tape recorder to a public place and to record his observations of the behavior of the people he saw.

Ed did a creditable job with his tape recording, but occasionally, at a loss for something to say and uncomfortable with silence, he burst into travelogue-style discourse about the beauties of his particular location in downtown Detroit. Though not intended to be, these digressions were hysterically funny, and the class laughed as each new rapturous description alternated with Ed's accounts of such things as how people filled up park benches and how they looked at him and his tape recorder.

Again people were laughing at Ed. He had a way of doing the wrong thing that was funny. And as I watched Ed, his behavior suggested that he was setting out to play the clown. He spoke softly and with excess formality. His language was almost always stilted. There was usually a grin on his face, as if he himself were mocking his own choice of words, using his language as a gag. Never again, after the arrest in the game, did Ed lose his cool. He was very cool, but at the same time he seemed determined to play every social situation for laughs.

My interest in feminist values was in sharp contrast with the commitments of most of the men in this class. We had long and lively discussions of many aspects of the war between the sexes, and various members of the class told of their experiences to make their points. Military service in Korea or Vietnam had been watershed experiences for many of them, and our conversations often dealt with those years. One day, and it was not out of context in the discussion, Ed began to speak of his life in Korea.

Ed had rented an apartment near the base for himself and a woman, and he spent most of his nights there. She lived in the apartment and was supported by him. Ed described it as the best relationship he'd ever had with a woman and as the happiest time of his life. I had no way, of course, of knowing anything about the relationship beyond what Ed said, and I had no interest in challenging Ed's interpretation of an important episode in his life. I wondered whether Ed was deceived or manipulated in thinking that the woman loved him, and I wondered whether a mutual relationship had developed between them in spite of their differences in wealth, culture, and power. But I did know—one could not help but notice—that Ed's manner changed as he told the story. He didn't grin, his language was less artificial, and his audience didn't laugh.

During the week between classes my mind kept going back to Ed. Not only was his story interesting, but his change in behavior was striking. And as I thought about all the other conversations he had participated in, I felt increasingly uncomfortable. His grin and self-mocking style began to seem like preemptive strikes. Perhaps Ed did not want to make people laugh. If it was inevitable, however, he might do better to laugh along, to pretend that the laughter was intended.

I always got to class early, and Ed was also usually one of the first to arrive. We happened to be the first two people in the room for the next week's class, and I broached the subject with him as gently as I could. I said that he seemed to make people laugh. Immediately and directly, again without a grin, he responded, "Yes, but I really don't know why they laugh." I told Ed that he appeared to be encouraging the laughter with his grin and his choice of words, as if he were trying to be funny. Ed said that he knew he had that habit, but that he wasn't terribly fond of the role of clown, even though he sometimes found it useful. Other students started coming into the room. Ed and I talked a little more, and he didn't seem uncomfortable. After another few minutes I asked him whether he wanted to stop, or if he would want to continue our talk in public in class. He said that he wouldn't mind continuing. I didn't quite know why Ed was the way he was. I really didn't understand what we were talking about. But the whole thing felt substantial to me and worth pursuing.

We told the rest of the group what we were talking about, and we thrashed around a little. I asked Ed whether he'd always made people laugh. He said no, it hadn't happened back home in the South. Ed, who was black, had come North looking for a good job after he left military service, just as David and several other members of the class had done. The conversation oscillated between general observations about the differences between the experiences these men had had in the North and South, on the one hand, and Ed's particular way of talking on the other. Slowly a conclusion emerged.

Each member of the group who had lived through the transition from small Southern towns to Detroit talked about the difficulties he had encountered. They spoke of embarrassments, mistakes, and uncertainties before they learned new ways of doing things and speaking. People had laughed at all of them, ridiculed them for their country ways, and now, no longer naive, they laughed at themselves for their former ineptness. Some of them were clearly not beyond mocking newer arrivals now that they were more or less at home in the North.

Ed said that he learned these things slowly. He was not adept at acquiring new ways of speaking and behaving. As soon as he made that statement, the rest of us realized its truth. Ed was simply not skilled at learning a new cultural style. He remained a rural person in his manners and speech. Out of place, he amused people. He was often awkward. His grin and his self-mocking ways helped him cope with frequent embarrassments. They were at once his protection and his trap.

An undercurrent of tenderness appeared in the treatment Ed received at the hands of the other men in the class. They had gone through similar ordeals, but most of them were better equipped to manage the kind of cultural learning required. Whatever happened to Ed outside of class, I think he met with a special kind of understanding in our class. The class had a fuller understanding of a cultural phenomenon that many had experienced, and perhaps Ed understood himself better.

288

Fourteen Men

AL

Al had blue eyes that sparkled, an incredibly endearing childish grin that he'd surely been capitalizing upon since early boyhood, and lots of energy and idealism. He was the radical unionist in the class, a grass-roots insurgent who wished to gain power in the United Automobile Workers and try to revitalize it. He felt that the union leadership was too comfortable and out of touch with its members. He contested and sometimes won elections in his local. Al had been a full-time college student in the 1960s and had been an activist. But college hadn't been right for him, and he'd dropped out and gone to work.

Al worked in the plant described by him and others in the class as the roughest in Detroit. Its workers were the youngest, had the least seniority, little discipline, and a reputation for being wild. This was all comfortable for Al. He liked chaos and excitement. He was starting a plant newspaper using his own money. He was a natural organizer, hanging around with coworkers after hours, drinking, and talking about the politics of the union and the plant. Al's talents were obvious to everyone, and the union leadership had already begun offering him positions and responsibilities. A major issue in his life, one which we discussed in class on several occasions, was whether he'd do better staying outside the union bureaucracy in a position of opposition, whether, in other words, the opportunity to advance in the union would lead him to being co-opted by the establishment.

As soon as Al heard about the structure of our class, he knew what he wanted to do. He came up with a project that he thought would help him better understand the union, particularly his adversaries. He looked forward to sharing his work with other class members, many of whom also belonged to the UAW and had perspectives of their own from which he could profit. Al also thought it would be fun. His plan was to do a series of tape-recorded interviews with key union officials; the main focus, though not the exclusive one, would be race relations in the UAW. Al was white, and he believed that his union suffered from strong racist tendencies. He intended to play the tapes, or excerpts of them, in class. He would discuss them with the rest of us, and get ideas and suggestions for future interviews. The idea was typical of Al, exhibiting one of his most attractive characteristics. The focus of his project was a group of people he considered his enemies, yet he knew he could learn from them and wished to approach them in good faith. He was respectful of the experience and knowledge of his opponents. I could detect no malice or guile in his approach to the project.

After a couple of weeks Al came to class with a tape recorder but no taped interviews. Nobody in the union would talk to him. He told the officials that he was going to college and doing a class project, but they simply wouldn't trust him. Al was, for them, a trouble maker, and they feared that the tape recordings were part of some scheme to set them up for a political attack. They saw Al was a nuisance at the very least and possibly as a real threat. None of us in the class could make a plausible suggestion for how Al might win the confidence of the people he wanted to interview. He had been honest with them, and they wouldn't believe him.

I was reluctant to see a group of interesting issues vanish from the shared domain of the class. Although I knew it would be a poor substitute for the real interviews, I suggested to Al that we do some role-playing. I asked him to tell us about the union official he most wanted to interview. He described one of the highest ranking black men in the union and told us the questions he wanted to ask and his reasons for wanting to ask them. He saw the man as a slick and sophisticated Uncle Tom.

I took the role of the interviewer, asking Al's questions. Al played the older black man. For our amusement, but to no clear purpose, we turned on the tape recorder. Amidst great merriment in the class, Al gave his version of the classic liberal answers: "If we go too fast, we'll lose all that we have gained." "A young fellow like you sees only the problems; you have no appreciation of the progress we've made." "In order to be effective we must understand the problems and limitations of our opponents." "Despite our shortcomings, our union is the most open, most democratic, least racist in the country." The class had a lively discussion when our little drama was over. As Al left I said, "Why don't you see if your man will listen to our tape." Al said, "I was thinking the same thing."

Al could charm even a hardened labor union official out of a tree. Tape recorder in hand, Al smiled his way into the man's office and said, "Just listen to the tape. You don't have to talk with me. If you want me to leave after you've heard it I'll go without another word." The man agreed. The recorded role play and the discussion that followed persuaded him that Al was indeed a student, that he was motivated by a desire to understand the union, and that he had no ulterior motives. He was, however, flabbergasted and amused by Al's version of him. Al's answers were, from his point of view, bizarre caricatures of his own positions, oversimplified, stereotyped, silly. He couldn't believe it. "Young man," he said, "come back next week with your tape recorder, and we'll have a real conversation. What's more, I will vouch for you with anybody else in the union you'd like to interview, and I'm sure they'll talk with you."

Al recorded a series of fascinating conversations, and we had a good class session listening to and talking about them. He brought into the classroom the voices and statements of people who were figures in the lives of a number of our students, but who were also usually rather remote, the objects of gossip and rumor. Discussions of the union tend to be ritualized, like discussions of religion and politics, with participants exhibiting well-worn views on the nature of the union, management, and industry. Al's tapes were a healthy influence because to some extent they shook us out of these normal conversational routines. The project was a great success for most of us in the class.

Although I knew he was pleased with his work, I was surprised by a final statement he made at the end of the course, which was only indirectly related to the interviews and our discussions of them. Al had worked, gone to school, and participated in union affairs with black people for years. His father, to whom he was very close, was married to a black woman, so Al had black half-brothers and half-sisters. When he spoke about our classes, however, he said that he had never before participated in discussions among blacks and whites that were as open in dealing with racial issues. He felt that this had allowed him to make important progress in his own life toward honesty and feeling natural in dealing with black people. Several of the other class members, black and white, said that the same thing had been true for them.

SAL

Sal was quiet and observant. You knew, just by watching him, that he was taking everything in. He said little and played his cards close to the vest. After a few weeks of the course, I think that almost every class member class would have said that he liked Sal, although we didn't know very much about him. Then it became clear that Sal's reticence could be broken. He volunteered nothing about himself, but he spoke openly and freely when he was questioned. It was almost as if he was waiting to be asked. Sal didn't remain a stranger to the rest of us for very long.

Sal was a family man. When he didn't work on weekends, he was occupied with maintaining and improving his family's suburban house. He lived near his parents and spent time each weekend with them. Sal was especially concerned about his father, who was, Sal thought, lonely in his retirement. He tried to offer him companionship, but the two men were not particularly close. Sal had two young sons to whom he was devoted. One of them was quite bright, with a gift for schoolwork, and Sal wondered what he should be doing for him. He often stayed after class to engage me in discussions of education, borrowing books and trying to figure out whether he should find enriching academic programs for his son, encourage him to read more, treat him in special ways because of his gifts, etc.

Like many men in our class, Sal was self-made, a person who had advanced on the basis of hard work and initiative. Somewhere along the line he had gotten a low-level job in the drafting department of one of the automobile companies. He began as a cleanup man. He watched and learned, took over a position as a drafting assistant, learned additional drafting by taking night courses, and eventually became operations manager of the department. It was easy to see how responsibilities would be given to Sal. It was self-evident to him that jobs had to be done no matter what obstacles arose. He worked until all hours of the day and night, demanding perfection for himself and his subordinates. He would do whatever was necessary to get the work done properly.

As I've said, our class often talked about the relationships between men and women. The discussions were sometimes provoked by my statement of issues from a feminist viewpoint. At other times they were occasioned by the men's desire to talk about developments at work like affirmative action programs and women in new workplaces. These conversations were always lively and high-spirited. They oscillated wildly between macho posturing and joking, on the one hand, and serious self-examination with its concomitant vulnerability, on the other. Sal spoke little during these discussions and not at all when talk turned to the sexual aspects of relationships. One got the impression that Sal was firmly rooted in his marriage and suburban family life. Certainly there was no mistaking the love in his voice when he spoke of his sons.

One day Sal, without being asked a question, said that he wanted to talk about something that had happened to him. It was the only time in our class that he had ever begun speaking on his own initiative. Sal spoke carefully and deliberately, with the air of someone who had decided to do something.

"I think it will do me good to talk about this, and it's connected with things we've discussed in class, so it might be interesting to you. Anyway, I want to get it off my chest.

"It started at a high school reunion. My wife and I went to the reunion about a year ago. I met a girl I had known in school. She really liked me then; I think she had a big crush on me. I was attracted to her, but there was something strange about her. She was different, and the real reason I never asked her out was that I thought the other guys would put me down or think that there was something wrong with me. I liked her, but I would have been embarrassed to be seen with her. I was part of an 'in' crowd at school, and that was extremely important to me. Everyone looked up to us. I didn't want to take any chances about remaining a member of that group. At the time, though, I knew I was hurting the girl, and in my heart I was ashamed of the way I avoided her. I also thought it was stupid, because I really liked her. But the clique was strong, and I went with it.

"When I saw her at the reunion, I was shocked. She had become beautiful. She used to be sort of funny looking, but now she was extremely attractive in a hippie kind of way. We talked for a long time. I told her about my kids and job. She was floating around, sometimes going to school, sometimes working at a job. She said that she wouldn't want to live the kind of life I did. Her view of it was that she wanted more freedom. We argued for a while. It was as if we were trying to show each other that things were going well for us.

"That was a year ago. After the reunion I started thinking about her a lot. I'd think of her during the day and when I went to sleep, and I found myself thinking of her when I woke up in the morning. I didn't even know where she lived. One day I called her parents and told them I was a friend of hers from school and asked for her address. They gave me an address in Ann Arbor. I put it in my wallet.

"A few weeks later I was driving to work in the morning like I always do. Without really thinking about it, I turned the car toward Ann Arbor. I stopped at a phone booth and called in sick. I haven't taken a sick day in ten years. I didn't call her, I just went. I didn't know what I'd say when I got there.

"She had moved, and I talked the landlady into giving me her new address. She didn't live there any more either, and I spent the rest of the day just walking around, thinking about her, and wondering whether I'd bump into her, which I didn't. I drove home to my family as if I'd spent a normal day at work.

"That's the end of my story. I've never seen her again. I haven't tried to call or locate her since that day. I haven't had an affair since I got married. I still think a lot about her, though maybe a little less as time goes on."

The class was stunned. It was evident that telling the story was a significant act in Sal's life, both because he generally spoke little about himself and because he almost always offered himself to us as a solid family man, undistracted by the temptations that were so attractive to others among us. Telling the story was also a clear act of trust and confidence in the class. A short and rather subdued discussion followed. It was made up mostly of other people's stories, addressed to Sal, dealing with similar examples of yielding to social pressure, as Sal had in high school, and of being fascinated by particular women.

Sal trusted the class and shared a secret with us. There wasn't much to do besides try to understand.

HAROLD

I taught this class at the start of my second year as a househusband, a life that was still new to me. Actually it's always new since the children change so quickly. In caring for them I always find myself a bit off balance, unsure of how much of yesterday's experience is relevant to today, and how much has suddenly been outgrown.

I was having some trouble with it all. It was summer vacation, so I had the kids at home for most of the day. I desperately wanted time for my writing and never felt that I had enough. The two boys, moreover, who are usually quite easy to care for, were in a period of squabbling. It seemed that as soon as they'd been fed, the dishes washed, some basic shopping done, etc.—that is, as soon as I could expect to have a few minutes to myself—I was needed to mediate a silly conflict, and we were all engulfed by bad feelings.

My commitment to nonviolent child rearing was being sorely tested. I felt

294

like throttling the kids. I didn't, but I was so disturbed and conflicted that I had several dreams about hitting them. I was thinking about all this one day as I drove to class. I decided to talk about it. I knew that few if any of the men would share my belief about not hitting kids, and the value disagreement might lead to an interesting discussion. Also, there was little chance, that day, that I might introduce the subject with a fatal air of moral superiority, because it was clear that I felt like climbing the walls. I thought there was a chance that important issues might be raised, issues concerning the nature of childhood and the relations between the generations.

I gave a short talk, sat back, and was enthusiastically attacked from every direction. The class, almost to a man, thought I was an idiot, and they had a wide variety of arguments to establish the fact, everything from appeals to scripture ("Spare the rod . . .") to appeals to popular psychology ("Children are asking for limits. . . .").

The discussion took an unexpected turn. The oldest member of the class was Clarence, in his fifties, a retired Air Force officer who had recently left the service and moved rather quickly into a middle-management position at one of the automobile companies.

Clarence was sure of himself and impressed by how much the younger men had to learn from him. To the utter horror of the class he told the story of the last time he'd beaten his daughter. (*Beaten* was his word, and it was, from his description, accurate.) It was when she came home late from a date at the age of nineteen. Clarence smiled, described his actions and rationale in great detail, and had absolutely no appreciation of the effect of his story on his audience. Since Clarence's arguments were very close to those of other men, his comments gave them pause. The reasoning was plausible when applied to a young child but preposterous when applied to a grown woman. Where was the dividing line properly drawn? The discussion ran its course, having provided some morbid moments. It was not at all clear that it had had much impact on anyone. We moved on to other matters. It was not one of our best classes, nor one of our worst.

About six weeks later I was approached after class by Harold. The most obvious thing about Harold was his body, which was enormous and muscular. He must have been a weight lifter. I remembered looking at Harold during our discussion of spanking, for I had thought at that moment that a number of these men were physically capable of inflicting considerable harm on other people. Harold said to me, "You know, Dick, I've stopped spanking my daughters." He had four young girls.

"How come?" I asked.

"Well, our discussion set me to thinking, especially when Clarence talked about hitting his daughter. It sounded terrible. It made me wonder when I would stop. I tried to think of how a spanking feels to a kid and then of how it might feel to a teenager. Also, I've been thinking about how you run this class. Almost everyone is working and learning, but it isn't out of fear. I thought I'd try it."

"How is it working out?"

Harold said, "It's been great. They're not as scared of me any more. I feel a lot closer to my daughters."

*

While I was teaching this course, I was also writing a column on education that was syndicated to college newspapers. The Wayne State University newspaper was one of my subscribers. That year I wrote two columns especially for the Wayne State paper. One expressed my anger at the shoddy programs being offered to the adult students. They were simply awful, and I felt that I had to speak out. The other was a public letter of gratitude to my fourteen students:

> *Disaster at the Weekend College*
> The sessions start late. The students are mature adults, but the lecturers treat them as if they have no significant experience. Films are scheduled, but they sometimes haven't been previewed by the professor in charge. Often they are irrelevant to the subject. The speeches are profoundly conventional; they all sound the same. Condescension and oversimplification abound. Imagination and intellectual stimulation are absent. Does all this sound familiar? It probably does if you're a student at Wayne State's Weekend College and you've recently attended one of its weekend conferences.
>
> I've attended four of these conferences as a part-time faculty member teaching a section of a social science course in the Weekend College. I suspect that I won't be asked to teach there again after this column is published. But it simply must be said: these conferences, at least the four I've attended, are awful. Two of the programs I participated in were on the family, and the other two were about science and society. They were among the very worst educational programs I've ever witnessed.
>
> Item: A professor talks for at least 90 minutes about Bertolt Brecht's

"Galileo." The group has just seen the film. His stated purpose is to "high-light the questions Brecht raises about the relationship between science and society." Yet he never mentions that Brecht was a communist, a fact that is absolutely essential to understanding the play's form and content. A familiarity with Brecht's Marxist aesthetic theory makes sense out of an otherwise puzzling work. Perhaps the professor wasn't sure that the students could handle the scandalous information. It was a little like neglecting to mention that Galileo was an astronomer.

Item: A very enjoyable old Alec Guiness film is shown at a conference on the family. It is a broad farce, and it illustrates absolutely nothing about the nature of the family. The principal character murders a lot of his relatives, and this fact probably caught the professor's eye as he desperately skimmed through the film catalog. The film, of course, hadn't been previewed by the director of the conference. He knew less about it than you do from having read this paragraph. Yet in tones of great profundity, he kept repeating, "Remember, this film is about an aristocratic English family." He was almost as funny as the movie.

Item: The director of a conference schedules 90 minutes for his own lecture, early on Sunday morning when most people with sense are sleeping it off or going to church. He talks for less than 30 minutes. He spends the time telling us what he would have said if he had given his originally scheduled lecture. His reason for not giving the real lecture is, he claims, that students have been asking for more time in group discussions. He is clearly lying to cover up the fact that he can't use the full 90 minutes well or that he hasn't prepared.

The Weekend College conferences are padded. The time is filled with professors who lecture about their favorite topics, whether or not they are relevant to the conference's subject. They also get an honorarium in addition to their regular salaries. The conferences are full of films, relevant and irrelevant. Showing films seems to be regarded as a way of keeping students occupied and entertained. The faculty, at least the important ones who run these things, seem to be more comfortable with the lights out. As a bonus, the organizers can appear to be progressive educators who use "the media."

Disrespect for students pervades these conferences. It is expressed by the lateness with which everything starts. People are kept waiting, their precious weekend time being frittered away while faculty, who do not really know what they want to do, chat with each other and delay the start of each session.

Disrespect is exhibited by the speakers who almost never seem to recognize that the students have experiences that are important. An auto worker knows something about the relationship of technology to society, but the professor of the history of science doesn't recognize this in his lecture. Nor does the professor of social work recognize that the working mother knows something about the relation of social services to the workplace. In these conferences the communication goes only in one direction, from the alleged expert/professor to the supposedly ignorant adult students. The arrogance of the professors is colossal.

Disrespect, most basically, is shown by the assumption that underlies these conferences. To be educated, it is assumed, is to acquire the language, style and dominant mythology (e.g., one of the speakers kept repeating, "Science is organized curiosity") of white upper-middle class academic culture. There is no sense that the culture of working people might interact with academia in an interesting and fruitful way. The goal is to initiate students into this very specialized academic culture without giving a damn about where they come from.

During my two quarters of teaching in the Weekend College I have come to admire my students. They are serious, ambitious, eager to learn, willing to meet an instructor more than halfway. I have only observed a small fraction of the Weekend College's program, and many people have told me that there are good parts of it. I believe them, but I also know that my students deserve better educational experiences than they have been getting at the weekend conferences. They get four credits for two weekend conferences. Their tuitions are paid by their veterans benefits, their employers, their unions or out of their own earnings. Someone is getting ripped off.

A Letter to 14 Men

Dear Al (both of you), Greg, Sal, J.C., Frank, Wally, Roy, David, Harold, Ed, Terry, Brown, and Clarence,

When I took the job teaching a course at Wayne State's Weekend College, I did it for the money. A year ago I stopped being a teacher and an educational administrator in order to try to be a writer. I didn't intend to return to a job at a college, at least for a while. But I needed the money. I was not sure that our class would be anything more than a chore at which I could pick up a few bucks. It turned out to be a wonderful experience for me, and this is a letter of thanks.

I keep thinking about the song by Leonard Cohen that includes the lines:

Like a bird on the wire,
Like a drunk in the midnight choir,
I have tried, in my way, to be free.

If I had to describe what was happening at the deepest level in our class, I would say that each of us, in his own special way, is trying to be free, and that we shared and discussed our struggles.

There are many things I will remember about our classes. Our discussions of race and discrimination were made vivid by the experiences of many of you, and especially by David's courage in demanding fair treatment in his job. When we discussed the contemporary family, you were honest in talking about your own quests for a fulfilling personal life and a happy family, often against the odds of modern life. And questions of politics and power were very well illuminated by your experiences at work and as members of unions. It will also be hard to forget Ed's observations of people in the park, Al's taped interviews with union officials, and all the dramatic moments in the simulation game, especially, of course, Ed's arrest.

I have been very aware of the differences between us. I spend most of my life dealing with words. Most of you do hard physical work. I have been moved by your interest and by your willingness to learn from me even though my experience is different from yours. It is unfashionable, in this era of "back-to-the-basics" in education, to talk about teachers learning from students. But I must say that I learned a great deal from you, perhaps more than in any of the dozens of other courses I've taught in almost two decades.

I would like to end this letter with a profound word of wisdom for you to remember. Instead, the best I can do is: Thank you.

Love,
Dick

34

The End / The Beginning

What makes a person choose one part of life, one value or process, and make it central? Why would one become obsessed, as I have, with the promises of educational freedom? Why should one infuriate colleagues and create programs that are almost certain to be destroyed along with the part of oneself that is invested in them? Why write a book expressing this obsession, full of extreme arguments and statements, laying oneself open to the infinitely clever attacks of the sophisticates of the academic world?

A commitment to educational freedom usually exists in the heart and mind as one in a complex web of related elements. Prominent among them are liberal values and beliefs about the world and human nature. Adopting such a world view is the result of some mixture of rational weighing and visceral responding, judgment and temperament. There are other things: we may find ourselves stubbornly bound on some idealistic or ideological course. Or we may relentlessly crave the admiration of someone or some group of people, a failure of which I have been accused by colleagues who believe me to be pandering to students. But still, why educational freedom?

No part of life is without its mysteries and hints of magic. One contemplates one's options, makes rational or irrational decisions, and then finds oneself surprised, pleasantly or unpleasantly, by unanticipated consequences in unforeseen realms. This is what has happened to me as an educator.

I have been very much taken by the powerful forces that can arise in teaching and learning. A student begins to glow with self-confidence and self-reliance where before there were fear and a yearning for dependence. A person becomes excited by the process of working close to the limits of his or her abilities instead of staying timidly near the center of reliable and proved competencies. One discovers the joy of achievements that are totally one's own, the satisfaction of pursuing and completing a task out of autonomous action, not coercion. There is the sense of adventure in the exploration of an area, even one that has been well traveled by others, without an externally imposed program. There are the endless surprises arising from the mixture of personality and subject matter, surprises that spring to the surface more often when personality is given some additional freedom to express itself in educational settings. And finally, there are the inspiration, feelings of renewal, and intimacy of educational relationships based on trust and collaboration rather than on the dynamics of power and control. I have found that these things have extraordinary value, and that, as unusual as they may be in experience generally, they are rather common consequences of educational freedom.

To the reader who has come this far, student, parent, teacher, administrator, the only thing I have left to say is, Try it. Trying is not in itself sufficient. There is much to be learned. But it is a beginning.